CW00541403

A TAILOR IN AUSCHWITZ

A TAILOR IN AUSCHWITZ

David van Turnhout and
Dirk Verhofstadt

Translation by
Kristien De Wulf and Jane Camerea

PEN & SWORD
HISTORY

AN IMPRINT OF PEN & SWORD BOOKS LTD.
YORKSHIRE – PHILADELPHIA

First published in Great Britain in 2022 by
PEN AND SWORD HISTORY
An imprint of
Pen & Sword Books Ltd
Yorkshire – Philadelphia

ISBN 978 1 39900 436 7

A CIP catalogue record for this book is available from the British Library.

Typeset in Times New Roman 11.5/14 by SJmagic DESIGN SERVICES, India.
Printed and bound in the UK by CPI Group (UK) Ltd.

Pen & Sword Books Limited incorporates the imprints of Atlas, Archaeology,
Aviation, Discovery, Family History, Fiction, History, Maritime, Military,
Military Classics, Politics, Select, Transport, True Crime, Air World, Frontline
Publishing, Leo Cooper, Remember When, Seaforth Publishing, The Praetorian
Press, Wharncliffe Local History, Wharncliffe Transport, Wharncliffe True Crime
and White Owl.

For a complete list of Pen & Sword titles please contact
PEN & SWORD BOOKS LIMITED
47 Church Street, Barnsley, South Yorkshire, S70 2AS, England
E-mail: enquiries@pen-and-sword.co.uk
Website: www.pen-and-sword.co.uk

Or

PEN AND SWORD BOOKS
1950 Lawrence Rd, Havertown, PA 19083, USA
E-mail: Uspen-and-sword@casematepublishers.com
Website: www.penandswordbooks.com

Contents

Family Kartuz

Moszek Kalma Kartuz (1884-1942/43) x Sura Kartuz (1882-1924)
|

Abram Kartuz (1908-1942/43)
Chaja Kartuz (1910-1942/43)
Itta Kartuz (1910-1912)
Zyskind Kartuz (1914-1942/43)
Ide Leib Kartuz (1905-1995) x Chaja Artman (1896-1942)
|

    Charles-Victor Kartuz (1931-1942)
    Simone Kartuz (1933-1942)

Ide Leib Kartuz (1905-1995) x Joséphine Vervloet (1927)
|

    Ellen Kartuz (1947-2009) x Henri Eyletters (1942)
    |

        Cathy Eyletters (1968)
        Nadine Eyletters (1969)
        Danny Eyletters (1972)
    Benno Kartuz (1948) – Greta De Voeght (1944) x| Andre Van Turnhout (1937-2019)
    |

        David Van Turnhout (1982)

Family Artman

Hejnoch Artman (1885-1942/43) x Hadessa Apelowicz (1882-1942/43)
|
    Chaja Artman (1896-1942) x Ide Laib Kartuz (1905-1995)
    |
        Charles-Victor Kartuz (1931-1942)
        Simone Kartuz (1933-1942)

    Litman Artman (1897-1992) x Deborah Zucker (?)
    |
        Elaine Artman (1930-1991)
        Mireille (Mimi) Artman (1932)
    Gitla Artman (1899-1942/43)
    Fajgla Artman (1903-1961) x Abraham Dzierlatka (1904-1988)
    |
        Lilliane Dzierlatka (1930-2019) x Nathan Shuman (1927)
        |
        Kip Shuman (1960)
    Laura Dzierlatka (1932-2008)
    Abram Artman (1904-1942/43)
    Jacob Artman (1906-1945) x Paula Singer (1910-1942)
    Mindla Artman (1912-1942/43)

Prologue

Grandpa

When I was about 6 years old, we sometimes drove through the city by car. A few times we drove to another neighbourhood, where, from the back seat, I saw strange people with big hats and long black coats. At the city park we drove down a street until we got to our destination – Grandpa's apartment.

In the apartment I played with cars on the floor, so I mainly remember the chair legs. I used to come out from under the chair to read my New Year's letter. Maybe I got a little money for that, but that was not the reason I did it. The bag with real Babelutte sweets from the seaside was a much nicer present. The kind old man who gave them to me almost always smiled. When the formalities were over, he would hug me warmly, after which I disappeared between the chairs with a Babelutte in my mouth. We hardly saw each other, but I still felt comfortable with him. Maybe I was used to him because he came to our house and was there on these enjoyable Sundays. Mama put in the extra effort then and, with her meagre budget, conjured up the tastiest things on her beautifully laid table. 'The tomatoes are nice and crisp,' he said.

His son Benno, whom I then called 'Papa', got angry and corrected him. 'It's crispy and tomatoes aren't crispy', after which they squabbled in a language I didn't understand. The relationship between Benno and my mother was anything but smooth. He didn't live with us, but when he was with us he spent half of the time arguing with my mother. One day I was at the centre of an argument. Benno shouted that I belonged to him and tugged at my arm, but mama didn't let go. I felt the heat of his cigarette on my face. After some pushing and pulling he left. As fast as she could, mama pushed me into the car and drove away.

These kinds of things happened a lot until one day Benno was no longer welcome. Mama had had enough of the arguments and decided to finish the relationship. When he was gone she reminded me that I should avoid any contact with that man. Later my eldest sister told me that they were all afraid that he would kidnap me and take me to Israel.

Although Benno no longer showed up at our house, he sometimes turned up at the school gates. Then I froze and couldn't say a single word. It was even harder when he appeared on the playground. The other children asked me who that man was. I didn't even know the answer myself. He wasn't my dad, but then who was he? After a barrage of probing questions, Benno sometimes pushed a toy in my hands, mostly things my mother would never have given me. My classmates thought his visits were peculiar, but fun. That somewhat diminished my shame. By accepting his gifts, I felt as if I were betraying my mother, but after a while his school visits decreased. School officials did not make it easy for him. They were wary of a man who just walked into the playground during school hours. Benno could not claim to be my father, because his name was Kartuz, and mine was Van Turnhout.

One day a birthday card from Benno got through to me in the post. But I wasn't allowed even to think about Benno Kartuz. But when I was 10 I started asking questions. 'We used to celebrate Christmas with Grandpa and Benno. Who is Benno actually, and who was Grandpa? Is Benno my father, or is it Andre Van Turnhout?'

I involved my eldest sister, Nathalie, as a mediator because I knew that this was a difficult subject for my mother. Nathalie was less emotional, so it was easier for me to talk about such things with her. With her I stood a better chance of getting objective answers. She promised me that she would discuss it with mama. Later she brought me the news, 'She's going to tell you on New Year's Eve.' In the hope of getting closure, I lay awake for nights on end. Mama and I were celebrating New Year's Eve together, simply at home. It was a celebration, so I was allowed to stay up to watch the fireworks. We ate canapés in the living room and clinked our posh glasses, mine filled with children's champagne and hers with Moët & Chandon. I showed restraint for a while, but quite early in the evening I realised I couldn't make an omelette without breaking eggs and I finally asked my question.

'Who is my actual papa, mama?'

Benno Kartuz turned out to be my real father. But why did I have a different name?

'Andre wanted to acknowledge you and Benno did not. Benno did not want to be your official father.' According to mama he was bad and I had to inform her if he came near me.

'What about Grandpa?'

He was Benno's father, hence my grandfather. Mum loved him very much, but because she wanted to break completely with the Benno chapter, she had also broken all contact with him. We watched the fireworks together and I accepted the situation as it was. I believed then that Benno was bad, but deep inside I stayed faithful to that kind Grandpa, with his soft smile and his Babelutte sweets from the seaside.

Polish Jew

Fifteen years later I walked with a fortune in diamonds to the Antwerp Diamond Bourse. Because of the nice weather Jews and Indians everywhere were doing business with each other on the street. A year earlier my stepfather had advised me to follow a diamond apprenticeship. 'You can earn a good living with that, little one.'

After an internship in Congo, I started working as a salesman at an Israeli diamond company. The firm of Israeli liberal and orthodox American-Jewish owners was active worldwide and well known in the United States. From their branch in Antwerp I had to sell what the markets in Hong Kong and New York did not want. I therefore sold little at the bourse. To do good business, I had to travel, away from the centre. Munich, Geneva or the south of France were on the agenda every month. If I wasn't traveling alone, there were usually Israelis or New York Jews with me.

The Israelis were quite aggressive and strongly focused on sales. The orthodox New Yorkers were calmer. One of the latter, Moshe, told me a story about a safari, and how God had meticulously linked everything together in nature like the workings of a watch. I did not believe in God, but I let Moshe continue. He was deeply convinced of it, and my job was more important than my opinion. When we went on a trip, he always brought a suitcase with food. 'Kosher food is not available everywhere, and I am definitely not going to starve,' he laughed. He was not the only one. All the devout Jews with whom I travelled always took two suitcases. One with clothes and one with supplies. With Moshe I ended up in strange places. In Switzerland we always spent the night in a Jewish retirement home. The bath towels there smelled of old people and during the day I could still smell the Dettol in my clothes, but the food was kosher. Moshe regularly interrupted his work to pray. I was used to him doing that, but one day, during an international jewellery fair, something special happened. Just before opening time, all the Jews from our team, including the Israelis, came together to pray. They honoured the victims of the Holocaust. That intimate moment when mature men bent their head and bowed down singing mourning songs touched my soul. 'I am of Jewish descent myself,' I confided to Moshe.

I was proud of that, but was afraid that real Jews would not believe me. How could I explain that my biological father was called Kartuz, my mother was non-Jewish, and that I was a Van Turnhout? With most people I didn't even bother to say anything about it, basically to save myself from a long and complicated explanation. My friend Jan had once laughed at me in the first year of secondary school. 'Haha, you are a Polish Jew. My family did business with the Germans.'

Fortunately, Moshe reacted differently. 'Have you never looked up your grandfather? If he has survived a concentration camp, there must be some kind of record?' With his tips I scoured the internet and finally came across the website of the Kazerne Dossin. Located in Mechelen, a city between Brussels and Antwerp, Kazerne Dossin served as a transit camp from which all Belgian Jews and Gypsies were deported to Auschwitz. In 2007 it was still not possible to search the image bank but the site did mention a general e-mail address. The only thing I had was a name: Ide Kartuz. I clicked on 'send' and waited for news. To my surprise, I quickly received a reply from Laurence Schram, senior researcher at Kazerne Dossin. She had found my grandfather in their database. The file was larger than I thought. It contained a photo, extracts from the Jewish Register and a summary with various dates. He looked like me when he was young, or rather I looked like him. His penetrating eyes looked at me, but I immediately jumped to the overview on the last page: 'Died in 1995'. I stared at the wall. I would never get to know him again.

Schoonselhof cemetery

A group of men stood in front of the diamond bourse. Two steps away someone was making a phone call. I didn't have to look twice, because even after ten years without any contact, I immediately realised that it was Benno. My heartbeat rose, my hands became clammy. Now, of all times! Now that I was looking so hard for anything that related to my Grandpa, he suddenly reappeared! I did not miss the opportunity and disregarded my mother's advice. When he finished calling, I approached him. My throat felt tight.

'Excuse me, sir, are you perhaps Benno Kartuz?'

He didn't recognise me.

'Yes, that's me.'

'I am David.'

I suggested going for a drink somewhere quiet.

We asked many questions. What about this, how about that? What do you do for a living? Are you married? Of course, I immediately asked him about his father.

'Grandpa died of a brain tumour in 1995,' said Benno. 'He's buried in the Schoonselhof cemetery, but I haven't been there yet.'

I told him about my search and about the file. He asked me if I could give it to him. It contained things that he did not know.

Benno went through a difficult time and we lost track of each other once more after that chance meeting. Occasionally we spoke with each other on the phone, but that was it.

I checked my note from the city services, on which I had quickly scribbled a burial plot number. Ide was buried there as a political prisoner. His grave was in a plot with hundreds of other graves; each one a person who had died for their country or who had performed a noteworthy act during the war. So, he was not with other Jews. His tombstone was part of a large group of war heroes and was at the front. He was one of the last to have been added to it. Although Ide had experienced the most dreadful things and was already 37 when he was deported, he had lived longer than most. He lived to be 90, but the epitaph was incorrect. It said he died in 1975 instead of 1995. I contacted the responsible department and asked if it could be changed. The country owed him that honour. The answer disappointed me. It would take too much effort and too much time to replace the bronze plate. Moreover, the person on the other end of the phone did not seem to think it was a big deal.

That made me angry. I left it for what it was. I bought some heather in a plant store down the road and put it next to his grave. Heather, he liked that, I thought. Mama had said that he often visited a friend in in a municipality north of Antwerp. He had a house next to the heath.

Meidl

I did not continue selling diamonds; the financial crisis in 2008 put an end to that. Anyway, the diamond business in Antwerp was already on the wane. Trade had moved to the East and the future of the diamond industry was no longer in our hands. In 2017, after some professional wandering I became a freelance copywriter. But I wanted to publish my own political and philosophical ideas as well as commercial texts. By spending time with like-minded people, reading a lot and forming opinions, I came in contact with Dirk Verhofstadt.

My contact with Dirk became closer. We also often exchanged book tips. Towards the end of June 2018, Dirk recommended I read the book *East West Street*, a whopping four hundred pages. In it, Philippe Sands describes the creation of the legal terms of 'genocide' and 'crimes against humanity', two terms which came into existence during the Nuremberg trials. These days, they are firmly embedded in international criminal law. They are aimed at punishing large-scale war crimes against civilians and were first used to describe the monstrous acts of violence that the Nazis had committed all over Europe. The book made a lasting impression on me. In particular, the lack of moral conscience with which Jews in Eastern Europe were wiped off the map between 1940 and 1945 stuck in my mind.

When Dirk asked me what I thought of the book, I told the story of Ide for the first time in ages.

'My grandfather was a Polish Jew. He survived Auschwitz because he was a tailor.'

Dirk e-mailed me immediately.

'When did he come to Belgium? When was he detained? What happened to his family? Tailor? That's unusual!'

I was able to answer most of the questions, thanks to the information from the Dossin Barracks, but I had no real details. The only thing I knew was that he was forced to make uniforms for the Nazis.

Dirk did not let it go. 'The quickest way to find out is to get in touch with your biological father. Would you be prepared to do that?'

Benno replied to my Messenger message quite quickly. He suggested having dinner together somewhere in Brussels, where he now lived. The last time we met had been more than ten years ago. Sitting at a pavement café, he again told me the story, most of which I already knew.

Ide Leib Kartuz was a tailor from Poland, who was forced to make uniforms in Auschwitz for the Germans. In the process, he was kicked and beaten and lost his wife and two children. I had hoped to learn more about Grandpa's first wife and children but, because he had told Benno very little about his life before the war, I did not discover very much more. He did give us the name of his mother, Joséphine, who had died a few years earlier. Ellen, too, Benno's older sister, about whom I had seldom heard people speak, had died in 2008 from a brain tumour. She could have told us a lot, since she was often with her father. In the last years of his life, she had visited him regularly in the rest home for war victims. After a bad fall, it was clear that Ide could no longer live alone, and he moved to Saint-Ode, which was a good distance away.

It turned out I had cousins too. Ellen had three children whom I quickly traced on Facebook: Cathy, Nadine and Danny. I sent all three of them a message through Messenger and went mad with impatience the rest of that weekend.

'Do they still have his papers? Will they want to get in touch with me? Are they interested in their grandfather's past?' Breaking my mother's cardinal rule of not having any contact with the Kartuz family also caused me stress. Nevertheless, Mama was also an important eyewitness. She knew Ide well and was on the same wavelength.

Mama said, 'Grandpa was such a sweet man. He was kind and gentle and wouldn't hurt a fly. Every now and then he would talk a little about the camps, but we didn't speak of it often. One day, his guards woke him up. They said it was a holiday, a festival with all the trimmings. When the prisoners went outside, they saw that their friends had been hanged. Those sadists made them look at them. Grandpa took care of his fellow prisoners and shared his bread with them.'

She also told me the same thing Benno had told me. That the guards had stamped on his stomach and that he had had problems with his stomach for the rest of his life.

My youngest sister turned out to know some things too. One evening, he had confided in her that the guards had shot at him. He tried to save himself by falling down and pretending to be dead. The Nazis had laughed, saying, 'You might as well get up, stupid. We know you haven't been hit.'

In the meantime, my new cousins had responded. All three, Danny, Nadine and Cathy, had been astounded. Understandable when you suddenly get a message from someone who claims to be related, after thirty-six years, by way of a secret relationship your married uncle had. I met Danny first. When he was small, Grandpa Kartuz used to whisper to him, just before he went to sleep, that people are not always kind and can do the most awful things to each other. Since Danny had spent most of his childhood with his father, he didn't know that much about Ide's war story. Danny knew Grandpa mostly as a loving grandfather, small in stature but with a very big heart.

A week later I met Nadine. It was already quite late, so she made me a tomato and mozzarella salad.

'After all, we're family,' she said.

As I ate, she told me with tears in her eyes about the death of her mother, Ide's daughter Ellen. She died in 2008 of a brain tumour. Personally, I had never known or seen her. Nadine showed me photos of her. She was a beautiful, elegant woman and Nadine resembled her. They both looked slightly Jewish, just as Benno and I do. Nadine's testimony was important. Not only had she kept a box of books and photos in the attic, but she also put me in touch with other eyewitnesses who might know more and who were probably still alive. She never went up to the attic, because of hip pain. So I climbed the little ladder alone.

'Which box is it?'

The heavier of the two boxes contained mainly old books. Every single one was about the Holocaust, but there was also a copy of *Mein Kampf* by Adolf Hitler. It wasn't clear whether the books belonged to Ide or Ellen. Maybe Ide was even mentioned in them somewhere. He had told Nadine once that one of his fellow prisoners in Auschwitz had written a book. When that man was made to clean out a cesspool, he had fallen in and drowned. No one knew what had happened to the manuscript. Benno also told me about a journalist who used to visit their house regularly. He was said to have written down my grandfather's stories.

Without some sort of direction, it was impossible to get started. Dirk and I delved deep into the books, but we could find no concrete trail or link. When I left, Nadine gave me an old photo album of Ide's. The photos showed a young Benno, Ellen and Mama Joséphine looking happy. They were gallivanting around Nice, Monaco and the Belgian coast and often posing in front of their large car, a Goliath.

Ide looked very good too. In almost all the photos, he wore a lovely suit, his hair was slicked back, and he was accompanied by his beautiful

Joséphine, twenty years younger than he was. They looked so carefree, with their many friends and their shiney new car. But in one photo, taken in Nice, Ide is wearing a short-sleeved shirt for once and you can vaguely see his camp registration number from hell. I found a close-up of it in Ellen's journal, which was also in the box: 61979.

State Archives

Number 61979 was also in the list from the Dossin Barracks, along with references to files in the State Archives. In the hope of discovering more there, I made an appointment with Filip Strubbe, an archivist who loves his work. He had prepared a file for us to look at. I had never held such an old archive file in my hands, and I carried it like a priceless treasure to the reading table. Obviously, I had no experience with archives, that much was clear. But this could be the holy grail that would finally be able to tell us the whole story.

As I opened the cover, Ide looked straight up at me from the photo, a copy of which Dossin had sent me. It was part of a foreigner's fiche. The document contained the names of his parents and his birthplace in Poland. All the address said was Pławno. I noticed the staples in the file. They were rusted through but still determinedly holding the photo in place, after eighty-nine years. I was in a hurry, because I was working for a client that day and I had promised to go back for a follow-up meeting. I didn't have time to go through it all thoroughly, so I started photographing the bulging file as fast as I could with my smartphone. Two hours later, I was finished.

I phoned Dirk from the train.

'We've struck lucky! The archive is full of details. He was even in the Resistance, in 1942!'

We did indeed manage to learn an awful lot from the photos, but we still couldn't reconstruct the whole story. Why did he come to Belgium? Was he here alone? Where were his parents and the rest of his family? We didn't find the answers to those questions in the State Archives, but where else could we look?

'We need to go to Poland.'

Part One

Treblinka

Poland

At five in the morning we leave by car from Antwerp to Poland. We will be spending a week there looking for Ide's roots, the places where he was born, grew up and went to school. Who were his ancestors and what happened to them before, during and after the war? Why did he apparently leave his native country in a hurry in 1929 for Antwerp? In the suitcase of our loyal Dacia Logan is a box filled with books about pre-war Poland. Ide grew up with his family in Pławno, but there were also many relatives in Żarki. Both were typical Jewish villages in central Poland, south of the city of Łodź.

We found the information about the family members after a long search on the website of CRARG, the Częstochowa-Radomsko Area Research Group of Daniel Kazez, a Jew with Polish roots who lives in Ohio. His non-profit organisation has existed since 2003 and manages a database with more than 800,000 files about people who lived in Pławno, Gidle, Żarki, Częstochowa, Radomsko and other small towns and villages in the area. The database contains Jewish archives on births, marriages, deaths, funerals, tombstones, synagogues, censuses, emigration, immigration, professions, elections, police, deportations, and the Holocaust.

As an introduction to his website we read a statement written by him:

> Whether you have just started a search or are an experienced researcher, I hope you will find something new on our website. Maybe 'new' cousins, your grandfather's profession, the street name for your family in Poland, the tombstone of a loved one or even details of your family before they changed their surname. I am the founder of CRARG and the chairman (an unpaid position). We put

1

all financial contributions towards finding and translating archive documents.[1]

The membership fee to access this information is $100 for one year, a figure that we are happy to pay. Immediately afterwards, Kazez sends us an e-mail stating that his grandfather was born in Radomsko, but that his family is from Pławno and Żarki. An hour later we have access to the database and receive various e-mails with more specific information about the Kartuz, Kartus and Kartusz families. We work all day long and gradually reconstruct a family tree that goes back to the middle of the eighteenth century.

Ide's father, Moszek Kalma Kartuz, was a salesman who was born on 23 June 1885 in Żarki. He married Sura Kartuz in 1904, who was born on 26 September 1882 in Pławno. Apparently, Moszek had joined his wife in Pławno where they lived in the bride's parents' house. After Ide, the couple had four more children: Abram (1908), the twins Chaja and Itta (1910) and Zyskind (1914). Mother Sura died in 1924, after which Moszek re-married Fajgl Kuperberg, who was born on 15 May 1897 in Pławno, and who was very religious. Moszek had two more children with her: Chaim (1925) and Ita (1927). Ide's grandparents all came from Żarki: Berek Kartus, salesman (1846), Chaja Szwimmer (1847), Izrael Kartuz, salesman (1855) and Minka Ruchla Kuperberg (1853, from Gidle). Berek, in turn, was the son of Abram Yitzchak Kartus, salesman (1811). His father Jakub Kartus Jakubowitz (1771) and grandfather Dawid Kartus Jakubowitz (1751) also came from Żarki.

In addition, the CRARG database contains hundreds of names of cousins, nieces, uncles, aunts and other relatives. The part of Poland where the family lived had been under Russian influence since the Vienna Congress in 1815. Congress Poland, or the Kingdom of Poland, was a puppet state of Russia, although it had a degree of sovereignty. After the Polish uprising of 1830, however, it lost its autonomous status and was incorporated into the Russian Empire. Although at first the country was allowed to continue using its own language, from 1860 Russian was the governing language and Polish nationalism remained deep rooted.

In the meantime, Kazez had informed the other members of CRARG that we were new members and this quickly resulted in an e-mail from a Michael Danziger from the United States. He wrote that he was the first in the group to look for relatives of the Kartus family. Based on the

2

family tree data, he turned out to be my cousin three times removed. Our common ancestor was Berek Kartus, Ide's grandfather.

The contacts with Kazez and Danziger greatly helped our research because we now knew exactly where and for whom to look. Ide's parental home was our first destination.

Sjtetl

The wide German and Polish motorways allowed us to make good time to Radomsko, where we booked four nights in the Zameczek hotel. It is a sinister building that is somewhat reminiscent of the hotel from *The Shining* in Stephen King's book. The owner bought it for the price of an Opel Kadett after the fall of communism. Today mainly Jewish tourists are staying there. We meet Maria Piekarska, project co-ordinator at the Forum for Dialogue in Warsaw. The Forum keeps the memory and history of Polish Jews alive and wants to encourage dialogue between Poles and Jews. The organisation is also actively committed to the protection of Jewish heritage and the fight against anti-Semitism. Maria speaks excellent English and assists us with our research into Ide's past.

After a short introduction, we set off for Pławno, a district of Gidle, a dozen kilometres south of Radomsko. We drive through fruit orchards and see two old men picking plums. One pulls a branch down with his umbrella while the other skilfully puts the fruit in a basket. Once there, Pławno actually turns out to be very small. There are only five streets and they all lead to the central square. There is a memorial for the seventeenth-century Polish King Jan III Sobieski and also a plaque for the Polish victims of the 1863 uprising against Russia and for the war against the Red Army in 1920.

Poland became independent on 11 November 1918. The fact that the flower hanging baskets on the square look like gallows was probably not intentional but that is the closest we get to an image of the village during the war. Nowhere do we see any reference to victims of the Second World War, not even to the Jews who were killed here. A ruin is all that is left of the old village synagogue. The former *yeshiva*, a Jewish school that was founded before the First World War by rabbi Yitzhak Rabinowitz, has disappeared. It's an extraordinary feeling to walk around the village where Ide grew up, especially since it seems so little has changed. The square, the main street, the small side streets, the houses ... it all looks exactly like the photos from before the war.

Where we live, old buildings have been demolished and renovated over the years, but not here; with the exception of a few television and satellite antennas, time has stood still.

We are looking for Kartuz's parental home which, according to our papers, is nearby. Młynarska number 5, that's the address. The former main street is now a dead end and is somewhat hidden behind the central square. In this neighbourhood, with only a few, low brick houses, the Jews of the village used to live together. According to CRARG information, Ide's cousins also lived in this street in a wooden house on the opposite side. The old, wooden barrack at number 9 is still there. With a lick of paint, it has survived the test of time. The hut of wooden beams is barely bigger than we are, but the discovery of it feels much bigger. We are face to face with a piece of David's family history.

At some later date Ide would have moved to number 27a in the same street. When we walk past the small houses and take pictures with our smartphones, a few residents show up. Maria says they don't trust us. And indeed, after a few minutes, three Polish women come outside and look suspiciously at us. *'Co tutaj robisz? Odejdź!'* 'What are you doing here? Go away!' they shout at us. Their dogs also growl and bark threateningly. With our foreign licence plate people look at us as if we are villains. Maria explains to us that in Poland there is a fear of Jews and their relatives coming to reclaim property. Such claims are more common in a large city like Warsaw. In the countryside they are rather exceptional. But how did the Poles end up living in the Jewish houses? In 1939 there were about eighty Jewish families, about 40 per cent of the total population of Plawno. Now there are none.

In the 1920s many Polish Jews, such as Ide, left the *sjtetls* to try their luck elsewhere. According to Maria, two factors were responsible for this: the poor economic situation and latent anti-Semitism. More and more people were motivated by the emerging Polish nationalism which came from anti-Jewish Christian thinking, in particular farmers from the countryside and smaller towns and villages.

One of the main perpetrators behind virulent anti-Semitism was Roman Dmowski, leader and ideologist of the right-wing National Democracy of Endecja.[2] He pushed for a boycott of Jewish shops, salesmen, pedlars, entrepreneurs and doctors, and for the exclusion of

Jews from higher education. Just like in Nazi Germany, members of the *Endecja* urged Poles to stop buying from Jewish stores. It often resulted in outbursts of violence. The cries from nationalist and racist groups grew ever louder for Jewish migrants to be prevented from entering, and even to be expelled en masse.

On 9 March 1936 this led to a real pogrom in the town of Przytyk, a *sjtetl* in Central Poland where several people were killed and many more were injured. In the years 1935 and 1936 around 150 smaller and larger pogroms took place, which took the lives of countless people, according to the German researcher Dieter Pohl.[3] It caused shock waves in the Jewish communities in numerous Polish cities and towns. The church also fed racism and anti-Semitism. Priests gave inflammatory speeches against Jews from the pulpit, portraying them as the murderers of Christ. The number of anti-Jewish acts of violence increased sharply in the years before the war. There were anti-Semitic riots in Gidle, the administrative district of Plawno. These happened after the celebration of St Hyacinth on 17 August 1936 in the Dominican monastery, which attracted many religious farmers from the area. They drank a lot and then smashed the windows of Jewish shops and looted them. As a result, young adult Jews in particular tried to leave the country as soon as they had the necessary financial resources. Ide did not wait that long. Apparently, he had enough money to get married in 1929, to get a travel pass to Belgium and to leave the same year. He never saw his parents, brothers, sisters and other family members again.

In Gidle we get a warm welcome from Jolanta Łęska. As a registrar she has access to the birth and marriage records of the Pławno district, including the period 1919-1942. She digs out three documents, which Maria translates for us. The first document is the death certificate of Izrael Kartus, the grandfather. He died on 31 August 1920 in Pławno. The document indicates that at some time he moved from Żarki to Pławno, probably because he wanted to be with his son Moszek Kalma in his old age and live closer to the family of his wife Minka Ruchla Kuperberg who also lived there. The second document is the death certificate of Minka, Ide's grandmother, who died in Pławno on 26 October 1936.

Jolanta tells us that she found no other death certificates. That is important for our research. It means that Ide's father, Moszek Kalma Kartuz, and his second wife Fajgl Kuperberg, and his brothers, sisters and cousins who lived in Pławno, were still alive in 1942 and that none of them died there.

The third document is the marriage certificate of Ide Leib Kartuz to Hela Artman on 22 March 1929, who then changed her name to Chaja Artman. In a beautiful, old manuscript the document states that Ide is a tailor and that it is a 'Hasidic marriage', which means that they are married according to strict Orthodox Jewish rules. That seems bizarre because, on the photo that Ide submitted for his travel pass, he doesn't look like an orthodox Jew. One post-war document indicates that Ide's stepmother was very religious, but that he did not follow these practices. Perhaps that explains his flight from Poland and his secular way of thinking as soon as he arrived in Antwerp.

From the town hall we go on to the Gidle library. We hope that the librarian there can help us to find out more about the Jewish history of the region. She cannot give us a conclusive answer as to where Ide attended school. Possibly he was at the *yeshiva* in Pławno, a religious school founded by rabbi Yitzhak Rabinowitz. But the old Catholic school was also a possibility. Up to a certain age, Jewish children were also obliged to go to lessons there. Most of them dropped out of school at the age of 14 and then became an apprentice with a family member who had a lot of experience in a certain craft. In Ide's case it may have been an uncle of his father who taught him the skills to be a tailor. That seems plausible because in this region, south of the textile city of Lódz, there were many Jewish tailors.

The librarian dismisses the generally accepted view that Poles and Jews lived at odds with each other. 'People of various religions lived here in peace,' she says, adding that discrimination against the Jews only started here after the Germans invaded. We doubt it.

The next place we visit is Żarki in the province of Silesia, about forty-five kilometres south of Pławno and fifty kilometres west of Katowice. Almost all of Ide's family came from here: his father, his two grandparents, great-grandparents and so on back to 1751. As a result, the vast majority of his uncles, aunts, nephews and nieces lived in Żarki. Before the war 2,500 Jews lived here, more than half of the total population.

We are warmly received by Katarzyna Kulińska-Pluta from the tourist office. She has searched the registry office for documents that mention the Kartuz family, but they are not there. To find these we have to go to the State Archive in the city of Częstochowa. Here we learn a lot more about Jewish life before the war, because the city is closely connected to Jewish culture: from the seventeenth century to the Second World War, Jews made up the majority of the population.

During the interbellum the city was a melting pot of people with various social, economic, religious and cultural backgrounds. They lived together and mixed with each other, and spoke different languages such as Polish, German, Hebrew, Yiddish and Russian. The photos of the market day in honour of St Stanislaus, which took place between the two world wars from 1 to 9 May each year, show how farmers from the area inspect, buy and sell animals as well as dozens of stands where artisans trade their wares and crowds of people shopping or just looking around out of curiosity.[4] During the year there was also a regular market every Wednesday that attracted both Poles and Jews. The two groups, however, largely lived separately. The Catholics had a church at the top of the Old Market and the Jews two synagogues, the larger of which was just around the corner. Jews bought their meat from the kosher butcher and their children went to the Hebrew school. Each group also had its own cemetery.

Wojtek Mszycca is our local guide and, like Maria, a member of the Forum for Dialogue. He is a Christian, but is actively committed to preserving the Jewish heritage in and around the city. He walks with us along the Old Market Square and the adjacent streets, where almost all the houses belonged to the Jews before the war. In 1921 they ran eighty-nine stores, workshops and small factories. Just about half of those were in the clothing industry. Mszyca shows us the book *Jewish Żarki, Lost photographs* by Polish photographer Josef Bacior. He survived the war and had a house near a forest in Żarki.

Most of his photographs were taken between 1937 and 1942, and show how the inhabitants of the town spent their free time in the green area behind Bacior's house. In numerous pre-war photographs we see not only simply dressed farmers and salesmen, but also nicely dressed and well assimilated Jewish townspeople. But other, less affluent, people are also wearing stylish shirts, trousers, cardigans and shoes. It is as if the entire city is benefiting from the creativity and productivity of the Jewish clothing industry. According to Wojtek there is a good chance that Ide's family members had a tailor workshop there, and that Ide received some sort of training there. In cramped spaces at the backs of the houses on the road to Chestochowa, young Jews learned the craft of the shoemaker, milliner and tailor. In so doing, they continued a tradition that had existed for centuries and that gave young newcomers the opportunity make something of their lives.

Ide, too, therefore, must have sat at a tailor's table from a young age, with a tape measure around his neck and with grey chalk in his hand. Tailors draw the patterns that they have to cut out with this. The photo of his travel pass to Belgium shows that he clearly got the hang of his craft. He is wearing an expensive fur collar, a stylish shirt with matching tie, a nice overcoat and a classic hat. We don't know if he made those clothes himself, but it does show that he took pride in his appearance, or even that he had ambition.

Here he met Chaja (Hela) Artman – probably through family. A beautiful, proud woman of Chassidic origin from Pławno, he married her and together they moved to a house in Pławno, near his parental home in 27a Młynarska. They appear to have followed the religious customs of their parents and ancestors, but in 1929 Ide decided to move away. Perhaps because he wanted to leave the suffocating traditional community behind, perhaps because of latent anti-Semitism, perhaps because the socio-economic situation was so bad and he barely made any money. Or, possibly, a combination of all three.

Częstochowa

We drive through Polish forests and watch buzzards and crows compete with each other in the sky. We believe that they symbolize the struggle between Jews and Poles in the country. After about an hour we reach Częstochowa, a city with more than a quarter of a million inhabitants, almost all Catholics today. On a hill near the city is the church of the Pauline Monastery with the famous Black Madonna. The painting shows the Virgin Mary with baby Jesus on her lap. Every year millions of pilgrims from all parts of the country come to see this work of art. Pope Saint John Paul II, the Polish Karol Wojtyła, also visited it during the communist period. The current pope, Francis, led an open-air mass there in 2016. He named Częstochowa the 'spiritual capital' of Poland.[5]

In the 1930s the city consisted of a majority of Catholics but also counted more than 30 per cent Jews, many of whom worked in the textile and food industries. From 1935 tensions with the Poles increased. This led to boycotts of Jewish shops and businesses, and even to small and larger pogroms in and around the city. The historian Yehuda Bauer describes the Częstochowa from just before the Second World War as 'a bastion of radical Catholic anti-Semitism. A local newspaper [*Ganiec Częstochowski*] from the *Endecja* published a list of Jewish homes that had not yet been looted.'[6] On 19 June 1937 a three-day pogrom took place under the impetus of Polish nationalists. Frenzied, bitter anti-Semitic citizens demolished dozens of Jewish shops and set fire to the local synagogue.

Once in the city, we immediately look for the State Archives. According to our sources, birth, marriage and death records can be found there for the entire Kartuz family. They could tell us more about relatives from Żarki, Gidle and Pławno. A large Polish flag flies next to a modernist building. That must be the State Archives. We are greeted by Michał Mszyca, the state archivist. He tells us that we can only request one document at a time. We can only touch them with white gloves, and wearing these we turn over the fragile, almost crushed sheets. We are ready for a journey into the deep past that is hidden between the letters, words and sentences written more than 150 years ago. We are not allowed to take photos with a flash. Michał shows us some timeworn books that we are allowed to go through carefully, document by document. The first dates from 1846. It contains the birth certificate of Berek Kartus, drawn up in Polish, with signatures under a Yiddish text. In that period Poland was a subject region of Russia, although the registry office still used Polish as its administrative language. The tsar imposed the use of Russian from 1867 to 1915. Berek was born in Żarki on 8 April 1846 and was the paternal grandfather of Ide. Below that we see that Berek was the son of Abram Kartus, who was also born in Żarki. Although Michał speaks Russian quite well, he has great difficulty reading the papers that follow. They are written in an ornate Old Russian handwriting. He translates the sentences for Maria into Polish and she translates for us into English.

It promises to be a long morning. But the time-consuming work yields some interesting results. The second document is from 1885. It is the birth certificate of Moszek Kalma Kartuz, the son of Berek, and Ide's father. He is also from Żarki. Strangely, here the name Kartuz ends with a 'z', while before it always ended with the letter 's'. The third deed dates from 1904. It mentions a marriage between Moszek Kalma Kartuz and Sura Kartuz on 9 October 1904. Moszek was 19 at the time and came from Pławno. His bride Sura was 20 and the daughter of Izrael Kartuz and Minka Rucha Kuperberg. She, too, was from Pławno. According to the document the marriage took place in the same village. Because almost the entire family came from Żarki, Michał says that there must have been a large group of relatives from Żarki at the wedding party.

The fourth document, which dates from 18 September 1905, is Ide Leib Kartuz's birth certificate. Father Moszek Kalma and mother Sura were both 20 at the time. The place of birth is Плавно, Cyrillic for Pławno. We carry on looking for the names of his cousins and come up trumps, the birth certificate of one Sura Kuperberg dated 16 March 1920. She was the daughter of Lejbus Kuperberg and Chaja Kartuz, who is the daughter of Moszek Kalma. So Sura was Ide's cousin. The certificate said she was born in Pławno.

When we get back to our hotel in Radomsko we find a message on our laptop from Michael Danziger who has gone through the documents on the CRARG website for us. 'Documents show that Moszek [Ide's father] was a salesman, but we found an interesting report that tells us that in 1929 he owned a *haberdashery* shop with a man called L. Guterman.' A haberdashery shop in British English sells articles for sewing like threads and yarns. In the United States, where Michael lives, it is the name for a men's clothing shop. His message raises new questions. Moszek, who came from Żarki, where many Jews worked in the textile industry, probably traded fabrics, yarns, buttons or other things used in tailoring. This backs up our theory that Ide grew up in this world of textiles and learned the craft there. But why did he leave his hometown in that same year? Why didn't he continue to work under his father's wing?

War

On 1 September 1939, at a quarter to five in the morning, sixty divisions with 1,800,000 German soldiers invaded Poland. On 17 September 1939 the Soviets struck from the east. It immediately became clear that the Nazi army had violated the international rules of war, as laid down in the Geneva Convention. Members of the SS, and also of the

Ordnungspolizei and the Wehrmacht, set fire to cities and villages, murdered thousands of Polish civilians, both Catholics and Jews, and raped women and girls. During the period to 25 October 1939 when Poland was governed by the Wehrmacht, German troops joined forces with the *Schutzstaffel* (SS) and the police in what Polish historians have called 'a merciless and systematic campaign of biological destruction. 531 Polish towns and villages were destroyed during this period of military rule. The provinces of Łodź and Warsaw suffered the heaviest losses.'[7] The invasion of Poland marked the start of the destruction of the Jews outside of Germany.

In a photo dated September 1939, we see a train with German soldiers who are ready to leave for the Polish front. On the outside wall of a carriage there are anti-Semitic images and the text *Wir fahren nach Poland, um Juden zu versohlen* [We are going to Poland to beat the hell out of Jews]. The soldiers knew the reasons they were being sent to areas populated largely by Jews. Numerous testimonies show that this was the first encounter for many German soldiers with the *Ostjuden*, Jews who, unlike in their *heimat,* had not assimilated and also differed in appearance to the local population. They were mostly poorly dressed Orthodox Jews with kaftans, beards and sidelocks. The Germans portrayed them as the enemy in Nazi newspapers and propaganda films. *Jud Süss* and *Der ewige Jude* are two typical examples. There are many photos of smiling SS men cutting the hair and beards of Orthodox Jews in Poland. To them they were *Untermenschen*, inferior beings.

Weeks before the invasion of Poland, Hitler had instructed the Reichsführer of the SS, Heinrich Himmler, to form special death squads that had to kill any opposition behind the front line. The *Einsatzgruppen* were instructed to kill Polish intelligentsia, Jews or so-called 'partisans' who had been resisting the invasion. In reality, the Poles and Jews were therefore outlawed. On 7 October 1939 Hitler also appointed Himmler as Reich Commissioner for the Consolidation of German Nationhood. The aim was to deport the *Untermenschen*, the Poles and Jews, from the areas annexed by Germany to make way for the settlement of Germans and *Volksdeutsche* [ethnic Germans]. The *Volksdeutsche* and other non-Jews often took the farms and houses of the expelled and murdered Jews.

The killing happened in different ways. In many places people were randomly killed with a shot to the neck. As revenge for a killed or wounded German soldier, dozens of innocent Poles were taken from their homes to be executed on the spot with machine guns. Between 15 and 18 October 1939, almost 200 psychiatric patients were taken from a hospital in Owińska to the *Konzentrationslager* Fort VII in Poznań. The SS – led by Rudolf Lange, who later attended the Wannsee Conference – poisoned the patients with carbon-monoxide gas that was dispersed from steel cylinders into a small plain space. The historian Richard Evans calls it the first mass murder in history through the use of a gas chamber.[8] In the end, around 15,000 people were exterminated here. During this period the Nazis experimented with new killing methods. The greatest emphasis was on efficiency and, more importantly, on a way to get rid of people (almost) invisibly.

The cities where Ide's family members lived were some of the first to suffer in the war. On 2 September 1939 Żarki came under heavy bombing from the Luftwaffe. They hit large parts of the city and destroyed many houses. Some residents fled to nearby forests, others hid in cellars, but 200 of them died instantly. A Jewish survivor, Jacob Fisher from Żarki, described this air attack as follows:

> German planes flew over. Suddenly we heard the explosion of a bomb. Everything around us became black with smoke and dust from the collapsing houses. The bombing lasted only a few minutes, but destroyed part of the city in one fell swoop. Fear and panic erupted. Everyone ran like crazy ... . The streets were covered with glass from broken windows. Everywhere lay corpses, dead horses, cows and overturned cars. Dozens of people were buried under the buildings.[9]

Meanwhile, the Wehrmacht with German Army Groups 8 and 10, led by Colonel General Gerd von Rundstedt, marched from the south to the cities of Łodź, Katowice and Krakow. On 3 September the Nazi troops occupied Żarki, where they arrested 102 people, especially Jews, and shot them. Soldiers looted the houses and then set them on fire. Before they blew up the factories with dynamite, they removed the machines. The soldiers loaded other usable items such as school desks into train wagons destined for Germany.[10]

A day later the existing Jewish self-governing officers were removed and the occupiers ordered the formation of a *Judenrat* (Jewish Council). This council had to unconditionally comply with and implement the orders of the Nazis. Jews were not allowed to leave the city and had to wear an armband with the six-sided Star of David on it. A Star of David was also painted on the windows and walls of Jewish houses, shops and factories, accompanied by the word JUDE. In the days that followed Jewish men, in forced labour, had to clear up the rubble of destroyed buildings and roads. They also had to repair or rebuild the houses running along the Old Market.

Concentrating Jews forcibly in ghettos from 1941 was a deliberate policy of the Nazis and took place in just about all Polish towns and villages. The aim was to isolate, identify and fully control them. In Warsaw 450,000 Jews were packed into an area of some 400 hectares, barely 2.4 per cent of the total area of the city. 'It was surrounded by three-meter high walls with thirteen heavily guarded entrances,' says historian Herman Vandormael, who describes the function of the ghetto as follows: 'The idea is for the Jews to be isolated, for the ghettos to be self-sufficient, to facilitate forced labour for the occupiers, and for as many people as possible to die.'[11] In Łodź, 160,000 Jews and 5,000 Roma Gypsies were housed in a few streets in the old town and the neighbouring Baluty district. Due to poor living conditions and an increasing lack of food, heating and medicine, thousands of them died, children first.

In smaller towns and in many villages Jews were similarly forced to live in a well-defined area, all with a view to the *Endlösung der Judenfrage* (Final Solution of the Jewish Question). Zarki's ghetto was located in a number of connected houses in the city centre, on the Old Market Square. It was considered an 'open ghetto' because it was not fenced off as in other cities, but its boundaries were demarcated by warning signs that made it clear to the Jews that they were not allowed to leave without permission – otherwise they would be shot. Numbering nearly 3,000, the surviving Jews were forced to live in buildings that were far too small. They were cold and hungry, had no medicine, and were at the mercy of the Germans. 'Healthy' men were selected on a daily basis to do forced labour. The elderly, women and children lived in appalling conditions, among them Ide's relatives. His grandparents, uncles, aunts, nephews and nieces could not go anywhere.

Częstochowa also suffered badly in the war. On 3 September 1939 the Werhmacht invaded with little opposition. Three days of killings and looting in the city followed. German soldiers from the regular army, not

SS men, arrested Poles and Jews and then randomly shot about 200 of them. They then drove thousands of Polish and Jewish citizens out of their homes and forced them to march to Magnacki Square opposite the cathedral. There, under the threat of a gun, they had to lie face down on the ground. Whoever moved was shot. In total there were around 10,000 people lying there, including many elderly people, women and children. In the end, nearly 1,000 men were killed.[12] The old synagogue was completely destroyed and Jewish schools were closed.

A Judenrat was also set up here on 1 October, after which the situation somewhat normalised although both Poles and Jews were still randomly murdered afterwards. The Germans increasingly targeted the Jews. They were humiliated, abused and robbed of their property. Anti-Semitism from the Poles increased. A delegation from the Catholic population of Częstochowa filed a petition with Governor General Hans Frank. In it they asked that all Jews be put in a ghetto. On 9 April 1941 the Nazis decided to set up an enclosed Jewish neighbourhood in the city. Other Jews from neighbouring towns and villages were added, including those from Żarki, which left it full beyond capacity. Soon more than 40,000 Jews were packed in together. Inside the ghetto the Nazis set up labour camps and turned former textile companies into munitions' factories where the Jews worked under forced labour. There was a sense of relief about this though because they believed that their importance to arms production would spare them from death.

However, the living conditions were harsh. In a report dated April 1942 from the Jewish self-help organisation we read: 'Thousands of children have not been able to get education for three years now. The housing conditions are usually dreadful. The houses are extremely crowded with an average of 5.85 people per room.'[13] The food also ran out. Fortunately, people were still able to smuggle in food, but the situation became ever more difficult and desperate.

After Żarki and Częstochowa, the German troops advanced farther south-east. The little *sjtetls* fell into their hands. Soldiers of the Wehrmacht captured Pławno on 4 September 1939 where the parents, brothers and sisters of Ide lived, along with about 460 other Jews. The Germans reduced the local synagogue to ashes and immediately shot dead Rabbi Rabinowitz and six other Jews. They tortured other residents. They later enslaved the younger, skilled Jews to excavate the channel of the Warta river. They were not allowed to go home in the evening. They spent their nights in nearby, cold and dirty farm stables. Among them were probably Ide's two brothers, the 32-year-old Abram and the 26-year-old Zyskind, and his 15-year-old half-brother Chaim.

In the first year of the occupation, Poles and Jews were still allowed to meet and do business. From the end of November 1939, however, the Jews of Pławno were also required to wear a white armband with a Star of David. That made them immediately identifiable. As the war progressed the living conditions of the Jews deteriorated. They barely had any money to buy food and care for the sick, there was a lack of sanitary facilities and the housing situation remained terrible.

In the archive in Gidle we take photos and copies of the correspondence of the Judenrat of the municipality of Pławno-Gidle and of the management of the *Jüdische Soziale Hilfe* JUS (Jewish Social Self-Help Organization) in Krakow. The latter was responsible for supplying and distributing medicines, food and clothing to the *sjtetls* in need.[14] The money for this came from Jewish associations in the United States, among others. With Maria we work on the translation well into the night, motivated by adrenaline and the desire to be able to put together new pieces of the puzzle.

The first letter, dated 11 April 1940, is from the Judenrat and addressed to the JUS in Krakow. It contains a list of destitute people from Pławno and tells of the miserable conditions in the Jewish communities in the villages. There was a great shortage of basic necessities such as food, as well as medicines and money. The Krakow reply is bureaucratic. 'We have received your request for help and will look into your concerns.' A second letter on 19 July 1940 repeats the request for help. Just like the previous one, it is written by hand and in Polish. Maria reads it out loud and is impressed by the beautiful handwriting. Similar requests for help follow on 19 July 1940, 7 October 1940 and 1 February 1941. Maria's translation sounds technical, but the words are dramatic. Whatever tone she uses to read out loud, we feel the depth of suffering of the Pławno community. 'Since the beginning of the war we received no money or other help. We are deeply affected by the situation. Orphans and poor people are starving. We ask for food and clothing for the poorest children. Help us!' On 31 July 1941 Icek Spaltyn, president of the *Judenrat* in Pławno, begged for help, but the answer was negative. Another letter was sent on 17 August 1941 requesting help and medication. This time the mayor of Pławno emphasised the urgency. Krakow responded in a business-like, almost indifferent, manner, and asked them to draw up a list of the medicines they needed. After sending the list, the small Jewish community in Pławno did receive medication, but it was no more than some dressings and aspirin. One more letter dated 25 August 1941 talks about 300 Jews in an open labour camp. They were all ill.

By 18 September 1941 the inhabitants of the village were no longer able to care for the sick. 'The nearest doctor is 10 kilometres away and we have no money for treatment,' they said. A few days later, 300 złoty [about £65 today] arrived from Krakow. Even for this small community that sum was totally inadequate. 'Thank you for the 300 złoty, but we now have more people who are ill. The cost of treatment at the Radomsko hospital amount to more than 1,000 złoty. We are unable to cover the cost for the sick.' The lack of food was also becoming more acute. On 30 October 1941 the council sent a letter to the JUS saying that they were no longer able to feed the 460 inhabitants and begged them to send food in kind. 'We don't have enough food. We need help.' On 28 November 1941 the Plawno Judenrat received the sum of 400 złoty from the American Joint Distribution Committee to buy food; but that, too, was insufficient. The situation worsened in December 1941. A new decree imposed by the Germans stated that the Jews were no longer allowed to leave the village, which meant that they could no longer trade with nor buy food from the farmers nearby. People now had to smuggle to survive, but if you were caught you were shot. T*he* Judenrat received 300 złoty from the JUS on two further occasions but then notice was sent that there was no more money. The Jews had to fend for themselves.

The last letter is no longer written in beautiful handwriting and the style is less dignified. It leaves a lump in our throats. There is no doubting that the writer had no strength, courage or even hope left to write a formal letter. The letter is powerfully worded, full of crossings out and exclamation marks, inscribed forcefully onto the page with a pen. We are all silent. Never before have any of us felt so close to the suffering in a small village eighty years ago, the village where Ide grew up and where his parents, brothers and sisters lived.

When the Nazis began to establish ghettos for all Jews at the end of 1941, the mayor of Pławno wrote, with the agreement of the SS, that it was not possible in Pławno.

It is impossible to create a Jewish neighbourhood (ghetto) within this local community because the municipality has 460 Jews and the village itself is too small to accommodate this crowd in one place. Moreover, we cannot displace the farmers who live here from their homes and farms. The only option is to transfer the Jews to the ghetto of Radomsko.[15]

Instead of this, the Jews living in Pławno were restricted to the confines of the village. Those who strayed too far from home were shot or arrested and 'tried' by the Germans. In a letter to Krakow dated 3 March 1942, the president of the Judenrat writes that eight residents were imprisoned for stealing potatoes from outside the village. Their case would go to trial. One of these eight was Sura Kuperberg, one of Ide's younger cousins. We came across documents referring to her mock trial during our research at the Czestochova archive. On 29 January 1942 she had left the area around Pławno, or rather she had fled. But a month later the Nazis arrested her. Official Nazi stamps confirmed that 'as a Jew she had left her assigned neighbourhood without permission', hence she received the death penalty. She was executed on 30 April at 5:00 a.m.

In September 1942, to have even greater control over the remaining Pławno Jews, the Nazis decided to send them to the ghetto in Radomsko. The Judenrat received an order:

The relocation of the Jews in Pławno to the Jewish neighbourhood in the city of Radomsko must take place on 22 September 1942 before 6:00 p.m. The Jews must take all their belongings and equipment with them. The houses will then be appropriated by the police. No Jew is allowed to remain in the village after the 22nd.

All the Jews, including the surviving relatives of Ide, prepared themselves. They collected up their scant possessions, put them in suitcases and left for Radomsko. Among the deportees were Ide's father, brothers, sister and other relatives. In that same period, a large group of Jews from the ghetto in Zarki was transferred to Radomsko. Several of Ide's relatives were amongst them too.

Radomsko

After conducting our research in Pławno, Gidle, Żarki and Częstochowa we go back to our hotel in Radomsko. There we meet Rachel Lea Kesselman, President-Founder of the first Jewish open-air museum in Europe in 2014. Rachel is a young, dynamic and, above all, lively creature. The Kesselman Museum in Radomsko is her life's work. With the museum she keeps the history of the Jews in this city alive and, in this way, she hopes to be able to warn young people in particular about the dangers of racism, fascism and anti-Semitism. She is the daughter of Henry Kesselman, a devout Jew from Radomsko, who survived the horrors of the Holocaust. Rachel was born in Nice in France, studied in Israel, and lived in Tel Aviv, Los Angeles and Buenos Aires. Having met Elie Wiesel and Stephen Smith of the Spielberg Shoah Foundation, she decided to return to Poland and set up this museum in honour of her father. She rents a studio in the hotel and is busy day in, day out. It's nice to see her getting people interested in her story and in her projects. She is fluent in Polish, Yiddish, Hebrew, French and English. She is surprised that Maria, who accompanies us, also speaks Hebrew.

Rachel tells us with as much sorrow as passion about the sad fate of the Jews who lived here. Radomsko is twelve kilometres north of Pławno and today is a city with almost 50,000 inhabitants. It lies along the busy railway line that runs from Katowice in the south to Lódz. Before the war, more than half of the population here was Jewish too. At the outbreak of the Second World War on 1 September 1939 the city, seventy kilometres from the German border, was the first to be bombed at 5 o'clock in the morning. The main targets were the central market and some local factories. Nearly half of the buildings on the Main Square, where Jews in particular lived, were destroyed. Hundreds of Jewish victims were killed. Polish anti-Semites looted the stores and warehouses while they burned. Two days later, on 3 September 1939 at 11:00 am, the Wehrmacht invaded and immediately began its brutal repression.

A number of Jews have recounted their stories about these dramatic developments in Radomsko. They are immortalised in the *Rodomsko Yizkor Book*.[16] The occupiers set a curfew immediately after the invasion. Jews were only allowed on the street between 8:00 am and 7:00 pm. Their shops and factories had to close down. A day later, many Jews in the more affluent areas were forced to leave their homes to make way for ethnic German (*Volksdeutsche*) families. In a rogue operation, members of the Gestapo, with the help of a group of Poles, dragged Jewish men out of their homes and gathered them on the central market square. They cut off the beard of some older Jews. Others were humiliated, kicked and heavily abused.[17] On 9 October announcements were placed on the walls of the city that all Jewish men between the ages of 15 and 60 had to register at the local sports stadium. Anyone who refused would be given the death penalty. Through this registration the Germans knew exactly where the Jews lived and who was living at each address. This way they didn't overlook women, children, parents and other relatives.

On 31 October the Nazis imposed the wearing of badges. Jews became recognisable by fabric patches and a large letter J. 'J' for *Jude*. This made Radomsko the first city where Jews were forced to wear an identification badge. The new *Judenrat* was then also forced to carry out the orders of the occupiers and to supply workers for the German war industry. At 6:00 am on 20 December 1939, announcements appeared on the walls in both German and Polish, that the Nazis had created a ghetto within a few streets in the centre of the city. Radomsko was to become Poland's second ghetto. That same day, about 10,000 Jews had to leave their homes and join the Jews who already lived in the demarcated area. The elderly, women, children, the sick and the disabled also went into the designated neighbourhood with their meagre possessions in suitcases. Some pushed carts or wheelbarrows to their new homes. They often lived with other families in single rooms, attics or in cellars.

Many Poles watched as bystanders to these events and even welcomed them. At the entrances to the ghetto, SS men seized any useful possessions from the Jews. Money, jewellery, even furniture and bedding did not enter the ghetto. At the same time SS officers and *Volksdeutsche* would be checking whether the Jews had actually left their homes or shops outside the ghetto. If they found someone they beat them severely. Some of them, however, had already fled to the forests in the area and were hiding there, Henry Kesselman being one of these. After a few days the Nazis placed white signs with red letters at the entrance to the ghetto: 'This is the ghetto. Entering is strictly prohibited. For Jews, leaving the ghetto without permission of the city commander is strictly prohibited.'[18]

The year 1940 started with a very harsh winter. The country was in the grip of freezing temperatures and snow showers. For the ghetto, this quickly led to a serious shortage of heating material, food and medicines. A newly established committee opened people's kitchens, where poor and starving Jews could eat and drink something. The committee received money for this from wealthy families who had already lived in this closed-off neighbourhood before the ghetto was created, and also from Jews who had smuggled money and jewellery into the ghetto. With the permission of the Germans the committee bought the food from Poles, who made a lot of money from it.[19] The *Judenrat* had its own police force that maintained order and guarded the exits and had to send workers to the work stations. Work stations were often sewing workshops in the ghetto. One of the Nazis' requirements, because of harsh winters, was that the streets be kept clear of snow. During one of those winters, a typhoid epidemic broke out in Radomsko. Both Poles and Jews died as a result, but due to the miserable living conditions the impact was much greater in the ghetto. It wasn't until April 1940 that the Germans provided typhus and dysentery vaccines because they were afraid that the diseases would also infect their soldiers.

The ghetto also had its own postal service. Jews were no longer allowed to make phone calls or send telegrams, but were allowed to send and receive letters and packages. These were often seized. At the beginning of June 1940 the Germans deported large groups of Jews from Lódz and other cities to the ghetto in Radomsko. The *Judenrat* had to take care of thousands, mostly weak and sick people, for whom there was barely any room left. They, too, had to wear a white armband with a blue Star of David. Cynically, they had to pay for these themselves.[20] By the end of 1940 the living conditions in the ghetto had worsened. Once more many residents were dying of typhus and other epidemics due to a lack of doctors and medicines. Slowly, but inexorably, people were starving to death due to the lack of food, which each day became evermore serious. In December 1941 the Jews were forced to hand over all their fur on pain of death. During the terrible winter of 1941-1942, numerous exhausted, starved and scantily clad Jews froze to death. Others fled and hid in the forests in the outskirts.

At the end of September 1942 the Germans ordered a further reduction in the size of the ghetto, leaving even less habitable space. The decision led to heartbreaking scenes of Jews evicted from their homes trying to find somewhere to live with their neighbours. Nevertheless, in this late summer of 1942, the Nazis were cramming still more Jews from surrounding towns and villages, including Pławno, Gidle and Żarki, into the overpopulated ghetto in Radomsko. Now all the surviving relatives of Ide, including his parents, were trapped in this futureless hell. Perhaps some of them had only survived until then because they had been useful to the occupiers as tailors or manual workers. Those skills no longer had any value in Radomsko. The final solution was imminent.

Endlösung der Judenfrage

It remains unclear when the Nazis decided to wipe out the entire Jewish population of Europe. Some historians follow the 'intentionalist' view of the Holocaust, namely that Hitler had had the intention to exterminate the Jewish people from the start of his political career. To back up this theory they reference a number of passages from his book *Mein Kampf* and his infamous speech of 30 January 1939:

> If the international Jewish financiers in and outside Europe should succeed in plunging the nations once more into a world war, then the result will not be the Bolshevization of the earth, and thus the victory of Jewry, but the annihilation of the Jewish race in Europe!

From the beginning of the war the Nazis gave orders to systematically kill Jews, making it evident that they were targeting them. Yet most historians follow the 'functionalist' view, which assumes that the extermination of the Jews developed into a definitive plan over the course of the Nazi regime. Even before the war, the Nazis tried to get a better grip on the Jews and to separate them from the German population. With hindsight we can now see the progression of events from the boycott of Jewish shops in Germany on 1 April 1933, the Nuremberg race laws on 15 September 1935 and the *Kristallnacht* of 9 November 1938. In the *Kristallnacht* pogrom, 267 synagogues and Jewish almshouses went up in flames, thousands of shops and businesses were destroyed, and houses, schools, and cemeteries were vandalised and destroyed. Large numbers of Jews were assaulted and killed. During the September 1939

21

invasion of Poland, the Nazi leadership ordered the murder of Polish intellectuals.[21] By the spring of 1940 more than 60,000 of them had already been killed, but the Jews were then increasingly targeted by the *Einsatzgruppen* operating behind the front.

The killings increased even more in 1941 when Nazi Germany invaded the Soviet Union. The invasion went so smoothly that it was expected that the Red Army would be conquered within twelve weeks. However, once the offensive had failed and the attack was halted, the slaughter of the innocent escalated.[22] The Wehrmacht had free rein to kill at random thanks to the Barbarossa Decree, which had been issued on 13 May 1941 by Field Marshal Wilhelm Keitel: 'Actions committed by members of the Wehrmacht and its supporting personnel against enemy civilians cannot be a matter for prosecution, even when those actions constitute a military crime or offence.'[23] Jews were often equated with the partisans who attacked the German troops behind the front and who could be killed as war enemies without any form of trial. The mass slaughter of Jews after the invasion of Russia became more systematic and on a much larger scale. Wherever the Germans captured towns and villages, they killed countless men, women and children, mercilessly. By the end of 1941 more than 600,000 Jews had been killed in the Soviet territories captured by the Germans. Yet Hitler still did not have a well-defined plan at that time. According to leading historian Saul Friedländer, the Führer wanted to wait for this final victory before deciding what should ultimately happen to the Jews.[24]

The outline plans for the systematic murder of Jews were now clearly in place. Hitler wanted to rid Europe of the Jews. Initially there was a plan to deport them to the African island of Madagascar, but that soon proved to have practical difficulties. In January 1941 the plan was to move hundreds of thousands of European Jews to the *Generalgouvernement* in occupied Poland. The plan to deport Jews to a sort of colony behind the Ural Mountains after a quick victory over the Soviet Union fell apart at the end of 1941. The Jews in regions formerly under Russian control suffered the most. Historian Yehuda Bauer investigated the situation in the Kresy (Eastern Borderlands), situated between Poland, Ukraine, Lithuania and Belarus. The area had been occupied by the Soviets since 17 September 1939 under the Molotov-Ribbentrop pact. In June 1941 it was recaptured by the Nazis.[25] The *Judenräte* had to supply specific numbers of people for forced labour. In addition to this the Germans demanded jewels and money from the Jews. They confiscated their furniture, clothing and household items and made their homes available to the non-Jewish population. Farmers from the surrounding villages collected the Jewish possessions by horse and cart. Nobody cared. The Jews were to be exterminated anyway. The vast majority of the Christian population was indifferent to the atrocities. Some even approved of the violence. Almost nobody wanted to help the Jews. Local farmers asked them for money to help them go into hiding, but then simply handed them over to the police. In extreme cases, farmers who had borrowed money from Jewish people they had hidden would then murder them. The killing of Polish Jews continued and increased with entire Jewish communities in the occupied territories being systematically wiped out.

Einsatzkommandos which originally had 3,000 SS men, used to end the lives of countless Jews with a gunshot. They were often helped by so-called *Hilfswilliger* or 'willing helpers', especially Latvians, Lithuanians and Ukrainians. Thousands of Jews were killed in a brutal way in a forest near the Lithuanian capital of Vilnius. Members of the Wehrmacht described the violent manner in which the Catholic Lithuanians in Kovno at the end of June 1941 killed the Jewish inhabitants with clubs and iron bars. Lithuanian women were applauding at the front with their children as they sang their national anthem. In just a few days, 4,000 Jews were murdered in this way. The SS officers called it spontaneous *Selbstreinigungsaktionen* (self-cleaning actions).[26] A similar operation took place on 10 July 1941 in the towns of Radziłów and Jedwabne in eastern Poland, which was captured by the Germans from the Soviets. 'After the Wehrmacht occupied the area, the inhabitants of these small towns exterminated most of their Jewish neighbours by beating them, shooting them, and burning scores or them alive in local barns.'[27]

By the beginning of July 1941 Ukrainian nationalists had killed more than 5,000 Jews in Lwów. To the south of Kiev, in the town of Tserkov, on 20 August 1941, Ukrainian auxiliary troops helped in the slaughter of ninety Jewish orphans under the age of five. The parents had already been killed. The German SS officer August Häfner described the massacre as follows:

> I went to the forest on my own. The Wehrmacht had already dug a pit. The children were brought by tractor.

The Ukrainians were quaking in their boots. The children were taken out of the vehicle. They were put next to the pit and shot so that they fell into it. The wailing was indescribable ... . What I remember most is a little blonde girl who took me by the hand. She was shot too.[28]

The German *SS-Obergruppenführer* Friedrich Jeckeln was generally known as one of the cruellest mass murderers. He came up with the sickening *Sardinenpackung* or sardine packing, which was later adopted by many murder squads. The first layer of victims lying at the bottom of a deep pit was shot. Then a new group of people was forced to lie down on top of the corpses, and were in turn shot. It went on like this until the pit was completely filled, after which a layer of earth was thrown over the corpses. Jeckeln had his men, assisted by Hungarian soldiers and the Ukrainian Auxiliary Police, murder 23,600 Jews in the city of Kamjanets-Podilsky on 27 and 28 August 1941. Farther south there were other huge mass exterminations. *Einsatzgruppe D*, led by *SS- Oberführer* Otto Ohlendorf, was responsible for 90,000 deaths. In the port area of Odessa Romanian troops, who fought alongside the Germans, killed many more Jews. After that they had their sights set on other towns and villages. 'Over a one-year period the Romanians were to massacre between 280,000 and 380,000 Jews.'[29]

One of the most detailed reports of the mass exterminations is that of *SS-Standartenführer* Karl Jäger, commander of *Einsatzkommando 3a*, a sub-unit of *Einsatzgruppe A*. He kept a very accurate record of the numbers of murdered Jewish men, Jewish women, Jewish children, communists, Polish and Russian prisoners of war, the disabled and others in Lithuania, Latvia, Estonia and Belarus for the period from 4 July 1941 to 25 November 1941. His astonishing nine-page list shows how the killing machine worked day after day. On 1 September 1941, the kommando went on a rampage in the Lithuanian city of Marijampolė. The army gathered together the Jews and locked them up in horse stables. The strongest men had to dig eight graves of 100- to 150-metres long, 4-metres wide and 5-metres deep. After every Jew had undressed, first the men had to lie in the pits in groups of 100 to 200 where they were machine-gunned to death. When they were all dead, the women and the children were next. They had to lie down on the warm corpses of their men or fathers, after which they were executed in the same way. Many of them were only wounded and were buried alive. After being covered with earth, a dull groaning was heard for hours. Jäger noted in his diary that on that day, namely 1 September 1941, 1,763 Jewish men, 1,812 Jewish women, 1,404 Jewish children, 109 mentally ill, a German woman who was married to a Jew, and a Russian were exterminated, a total of 5,090 people.[30]

On 29 October 1941 a *Grosse Aktion* (Big action) took place in the Lithuanian city of Kovno where 2,007 Jewish men, 2,920 Jewish women and 4,273 Jewish children, a total of 9,200 people from the ghetto, were murdered.[31] And so it went on in every city and every village, often with the help of the local population. In less than five months 57,338 Jewish men, 48,592 Jewish women, 29,461 Jewish children and 2,058 unidentified people were killed, 137,346 people in total. Jäger wrote at the end of his report: 'Today I can confirm that our goal, the solution to the Jewish problem in Lithuania, has been achieved by *Einsatzkommando 3*. There are no more Jews in Lithuania except for Jewish forced labourers and their families.'[32]

The other *Einsatzkommandos* did the same. In Latvia, the Germans, with the help of Latvians, went on a rampage. Tens of thousands of Jews were massacred in the forests surrounding the towns and villages. In a letter home the German soldier H.C. wrote: 'The city of Dünaburg [Daugavpils in Latvia] is a bombsite. Nearly 75% of the population here was Jewish. ... 30,000 Jews were then shot, not far from the city.'[33]

In Ukraine, on 29 and 30 September 1941, the massacre of Babi-Jar near Kiev took place, led by *SS-Brigadeführer* Otto Rasch, commander of *Einsatzgruppe C*. The German army, together with Ukrainian collaborators, killed with machine guns 33,771 Jews from the Kiev ghetto. In correspondence to his wife in Vienna, Walter Mattner, an SS and police commander, describes the horrific nature of the act. On 5 October 1941 he wrote:

> I have to tell you something else. I participated in a mass murder yesterday. When we shot the first consignment of Jews, my hand shook a little while shooting, but you get used to it. By the tenth time, I started firing with a steady hand and shot the many women, children and babies with great precision. ... The babies went flying through the air in a big arc and we shot them down as they flew, before they fell into the grave or into the water.[34]

By the winter of 1941-1942, the various groups had their first global 'results'. Group A spoke of 249,420 exterminated Jews, Group B of 45,467, Group C of 95,000 and Group D of 92,000.[35] In total about half a million people.

During the remainder of the war, the *Einsatzgruppen* would slaughter an additional one to one and a half million Jews in a similar way. The commanders were in competition with each other to record in their reports to Berlin the highest possible numbers of exterminated Jews. Some soldiers and policemen who participated in the mass killings quickly got used to it. Holocaust researcher David Cesarani writes that the killing of innocent men, the elderly, women, children and babies was not very problematic for most involved. For many of the perpetrators this was after all a race for the survival of the German people. 'Almost all policemen, troops and those in the civilian echelons shared this outlook to some extent,' says Cesarani.[36] Nevertheless, the psychological pressure on the men on the ground increased rapidly. First, the victims were shot at close range, causing their brains to burst open and stain the uniforms of the killers. 'The shooters were gruesomely besmirched with blood, brains, and bone splinters. It hung on their clothing.'[37] Later, groups of Jews were lined up to be executed from a distance. Some were injured rather than killed and had to be shot through the neck. It was a slow process; because then a group of Jews who had been picked out had to remove the corpses. The need to accompany the Jews in small groups to the edge of or into the pits, the loading and aiming of the guns, the shooting of the men, women and children, the stacking of the corpses, the killing of those who were injured, and the assembling of the next group of Jews was time-consuming. Even the hardiest soldiers didn't last a full day. As is also clear from Jäger's reports, some Jews were still alive after the mass slaughter. The SS men would sometimes shoot them in the neck, but that did not always happen. Often some chalk and soil were thrown over the bodies. Because the wounded sometimes tried to crawl out of the mass graves of corpses, the ground would move. There are even testimonies of Jews who did manage to escape from the pit full of bodies.[38] To relieve the psychological pressure, the perpetrators often consumed large amounts of alcohol. On the one hand they drank for extra courage, on the other hand the alcohol numbed any feelings.

In the wake of the advancing German army, units of the *Einsatzkommandos* killed hundreds of thousands of people in the forests of Eastern Poland, the Baltic states, Ukraine and Belarus. On 15 August 1941 Heinrich Himmler was on a working visit to Minsk. *Einsatzgruppe B* was active there under the leadership of *SS-Gruppenführer* Arthur Nebe. In a forest around Minsk, Himmler attended the executions of Jews and saw how much the killings weighed on the minds of the SS-men. Some soldiers began to report sick or refused to perform their duty, but there were others who thrived on it. There is a reference to this in a statement by Gustave Fix, a member of the *Einsatzkommando 6*:

> I would also like to report that due to the enormous psychological pressure there were a lot of men who were no longer able to carry out executions and therefore had to be replaced by other men. On the other hand, there were men who relished the opportunity and often volunteered for these executions.[39]

The killings often took the whole day. Reports from *Einsatzgruppe B* show that the Germans and their helpers sometimes got up at six in the morning and drove to a ravine where the Jews were already lined up. They had to descend into the ravine and lie down. Then some of the men who were down in the ravine shot the desperate victims one by one. The shooting lasted until noon. Then the men ate something and swapped roles. Whoever had carried out the shootings in the morning now had to escort the Jews, while the others descended into the ravine to carry out the shootings. That lasted until five or six in the afternoon. Then they returned to their quarters where they received copious amounts of *schnapps*.[40]

Walter Stahlecker, commander of *Einsatzgruppe A*, was the first senior SS officer to report on psychological problems among the men. He wrote as early as July 1941, a few weeks after the invasion of Russia, how damaging the burden of killing was for his men. Even several senior SS officers could not handle the psychological pressure. Karl Jäger, the commander of *Einsatzkommando 3,* a division of *Einsatzgruppe A*, who had countless Jews murdered in the Baltic States, sank into a deep depression in 1942. Erich von dem Bach-Zelewski, supreme commander of the SS in Central Russia and a particularly cruel Nazi executioner, had a nervous breakdown in February 1942.[41] Himmler himself also felt nauseated during the massacre in Minsk when one of the victims' brains splattered over his overcoat. He ordered Nebe to find other, less burdensome methods to kill the Jews efficiently and in much larger numbers. Near the city of Konin, in the centre of Poland, experiments were carried out using boiling water. The Jews had to undress and step into a deep pit. When the pit was full, the Germans started pouring some sort of liquid over the victims. Then they added quicklime to burn alive the people in the pit. 'The screaming was unimaginable. The entire process lasted two hours.'[42] The experiment was a failure. Nebe later tried to kill a group of psychiatric patients from Minsk with explosives, but cleaning up the torn-apart bodies and limbs was just as bad. Nebe described it as 'utter rubbish'.[43] Some body parts even had to be picked from the trees.[44] Afterwards he experimented again on psychiatric patients by exposing them to toxic exhaust gases from vans. That seemed to work more efficiently. During the course of 1941 each *Einsatzkommando* received such a gas van. There were two types: a large *Saurerwagen* weighing seven tons and the smaller Opel Blitz with a weight of three to five tons.[45]

T4 Programme

The use of carbon monoxide to gas people had been practised before in the T4 Programme, albeit with gas cylinders in small confined spaces. The insight that doctors and other Nazi members gained from that notorious euthanasia programme was crucial in determining the killing methods used in the subsequent concentration and extermination camps. In the autumn of 1939 the Nazi regime launched a euthanasia programme to eliminate people who were severely disabled, mentally retarded, or had a psychiatric illness. In addition, they also targeted people with severe neurological diseases, epileptics, syphilis sufferers and anyone who needed hospital care for more than five months. The goal was clear: to guarantee the genetic purity of the Germanic people. People with such disabilities had to be sterilized or killed as quickly as possible; they were, after all, regarded as *unwertes Leben* (lives with no value) or *volksbelastende Kranken* (burdensome sick people). The aim was to prevent further offspring, which would eventually lead to a race with no mental or physical disabilities. Another important goal was to make sick beds available for the soldiers by eliminating the mentally ill. The T4 Programme was led by *SS-Oberführer* Viktor Brack, *SS-Obergruppenführer* Philip Bouhler and Karl Brandt, the personal physician of Adolf Hitler. Their headquarters were in Berlin, at 4 Tiergartenstrasse. Hence the name 'T4 Programme'. On 3 October 1939 registration forms were sent to all psychiatric institutions in the Reich, mostly monasteries and Christian care homes. After a few weeks, the T4 head office received around 200,000 completed forms. Experts then decided which patients would live. A simple plus sign before or after their name meant live or die. Patients were picked up in grey-painted buses with blacked-out windows. They transported the patients to one of the six killing centres.[46]

Between December 1939 and August 1941 Nazi Germany secretly exterminated more than 70,000 nationals in this way. The techniques they used were starvation, lethal injections, poisoning or gassing. There were at least 6,000 children and young people under sixteen in this figure. These murders took place in the extermination centres of Grafeneck, Schloss Hartheim, Hadamar, Bernburg, Brandenburg an der Havel and Pirna-Sonnenstein. Gas chambers were also used in the latter. After the invasion of Poland a similar euthanasia centre was added in Meseritz-Obrawalde. Thousands of mentally ill people were killed with lethal injections. Nazi doctors and nurses carried out the murders in the greatest secrecy and going directly against the Hippocratic Oath. They signed a document that ensured their silence. The euthanasia centre in Brandenburg an der Havel, headed by *SS-Untersturmführer* August Becker, was set up for the killing of the mentally ill and large numbers of children. In the first half of 1940 a kind of 3-by-5-metre shower room was built there. The space was filled with carbon monoxide via small holes in a pipe. For the first gassing, eighteen people had to undress and then enter the shower room. After a few minutes the victims fell to the ground. The staff took them to an incinerator on stretchers; 9,772 people had been killed in this way here.

Another killing centre, located in Hartheim, was run by Rudolf Lohnauer and Georg Renno, both doctors. They assessed the 'patients' not only on the basis of their illness but also on their capacity to work and whoever was not fit enough was killed. They extracted their gold teeth and cremated their bodies. In Hartheim the Nazi-regime also trained staff to 'treat' patients. In reality, they learned how to kill 'worthless people'. Here 18,269 mentally and physically disabled people were killed in a gas chamber. One of the staff there was Franz Stangl, a former police officer from Linz, Austria. From November 1940 to February 1942 he worked at the institute for euthanasia in Schloss Hartheim.[47]

In Grafeneck, hundreds of disabled and psychiatric patients, often referred to as *unnütze Esser* or 'useless eaters,' were eradicated to ensure the purity of the Aryan race. In the end 9,839 people were killed. The management was in the hands of *SS-Obersturmführer* Christian Wirth, who later worked in Brandenburg and Hartheim and who from 1940 became inspector of all euthanasia centres. Sonnenstein Castle soon became known as the 'Euthanasia Institute'. Doctor Horst Schumann and his team gassed 13,720 people. There was a crematorium and a bone mill next to the gas chamber. In Hadamar Alfons Klein and his team gassed more than 10,072 people between January and September 1941. One of his most important employees there was *SS-Unterscharführer* Willi Mentz. In Bernburg 8,601 sick and disabled people were killed in gas chambers using carbon monoxide in the space of ten months. *SS-Obersturmführer* Irmfried Eberl was in charge there. SS man Siegfried Graetschus assisted him. The six centres were connected and SS members drove employees from one place to the other.

The German population gradually became aware of the industry for extermination. Family members were sent a pre-printed death certificate with a false cause of death and an urn filled with ashes. The stated cause of death was actually impossible in some cases. One letter said that a young man had died of acute appendicitis, but his appendix had already been surgically removed before being admitted to the institute. Several families in the same city received obituaries on the same day, which caused quite a stir. The rumour mill started and more and more parents refused to hand over their disabled children to the government. Citizens saw patients from the blacked-out buses being carried into buildings with chimneys, which were constantly belching black smoke and emitted a horrible smell of burning. In Hartheim ash containing human hair sometimes rained down over the city.[48]

The Germans reacted differently. For some, the murder of the disabled was a mercy killing; others did protest. By 3 August 1941, when 70,000 disabled people had already been killed, the Bishop of Münster, Clemens August von Galen, belatedly condemned the murder of the mentally and physically disabled. On 24 August 1941, when Germany had been at war for two years, Hitler officially ordered the end of the

Euthanasia Programme. However, that quietly turned into a system of *ad hoc* euthanasia in nursing homes, the so-called *Aktion 14f13,* whereby sick, older and worthless prisoners were selected from concentration camps, and killed in three of the six T4-centres (Hartheim, Bernburg and Sonnenstein). The former T4 employees carried out these murders. Sick, disabled and Jewish prisoners were gassed here because the camps were not yet set up with the necessary 'extermination facilities'. The number of deaths was between 15,000 and 20,000 people. In Hartheim alone 12,000 people were killed under the *Aktion 14f13*, mainly prisoners from Mauthausen and Ravensbrück. Dozens of employees from the T4 Programme and *Aktion 14f13*, such as Franz Stangl, Christian Wirth, Irmfried Eberl, Werner Heyde, Lorenz Hackenholt, Ernst Zierke, Heinrich Barbl, Karl Gringers, Siegfried Graetschus, and Willi Mentz and Erich Bauer, became directly involved because of their 'expertise' in the systematic extermination of the Jews in Bełżec, Sobibor and Treblinka. The notorious doctor Horst Schumann, who worked for the T4 programme, carried out sterilisation and castration experiments in Auschwitz from 1942.

Extermination camps

The crucial decision about the murder of all European Jews was probably taken in the summer or autumn of 1941, although it is not entirely certain. There are detailed plans about Auschwitz, signed by Himmler in November 1941, with the word 'gas chamber' written next to the drawing of a building. However, a specific written order for the extermination of the Jews has never been found.[49] It is clear, however, that the specific implementation of this was discussed during the infamous Wannsee conference on 22 January 1942. It was originally planned for 9 December 1941, but was postponed by the Japanese attack on Pearl Harbor and the subsequent entry of the United States into the war. Wannsee is a green city district in south-west Berlin, on the Havel river and Wannsee Lake. SS leader Reinhard Heydrich assembled fifteen senior Nazi officials in the beautiful Villa Marlier. The purpose of the meeting was to brainstorm about the *Endlösung der Judenfrage*, or the definitive solution to the Jewish question. Among those present was Adolf Eichmann, who was responsible for organising the deportation of the Jews who lived in Europe and who took the minutes at the meeting. The minutes showed that the idea of a mass deportation of the Jews to the island of Madagascar or far beyond the Urals in Russia had been abandoned. It was no longer about 'expelling' the Jews but about a 'final solution' to the Jewish problem. Eichmann noted:

> Instead of emigration another solution has been proposed – following the prior approval of the Führer – to evacuate the Jews to the east. These actions can only be considered a temporary solution though; practical experience of great importance to the imminent final solution to the Jewish question is already progressing.[50]

The term 'final solution' (*Endlösung*) was clearly a euphemism for extermination here, as was also shown during the Eichmann trial in 1961. And the target was all eleven million European Jews, including those who lived in (not yet) occupied countries such as the UK, the Soviet Union and Switzerland. 'None would escape or be allowed to survive.'[51]

Also present at the Wannsee conference was Joseph Bühler, who, on behalf of Hans Frank, head of the General Government of occupied Poland, insisted that the 'final solution' should begin in that part of Poland. According to Bühler, the Jews in the full-to-capacity ghettos were a public health hazard. The systematic deportation of Jews from the German Empire, the Czech Republic and Slovakia to the overcrowded Polish ghettos in 1942 increased the need to get rid of large numbers of the ghetto residents. Preparations for the large-scale extermination of the Jews had already begun. In a speech to his co-directors, Frank left no room for any misunderstanding: 'Gentlemen, I must request that you put aside all feelings of pity. We must destroy the Jews wherever we find them and whenever it is possible.'[52] Himmler sent the same message. On 7 May 1942, he told senior SS officers that a death sentence had been pronounced on all European Jews.[53] At the same time SS leaders were still feverishly looking for methods to kill large numbers of Jews, without overly burdening their men psychologically.

In the city of Chełmno (Kulmhof), close to the Ner river and about fifty kilometres west of Łodź, the Nazis had been experimenting with the killing of people in gas vans since December 1941. Jews from the immediate surrounding area were the guinea pigs. Later, thousands of residents of the Łódź ghetto became victims. A road led them to the 'castle'. There they had to undress in a warm room. Members of the SS told them they could take a shower, that the men would be working in factories, that the women would be performing housework, and that the children would be going to school.[54] It was nothing more than a false re-assurance. After undressing, they went into the loading area of a large truck via a closed corridor. This was then quickly hermetically sealed. The exhaust pipes of the truck filled the airtight cargo space with carbon monoxide, causing the unfortunates to suffocate. The truck then drove on a further eight kilometres to a pit in the nearby Lubrodz forest. A Jewish *Sonderkommando* dragged out the corpses, stripped the bodies of any gold teeth, cleaned up the cargo space and dumped the bodies in a pit. A group of grave-diggers then had to camouflage everything. There were three trucks with wooden structures and zinc coatings.[55] The largest truck had space for more than 100 people. The other two had a capacity for fifty. They went back and forth all day between the castle and the forest.

In the first four months of 1942 alone, 50,000 Jews from the Łódź ghetto and about 5,000 gypsies from the area were killed in this way. Eichmann testified in 1960 about the procedure in Chełmno:

> I drove out to the designated place where a thousand Jews were about to board buses. The buses were normal, high-windowed affairs with all their windows closed. During the trip, I was told, the carbon monoxide from the exhaust pipe was conducted into the interior of the buses. It was intended to kill the passengers immediately. A doctor who was there suggested that I looked at the people inside one bus through a peephole in the driver's seat. I refused. I couldn't look. I had been told that the whole process took only three minutes, but the buses rode along for about a quarter of an hour. We reached our destination and hell opened up for me for the first time. The bus in which I was riding turned and backed up before a pit about two meters deep. The doors opened. Some Poles who stood there jumped into the buses and threw the corpses into the pit.[56]

He continued: 'Another Pole with a pair of pliers in his hand jumped into the pit. He went through the corpses, opening their mouths. Whenever he saw a gold tooth, he pulled it out and dumped it in a small bag that he was carrying.'[57] Apparently Eichmann said that this whole experience had shocked him, but that at the same time he felt inspired. Seemingly for the first time he saw that it was possible to destroy Jews in large numbers without causing too much 'trouble' for the SS. But he was not convinced by this system. He told his superior, Heinrich Müller, head of the Gestapo, that they could not continue down this route because it was too horrendous. The search for a more suitable way to exterminate Jews continued, but in Chełmno the deadly gas trucks kept running until April 1944 and were the cause of death for about 320,000 victims in total.

In Majdanek, close to the city of Lublin in eastern Poland, a work and extermination camp had been operating since October 1941 where not only SS men, but also Lithuanian guards worked. As well as Russian prisoners of war, the Jews from the Lublin ghetto and the surrounding towns and villages were also systematically shot and dumped in mass graves there. Majdanek was the most primitive Nazi camp, with dreadful living conditions. Many prisoners died of exhaustion, hunger and cold. The wooden barracks hardly offered any protection against the harsh weather, especially during the winter of 1941-1942. Georg Pfeffer was one of the few survivors. He testified about the inhumane treatment in the camp:

> You get up at 3am. You have to dress quickly, and make the 'bed' so that it looks like a matchbox. For the slightest irregularity in bed-making the punishment was 25 lashes, after which it was impossible to lie or sit for a whole month. Everyone had to leave the barracks immediately. Outside it is still dark, unless the moon is shining. People are trembling because of lack of sleep and the cold. ... We went in groups, some to build railway tracks or a road, some to the quarries to carry stones or coal, some to take out manure, or for potato-digging, latrine-cleaning, barracks or sewer repairs. All this took place inside the camp enclosure. During work the SS men beat up prisoners mercilessly, inhumanly and for no reason. ... Another customary SS habit was to kick a Jew with a heavy boot. The Jew was forced to stand to

attention and all the while the SS man kicked him until he broke some bones. People who stood near enough to such a victim, often heard the breaking of the bones.[58]

In September 1942 the Nazis started killing prisoners in three gas chambers, first with carbon monoxide from engines, later with Zyklon B. These installations, too, were primitive. Anyone could see the buildings with the gas chambers and this news must have quickly reached the Jews in the nearby ghetto of Lublin. But escape was difficult. Whoever tried was immediately executed. Moreover, the Poles in the surrounding area received a fee if they captured fleeing Jews and brought them to the police. After several attempts at resistance by the Jews in the ghettos of Vilnius and Białystok, and an attempted uprising in the camp, the SS decided to kill all Jews from Lublin during the *Aktion Erntefest*. 'On November 3, 1943, the SS killed 18,400 inmates in Majdanek while music was played over loudspeakers to cover the sounds of shooting and the cries of the dying prisoners.'[59]

It is estimated that around 60,000 Jews were killed in Majdanek.[60] On 23 July 1944 the Red Army captured the camp and found only a few hundred living prisoners. The barracks and grounds were full of corpses. The SS men had not had enough time to destroy everything. As a result, one gas chamber and the crematoria were in the hands of the liberators. Photos of the Nazis' crimes and the methods they used appeared in the Soviet newspapers. For the first time, the extent and manner of the Nazis' genocide came to light.

In Bełżec, on the border between the Lublin and Galicia districts, the construction of an extermination camp with three fixed gas chambers was started in November 1941. From March 1942 Jews were being exterminated there, principally residents from the ghettos of Lemberg (Lwów) and Krakow. In his diary Polish historian Zygmunt Kowalski described how two trains with twenty wagons each came to Bełżec every day, one from Lublin and the other from Lwów.[61] Kurt Gerstein was an eyewitness to the mass murders. He volunteered for the Waffen-SS in March 1941 after his sister was murdered in the T4 Programme. She stayed at the institution for the mentally disabled in Hadamar. Kurt Gerstein rose to become the *Obersturmführer* of the SS Health Corps and was instructed in June 1942 to take a quantity of prussic acid from a factory in Prague to Lublin in Poland. There, on 18 August 1942, he saw with his own eyes how Jews were gassed in Bełżec. He wrote about this later in his report:

> The next morning, shortly before 7 a.m. someone announced to me: 'In ten minutes the first transport will come!' In fact, the first train arrived after some minutes, from the direction of Lemberg. 45 wagons with 6,700 people of whom 1,450 were already dead on arrival. Behind the barred hatches children as well as men and women looked out, terribly pale and nervous, their eyes full of the fear of death. The train comes in: 200 Ukrainians fling open the doors and whip the people out of the wagons with their leather whips. A large loudspeaker gives the further orders: 'Undress completely, also remove artificial limbs, spectacles etc.' handing over valuables at the counter, without receiving a voucher or a receipt. The shoes carefully bound together, because on the almost 25-meter-high heap nobody would have been able to find the matching shoes again. Then the women and girls to the barber who, with two, three scissor strokes is cutting off all hair and collecting it in potato sacks. ... So they climb the small staircase, and then they see everything. Mothers with little children at the breast, little naked children, adults, men, women, all naked – they hesitate but they enter the death chambers, pushed forward by those behind them or driven by the leather whips of the SS. The majority without saying a word. A Jewess of about 40 years of age, with flaming eyes, calls down vengeance on the head of the murderers for the blood which is shed here. She gets 5 or 6 slashes with the riding crop into her face from Hauptmann Wirth personally, then she also disappears into the chamber. Many people pray. I pray with them, I press myself in a corner and shout loudly to my and their God.[62]

Gerstein then testifies about the gassing itself:

> The people stand on each other's feet. 700 - 800 on 25 square metres, in 45 cubic metres! The SS physically squeezes them together, as far as is possible. The doors

close. At the same time the others are waiting outside in the open air, naked. Someone tells me: 'The same in winter!' 'Yes, but they could catch their death of cold,' I say. 'Yes, exactly what they are here for!' says an SS man to me in his Low German. Now I finally understand why the whole installation is called the Hackenholt-Foundation. Hackenholt is the driver of the diesel engine, a little technician, also the builder of the facility. The people are brought to death with the diesel exhaust fumes. But the diesel doesn't work! Hauptmann Wirth comes. One can see that he feels embarrassed that that happens just today, when I am here. That's right, I see everything! And I wait. My stop watch has honestly registered everything. 50 minutes, 70 minutes – the diesel doesn't start! The people are waiting in their gas chambers. In vain! One can hear them crying, sobbing ... After two hours and 49 minutes – the stop watch has registered everything well – the diesel starts. Until this moment the people live in these 4 chambers, four times 750 people in 4 times 45 cubic meters! Again 25 minutes pass. Right, many are dead now. One can see through the small window in which the electric light illuminates the chambers for a moment. After 28 minutes only a few are still alive. Finally, after 32 minutes, everyone is dead![63]

Between March 1942 and December 1942 around 435,000 Jews were killed in Bełżec. After the war, archaeologists found thirty-three mass graves, the largest of which was 24 meters long, 18 meters wide and 5 metres deep.[64]

The Wannsee Conference also led to the construction of other new camps. From April 1942 the Nazis started using the Sobibor extermination camp. Partly under the orders of camp commandant Franz Stangl, Jewish forced labourers from the surrounding ghettos built a concrete building there with first three and later six gas chambers with a gassing capacity of 500 people. The corpses were subsequently thrown or burned in mass graves by a *Sonderkommando*.[65] According to Stangl, a transport of thirty freight wagons with 3,000 people was disposed of in this way in three hours. *SS-Scharführer* Erich Fuchs witnessed this at first hand. The driver had previously worked for the T4 Programme, and was later active in Bełżec and Sobibor. He testified that in the spring of 1942, under the orders of Christian Wirth, he had to drive a truck to Lemberg (Lwów) to pick up a Russian engine for the gas chambers.

> Upon arriving in Sobibor I discovered a piece of open ground close to the station on which there was a concrete building and several other permanent buildings. Amongst the SS personnel there were Floss, Bauer, Stangl, Schwarz, Barbl and others. We unloaded the motor. It was a heavy, Russian petrol engine (presumably a tank or tractor engine) of at least 200 HP (carburettor engine, eight-cylinder, water-cooled). We put the engine on a concrete plinth and attached a pipe to the exhaust outlet. Then we tried out the engine. At first it did not work. I repaired the ignition and the valve and suddenly the engine started. The chemist whom I already knew from Belzec went into the gas chamber with a measuring device in order to measure the gas concentration. After this a test gassing was carried out. I seem to remember that thirty to forty women were gassed in a gas chamber. The Jewesses had an undress in a clearing in the wood which had been roofed over, near the gas chamber. They were herded into the gas chamber by the SS members and Ukrainian volunteers. When the women had been shut up in the gas chamber, I attended to the engine together with Bauer. The engine immediately started ticking over. We both stood next to the engine and switched it up to 'release exhaust to chamber' so that the gases were channelled into the chamber. On the instigation of the chemist I revved up the engine, which meant that no extra gas had to be added later. After about ten minutes the thirty to forty women were dead. The chemist and the SS gave the signal to turn off the engine. I packed up my tools and saw the bodies being taken away. A small Lorenbahn wagon on rails was used leading to an area farther away.[66]

To re-assure the Jews, SS men would ask if anyone was a baker, electrician, tailor or shoemaker. Many of the prisoners came forward in the belief that they would be employed as craftsmen. They were then led to the gas chambers in groups and killed. During the third Sobibor trial in 1965, SS *Oberscharführer* Kurt Bolender testified about these gassings in the extermination camp:

> Before the Jews undressed, *Oberscharführer* SS-Sergeant Michel made a speech to them. On these occasions, he used to wear a white coat to give the impression that he was a physician. Michel announced to the Jews that they would be sent to work, but before this they would have to take baths and undergo disinfection so as to prevent the spread of diseases. ... After undressing, the Jews were taken through the so-called 'Schlauch' [sluice]. They were led to the gas chambers not by the Germans but by the Ukrainians. ... After the Jews entered the gas chambers, the Ukrainians closed the doors. The motor which supplied the gas was switched on by a Ukrainian named Emil Kostenko and by a German driver called Erich Bauer from Berlin. After the gassing, the doors were opened and the corpses removed by a group of Jewish workers.[67]

In addition to Polish Jews, tens of thousands of Jews from the German Empire, Slovakia, France and the Netherlands were also deported here. In total, around 170,000 people were killed in Sobibor. On 14 October 1943 a number of prisoners rebelled and were able to escape. Himmler then decided to dismantle the camp and conceal as much as possible.

The construction of the Treblinka extermination camp started in May 1942 about 120 kilometres north-east of Warsaw. Gassings had been taking place in Auschwitz, 60 kilometres from Krakow, since December 1941. The first victims were Russian prisoners of war; later it was mainly Jews and gypsies. In the same period the construction of a much larger extermination camp began: the adjacent Birkenau. All these camps were part of *Aktion Reinhard*, named after Reinhard Heydrich, who was murdered in Prague on 4 June 1942 by Czech resistance members. It was the codename for the large-scale eradication of European Jews as discussed at the Wannsee Conference. From the summer of 1942 it was already running at full speed. The first stage was the disposal of the ghetto residents. From that time the *Judenräte* had to collect large numbers of Jews at regular intervals who, according to the letters from the German authorities, would be employed elsewhere. It was soon suspected that this was incorrect. In reality the ghetto residents were taken to Chełmno, Bełżec, Majdanek, Sobibor, Treblinka and Auschwitz-Birkenau.

Ghetto

We walk through the streets of Radomsko with Rachel Kesselman. She shows us where the ghetto used to be, where, behind the grandiose mansions with their large inner squares, the Jews were packed in like sardines. Then we visit the Muzeum Regionalne w Radomsku, where historian Kamil Rutkowski shows us around. The many photos and documents give us an incisive image of pre-war Radomsko, of life during the occupation, the living conditions in the ghetto, and the definitive extermination. The Jews from Pławno and Gidle were taken to Radomsko at the end of September 1942. The extermination of Jews in Żarki's ghetto began on 6 October 1942. About 300 people were shot immediately. Smaller groups of employable men were deported to the larger ghettos of Częstochowa and Radomsko. But the largest group of Jews, consisting of 800 elderly people as well as men who were not useful, women and children, all went on foot to Złoty Potok train station on 6 October under the surveillance of SS men. From there they left in cattle wagons for the Treblinka extermination camp. Fellow Polish townsmen immediately moved into the empty houses. This was the beginning of the end for the Jews in Pławno, Gidle and Żarki. They had lived there for generations, built houses, worked and helped build the region. Now they were gone, as if they had never existed.

Although the influx of Jews from poor shtetls in the area reinforced the rumours in Radomsko that a 'Action' was about to begin. Some Jews went into hiding with Poles, to whom they gave money and jewellery. Others managed to escape to the nearby forests. Many, in desperation, committed suicide.[68] Most people awaited their fate in a defeated and passive manner.

On Thursday 8 October 1942 the Polish police together with Ukrainian and Lithuanian SS auxiliary troops hermetically sealed off the Radomsko ghetto. 'People said goodbye, cried and kissed, and the heartbreaking screams went far beyond the boundaries of the guarded ghetto.'[69] The next morning, at 5 o'clock, the *Judenrat* was informed that the Special Action would start at 6 o'clock. German police entered the ghetto with cars and fired in the air. The Jews were forced out of their homes and were only allowed to bring their leftover money and jewellery together with some food and clothing. Those who did not answer quickly enough were dragged out of their houses. People who were too sick or too weak were shot on the spot.

The 14,000 Jews had to gather on the square at the northern border of the ghetto. They arrived with their belongings packed into bags, suitcases and school bags. Tired, tormented and anxious, they waited for what was about to come. Guards took their money and jewels.[70] Around noon the Jews were lined up in rows of five. In the pouring rain the Germans removed 350 people from the rows. They included members of the *Judenrat* and police officers who had to return to the ghetto. The others were forced to go to the station in groups of 500. There, everyone again had to wait for hours, soaked and frozen. Late in the evening, around 10:00 pm, a freight train arrived with dozens of cattle wagons. A barrage of blows drove the Jews, a hundred at a time, into the cattle wagons, after which the doors closed inexorably. It led to heartbreaking situations in which men, women, children and parents were separated. Filling the wagons took hours. Because there was not enough space, thousands of Jews were brought back under heavy surveillance. Finally, on Friday 9 October 1942, the train left for Treblinka carrying about 10,000 Jews. Three days later the train was back. The 4,000 remaining Jews went to the station again, where the same scenes occurred. When the train left, the ghetto was almost clear of people with the remainder locked up in a smaller area of the city.

The Germans realized that there were still hundreds, perhaps even thousands, of Jews hiding in the surrounding forests, in bunkers, in the houses of Polish people and even in enclosed cellars in the old ghetto. As time went on, totally exhausted and starving, the Jews returned, increasing their numbers in the ghetto. Hundreds also came from other areas, such as Lódz and Częstochowa. The Germans did not get involved and it seemed as if the situation had normalised with no more serious incidents. As a result, many more Jews who were still hiding, or had fled, re-appeared. By the end of 1942, once again more than 4,000 people were packed together in the small ghetto; sometimes twenty people were living in one room. On 6 January 1943, like cornered animals, they, too, were put on the train to Treblinka. Two days later, the Germans shot 300 people who were left behind, including eighty-four children, at the Jewish cemetery.[71] Radomsko was now as good as *Judenrein*.

Treblinka

After a long drive on the motorway, we arrive in a sparsely populated and densely wooded area. The evening before we had said goodbye to Maria Piekarska and Rachel Kesselman. Rachel did not understand why we had an overwhelming desire to visit Treblinka, even though more than 200 members of her family were killed there, including her niece Ruchel-Laja Kesselman, 23 years old. 'I'm not a masochist,' said Rachel. She preferred to pray at the Radomsko cemetery. But we want to complete our search to know what happened to the Kartuz family and where this terrible torture finally ended for them. Our search is not complete without the final destination of Treblinka.

Along the way we come across numerous little chapels and we see metre-high crucifixes in the green landscape, which bear witness to the godliness of the Polish villagers. Beside a cottage with a chapel is a large stone with the ten commandments on it. Hopefully, someone also knows their way around here. An old woman looks at us and, speaking incomprehensible Polish, gestures at us to turn right. A forest track takes us deep into a forest where not a soul can be seen. The GPS no longer works. We navigate our car in between all the potholes and we almost get stuck in a puddle. We decide to turn back and find the main road again. After driving a couple of dozen metres, we find another road, which does lead to Treblinka. Everything here seems to be hidden behind dense forest. A small sign takes us to a large, abandoned parking lot with markings for buses and normal-sized vehicles. Nobody is there.

'It is easier to arrange one-day visits to Auschwitz-Birkenau, where an estimated 960,000 Jews were murdered, than to Treblinka, where some 860,000 Jews were killed in a shorter space of time,' wrote historian David Cesarani.[72] Unlike Auschwitz, you don't see full buses or chip stalls in the parking lot here. The silence is overwhelming; we don't even hear the birds; everything seems dead here. On the right there is a somewhat dilapidated stone building with a sign saying 'Tourist Centre', but nobody is there. We walk to a low building that serves as a museum. We finally encounter a member of staff of the museum. He says that we can look around and that information is available if we wish to see it. He eventually accompanies us during our visit. He may well be happy to see someone.

The first camp in Treblinka dates from July 1941. Polish, Ukrainian and Jewish prisoners had to work in a quarry. As part of the *Aktion Reinhard*, whose aim was the total extermination of the Jews, the Nazis built a new extermination camp a few kilometres away. Under the direction of *SS-Obersturmführer* Irmfied Eberl, who had previously worked on the T4 Programme in Germany, the construction of Treblinka II began in May 1942 and was completed two months later. Treblinka is located in north-east Poland, close to the important Warsaw-Białystok railway line. About halfway along this is the Malkinia Górna junction, where the line east meets at the river Bug. There was no railway bridge in that direction which used to be in the hands of the Russians before the First World War. They had laid tracks there, but they were wider than in the rest of Poland. Trains from the west could not run on those tracks. This was one of the most remote places occupied by the Germans that could be reached by trains from the west. From Malkinia Górna there was a single track to the village of Treblinka, four kilometres away, with a side track into the camp.

In the museum we bend over a large maquette, which represents the new camp as it looked in 1942, 400- by 600-metres, completely fenced in with barbed wire and camouflaged with pine branches. At one end we see the railroad next to an elongated wooden platform that opens onto a large space for gathering the Jews. Here they took the last of their possessions. In a corner of the sorting area was the *Lazarett* (hospital), where a flag with a red cross was hanging. In reality, the elderly and sick who were still alive when they arrived were immediately shot. As soon as they were off the platform, the men had to undress outside. On one side was a barrack for women. They too had to undress there. Their hair was cut off in a room at the back. There was a narrow path beyond this barrack. Above it was a beautiful sign with the word *Himmelstrasse* or 'the road to heaven'. The winding path was hidden from view and separated by a green hedge and barbed wire. It was 80 metres long and about 4 metres wide. The maquette resembled a theme park from another era, where people queue in a long line to go on a ride. It says something about the deranged manner in which the Nazis operated. Perhaps such methods made it easier for them to commit mass murder. They just wanted as little trouble as possible to calm the crowds. The naked Jews ended up at a stone building with the sign *Badeanstalt* (bathhouse). Initially there were three gas chambers of 5- by 5-metres and a height of

2.6 metres in the building. They had a capacity of up to 600 people per hour. They were gassed with the toxic exhaust fumes from a tank engine that were pumped into the chambers through pipes. There were barracks for 120 Ukrainian and thirty SS guards in the left wing of the camp (in the early days). There were also barracks for the working Jews, a real hospital, a relaxation room, a tailor's workshop, a forge, a workshop for carpentry, latrines, a kitchen, a bakery, a vegetable garden, a few pigsties and even a small zoo. There were barracks in the right wing for storing stolen, valuable items. Behind the sorting area, protected by high hedges, there were huge burial pits about 50-metres long, 20-metres wide and 10-metres deep.

The first transport arrived on 23 July 1942 with 6,500 Jews from the Warsaw ghetto in sixty cattle wagons. It was very hot and the unfortunate people screamed for water. The locomotive stopped at Malkinia Górna station, disconnected some wagons and continued on with about twenty wagons via the side track to Treblinka. There the Ukrainian guards opened the doors and, with much violence and shouting, forced the Jews to disembark. They drove them to the courtyard where SS officers ordered them to undress, leave their things behind and take a shower. The gassing lasted twenty to thirty minutes, after which 200 working Jews from the *Sonderkommando* dragged the corpses out of the gas chambers, extracted their gold teeth and threw them into mass graves. The whole extermination process lasted until the evening, which meant that many Jews had to wait for hours in the blazing sun until their wagon was next. Everyone who was still alive was killed. The next human cargoes also came from the Polish capital and underwent the same process. On some days multiple transports would arrive with more than 10,000 Jews. The notorious SS *Unterscharführer* Franz Suchomel was active in the camp from 18 August 1942. He described the influx as follows.

> The Warsaw ghetto was being emptied then. Three trains arrived in two days, each with three, four, five thousand people aboard, all from Warsaw. But at the same time, other trains came in from Kielce and other places. So three trains arrived, and since the offensive against Stalingrad was in full swing, the trainloads of Jews were left on a station siding. What's more, the cars were French, made of steel. So that

while five thousand Jews arrived in Treblinka, three thousand were dead in the cars. They had slashed their wrists, or just died. The ones we unloaded were half dead and half mad. In the other trains from Kielce and elsewhere, at least half were dead. We stacked them here, here, here and here. Thousands of people piled one on top of another on the ramp. Stacked like wood. In addition, other Jews, still alive, waited there for two days: the small gas chambers could no longer handle the load. They functioned day and night in that period.[73]

Gerstein too saw what went on:

On another day – August 19, 1942 – we drove the car from Hauptmann Wirth to Treblinka, 120 kilometres north-east of Warsaw. The layout was about the same, but much larger than Bełżec. Eight gas chambers and proper mountains of suitcases, textiles and linen. A banquet had been organised in the canteen in our honour in the typical Himmlerian old German style. The food was simple, but there was plenty of everything. Himmler himself had ordered that the men of these Kommandos be given as much meat, butter and alcohol as they wanted.[74]

By the end of August, more than 300,000 Jews had died barbarically. Most came from the Warsaw Ghetto, others from the ghettos in Radom, Kielce, Otwock, Mińsk Mazowiecki and Międzyrzec Podlaski. The gas chambers were running to full capacity, day and night. Before long, however, the camp was unable to handle the numbers arriving. The full cattle wagons sometimes remained on the track for days, occasionally the engine tanks shut down, the gas chambers were difficult to open and rotting corpses were lying everywhere. The smell was unbearable. As a result, there was a risk that these secret operations would become known in the area. Franz Suchomel, who was responsible for handling the incoming transports and confiscating the valuables, testified in *Shoah*, the documentary film by Claude Lanzmann, as follows:

The smell was infernal because gas was constantly escaping. It stank horribly for miles around. You could smell it everywhere. It depended on the wind. The stink was carried on the wind. Understand? More people kept coming, always more, whom we hadn't the facilities to kill. The brass was in a rush to clean out the Warsaw ghetto. The gas chambers couldn't handle the load. The small gas chambers. The Jews had to wait their turn for a day, two days, three days. They foresaw what was coming. ... They heard the engine feeding the gas chamber. A tank engine was used in that gas chamber. At Treblinka the only gas used was engine exhaust. Zyklon B gas – that was Auschwitz. Because of the delay, Eberl, the camp commandant, phoned Lublin and said: 'We can't go on this way. I can't do it any longer. We have to break off.' Overnight, Wirth arrived. He inspected everything and then left. He returned with people from Belzec, experts. Wirth arranged to suspend the trains. The corpses lying there were cleared away. That was the period of the old gas chambers. ... Because there were so many dead that couldn't be gotten rid of, the bodies piled up around the gas chambers and stayed there for days. Under this pile of bodies was a cesspool three inches deep, full of blood, worms and shit. No one wanted to clean it out. The Jews preferred to be shot rather than work there.[75]

The entire extermination process in Treblinka was flawed, but camp commander Eberl remained true to his mission to destroy as many Jews as possible and did not stop the transports. .

SS-Obergruppenführer Odilo Globocnik replaced Eberl with Franz Stangl who, at that time, was still working as commandant in Sobibor. When Stangl arrived in Treblinka, he was witness to the terrible conditions. He described them in his conversation with journalist Gitta Sereny:

I drove up there with an SS driver. We could already smell it miles away. The road ran alongside the railway track. When we were 15 or 20 minutes away from Treblinka, we saw bodies lying alongside the tracks, first two or three, later on more and when we arrived at the station, there were hundreds of them – they just lay there – obviously for days in the heat. At the station was a train full of Jews, some dead, others still alive ... that train looked like as if it had already been there for days. ... When I arrived in the camp and got out of the car on the platform, I am up to my knees in money. I did not know where to walk. I waded through bank notes, coins, gemstones, clothing. The whole platform was littered with it. The stench was indescribable. Hundreds, no thousands of bodies were lying around, decomposing, rotting. Across from the platform, in the forest on the far side of the barbed wire there were tents and bonfires. There I saw groups of Ukrainian guards and girls – whores I discovered later – from the entire region, dead drunk, dancing, singing, making music ... .[76]

Globocnik stopped transports to Treblinka at the end of August 1942 and immediately set Stangl to work. He restored order in the camp and had the corpses that lay along the railroad and in the camp removed and burned. He also had a wooden station built with signs above the doors saying 'first-class waiting room', 'second-class waiting room' and 'restaurant'. There was a large fake clock with hands that didn't move, and there were even flower pots to cheer things up and re-assure the Jews. At the beginning of October 1942 he also had new gas chambers built. A new brick construction comprised ten blocks, each 7-by-7- and 2-metres high. A corridor divided the length of the entire building in half, with five gas chambers on either side with one or sometimes two petrol engines to pump in their suffocating gas. The old and the new gas chambers together had a gassing capacity of 12,000 people every day.

From 3 to 12 September 1942 at least another 50,000 Jews from the Warsaw Ghetto were exterminated. After that, the other ghettos in other towns and villages were emptied, often with several trains a day. Almost nobody survived this hell.

One of the few survivors of Treblinka was the Czech Jew Richard Glazar, who was deported from the Theresienstadt concentration camp on 8 October 1942. In his book *Trap with a Green Fence: Survival in Treblinka* he describes the train's arrival at the extermination camp.

Shortly after midday we stop again. There is a small station house identified as 'Treblinka'. A part of the train is uncoupled. At the curve we can see the front cars turning into a one-track spur. Forest is on both sides. But no one dares look out. A high green fence, an open gate – our car passes easily through it. 'Out, everyone out, hurry up! Leave the heavy luggage. It'll be delivered later!' A platform, behind it a wooden barracks – people on the platform wear boots but are in civilian dress. … Everyone is being directed down off the platform through another gate and into a square. Wooden barracks are along both sides. 'Men to the right, women and children to the left! Leave the luggage. Clothes off, everything off, strip!'[77]

Everyone did. A tall SS man then instructed Glazar to get dressed again, take off his Star of David, and go to a barrack with huge piles of items. From then on, he was part of a *Sonderkommando* that had to remove the suitcases, clothes, shoes, food and other possessions from the new arrivals in the courtyard.

The German-Jewish survivor Abraham Bomba was also in that group of working Jews. He described how quick and efficiently everything was dealt with.

Then they told us to make clean the whole place. There were about two thousand people who had undressed on the outside, to take the whole thing away and to clear up the place. And that was done in minutes. Some of the Germans, some of the other people that were there, the Ukrainians and other ones, they start shouting and hitting us that we should do it faster, to carry the bundles to the main place where there were big piles of clothes, of shoes, of other things. And in no time, this was as clean as though people had never been on that place. There was no trace, none at all, like a magic thing, everything disappeared.[78]

By that time the naked Jews were already in the gas chambers. After about twenty minutes, the doors to the outside opened and another *Sonderkommando* had to drag the corpses out. 'Then slaves immediately reach for the naked, tightly packed, ashen and violet-colored results.'[79] Samuel Willenberg, a survivor of Treblinka, described the removal of the dead bodies from the gas chambers as follows: 'They're still warm. They're all crushed into one great mass of meat. We throw them on the ground, and then it's the turn of the prisoners known as "dentists", who pull the gold out of the corpses' mouths.'[80] Imprisoned dentists, even butchers, then went to work to pull the gold from the open or clenched mouths or break it off the jawbone. After that the corpses were taken to the large prepared mass graves where they were thrown in. A bulldozer worked continuously to dig new pits and to cover the corpses with sand. Sometimes the earth began to move due to explosions from the fermenting and decaying bodies. The stench from this was overwhelming. In the meantime, another load of Jews arrived and the whole process started again.

According to the latest calculations, over 900,000 Jews were systematically murdered over thirteen months in Treblinka, probably even more. The extermination camp was therefore, just like Auschwitz-Birkenau, a place where the Jews were murdered with incredible speed, in a well-thought out, insidious, systematic and particularly horrific manner.

We stare at the numbers in the museum which are unimaginable. They come to many hundreds of thousands, almost a million Jews. The Germans deported between 21 September and 8 October 1942 the 40,000 Jews from Częstochowa, on 6 October 1942 the 800 remaining Jews from Żarki, and on 9 and 12 October 1942 over 14,000 Jews from Radomsko. On 6 January 1943 another 4,500 Jews from Radomsko arrived in Treblinka. It is certain that nearly all members of the Kartuz family and in-laws were exterminated there. The only member of the family who was still alive at that time was Ide, who had come to Antwerp in 1929. Photographs of huge numbers of deportees boarding the trains to the extermination camp hang on the walls of the museum. We think about of Ide's father, brothers and sisters, uncles and aunts, cousins, all squeezed together in the wagons, standing because sitting is impossible. Then the long train ride; stop, start, then stop again. Wagons that are unhooked and disappear, while the rest are left in the heat for hours. Then, with a jolt, moving again. Through the cracks all you can see are green bushes and one tree after another. There's a sudden braking, and the bodies are thrown forward altogether. The latches are unlocked and the shutters open. There is turmoil, soldiers yelling and shouting, beating the Jews. They yell that they must leave their possessions and undress, quickly, quickly. How did Ide's aunt Laja endure this as an 81-year-old? His father Moszek at the age of 57? His brother Zyskind at the age of 28? His half-sister Ita as a 15-year-old? And his nephew Enoch at the age of 5? They have to take off their clothes, covering their genitals in shame. The women's hair is cut off and their bodies are searched for hidden jewels. Some cry, scream and get a beating. They must take a shower, that is an order. Eventually, as if in a trance they go through the winding *Himmelstrasse* into a dark room. The first ones enter hesitantly, the ones in the middle push forward, the last ones begin to scream. The door closes. An engine starts and the gas spreads. Half an hour later the bodies lie in one of the huge pits.

We leave the Treblinka museum and walk from there to the place where hundreds of thousands of Jews arrived by train, were forced out of the cattle wagons, then were gassed, buried and then later on burned; it was indeed, at the end of February 1943 that Himmler had decided to exhume the mass graves and burn the bodies, which had long been in a state of decomposition. That happened on huge pyres made out of iron grills from train rails. When the burnings ended at the end of July, partly because the number of transports began to diminish from March 1943 – when the deportations to Birkenau started – the fear that they themselves would be murdered grew among the members of the *Sonderkommando*. After all, they were well aware that the Nazis wanted to get rid of all witnesses.

On 2 August 1943 there was a well-prepared uprising, involving around 300 prisoners. They stole weapons from the ammunition depot and stormed the main gate but they did not succeed in killing the SS guards in the watchtower who shot and killed more than 200 insurgents. Barely eighty Jews escaped successfully and only about sixty survived the camp. In mid-August two last transports with 7,600 Jews from Białystok were killed.[81] After the uprising, Franz Stangl left the camp and was replaced by *SS-Untersturmführer* Kurt Franz as commandant, who was instructed to dismantle the camp and erase or destroy all evidence. The remaining Jews, who had to help with this, were shot and afterwards burned. The Nazis subsequently destroyed the buildings and installations. Trees were planted in their place. Only the Ukrainian guard Streibel and his family were allowed to live in this dreadful place where they farmed the land.

Elsewhere, too, when the chance of a German victory was beginning to be lost, the Nazis had begun to erase the evidence of the mass murders. For this purpose, the *Sonderkommando 1005* was founded in June 1942 under the direction of *SS-Standartenführer* Paul Blobel for an *Enterdungsaktion* (Exhumation Action).[82] He was instructed to excavate the mass graves of the *Einsatzgruppen*, to dig up the bodies and burn them on the pyres of railway sleepers. Any remaining bones were ground. The Germans deployed newly-imprisoned Jews to do this, who were then killed after completing the work.

As well as Richard Glazar, Samuel Willenberg also survived. They wrote down their testimonies in a book. Other than accounts from SS guards, Polish train drivers and farmers who lived in the area around the camp, there are barely a handful of other eyewitness accounts. As a result of the small number of surviving testimonies, Treblinka threatens to sink into oblivion. However, it deserves as much attention as the much-visited Auschwitz-Birkenau.

We walk in the direction of the former single track, where the wooden sleepers have been replaced by heavy rectangular granite specimens. They represent the railway line and end at the wooden platform. Over a huge surface there are boulders with the names of the countries where the victims came from. On the site of the gas chambers there is now a metre-high, massive granite obelisk with a menorah at the top, the seven-armed candlestick which is a symbol for the Hebrew people. The monument is surrounded by a grass area with 17,000 jagged boulders that seem to come out of the earth like flames. More than 700 of them each represent a city or village from where the Jews were sent to their death in Treblinka.

After some searching, we find the stone for Radomsko, another for Żarki and then one for Częstochowa, the three cities where the family and friends of Ide Leib Kartuz were brought to the ghettos and from where they were deported here. A large rectangular pit, full of chunks of molten basalt, symbolizes the place where their bodies were burned after the gassing. It makes a deep impression on us. Completely and utterly in a state of shock we return to the parking lot. Treblinka is a body blow.

Jewish graves

We drive along the motorway to Warsaw, our next stop. We chat about our findings and talk about Rachel, who had prayed for us at Żarki's cemetery. Although we are both liberal humanists, we very much appreciate her gesture. It was a moment of peace after a difficult and eventful journey. We now understand better that an indescribably horrific tragedy took place in Poland. Here a whole culture, a whole society of millions of people was erased in a few years. The country that had 3.3 million Jews before the war is now almost *Judenrein* thanks to the Nazis and their supporters. Poles now live in their houses. The synagogues have disappeared in many places, their existence erased.

After the war some Jews who survived the camps returned to the places where they grew up, worked and lived. Most of the time they were told that they had should leave; sometimes they were driven away by force. The hatred of Jews remained particularly great even after the war with pogroms happening in Białystok, Krakow, Warsaw, Łódź, Lublin, Rzeszów and dozens of other Polish cities and villages. One of the most striking examples was the pogrom in Kielce in the summer of 1946. There, dozens of Jews were killed by the local population with the full knowledge of the Polish police. The Jewish inhabitants of Kielce had already been hit badly during the war. More than 20,000 Jews died in various actions during the war. In his book *Fear: Anti-Semitism in Poland After Auschwitz*, the historian Jan Gross talks about this post-war pogrom.[83] The cause of the mass murder was the sudden disappearance on 1 July 1946 of an 8-year-old Polish boy. He had been hitchhiking back to the village where he had once lived. Two days later he returned unharmed. Meanwhile, the father had reported the disappearance of the child to the police. When the son returned, he made up a story that he had been abducted by Jews but that he had managed to escape. He further claimed that Jews kept the bodies of murdered Christian children in a house. Rumours in the town grew and soon the Polish Catholics announced that the Jews had ritually killed a Christian child. On 4 July 1946 policemen and soldiers broke into a house where Jews who had returned from the concentration camps lived. They handed them over to the crowd, who began to kill them. Following this, Jews in other parts of Kielce were attacked with clubs and stones and either seriously wounded or killed.

A lot of Poles refused to give back houses and properties to Jews who returned from the concentration camps. According to Gross, this is a public secret. He emphasises that whoever 'acquired' any of the 'former possessions of the Jews' are still known today in every small town or village. Opportunism by many Poles meant that they were to some extent complicit in the mass murder organised by the Nazis. This attitude was only possible 'as Poland's fundamentally anti-Semitic clergy' proved unwilling to step in and prevent their flock from getting involved, as British ambassador Cavendish-Bentinck stated.[84] The pogrom in Kielce was no exception. A year earlier there had been a pogrom in Krakow. The fact that anti-Semitism in Poland is far from eradicated is evident from the fact that Jewish cemeteries have been increasingly the target of Jew hatred in recent years.

The extent to which the Jewish presence has been erased can be seen from the ruins of Jewish cemeteries that we visited. Behind a quiet residential area in Żarki are hundreds of pillars, crooked and weathered, that criss-cross in a seemingly desolate landscape. The Germans randomly took gravestones from the cemetery to build roads. After the war, the communists also stole Jewish gravestones.

In Pławno it was even worse; hardly anything is left of the old Jewish cemetery. We only found three gravestones in the middle of a forest. A little further on were some more stones, but they were overgrown or partly destroyed. The Jewish presence in Pławno has been completely erased. There is also a large Jewish cemetery in Radomsko. Rachel Kesselman showed us around, but the graveyard was very poorly maintained and completely overgrown. She does not have the money for the maintenance of the grounds. The ancient gravestones remain impressive. We also found larger gravestones that commemorate the place where Jews were thrown into a mass grave. Taking courage from desperation, Rachel is trying to raise some money to put new memorial stones in the city which will bear witness to the former Jewish society. The old ones were of poor quality and the engravings had gone. We decided to help Rachel and we financed together a new memorial stone.

The Warsaw Ghetto

Unable to speak and deeply moved we drive from Treblinka back to Warsaw. There we have an appointment with historian Katarzyna Person at The Emanuel Ringelblum Jewish History Institute, which was founded in 1947. The institute conducts research into the historical Jewish presence in Poland, the Holocaust and its aftermath in Eastern Europe. The Warsaw Ghetto Archive (Ringelblum Archive) is the most important part of the collection and contains around 6,000 documents. There are also collections with testimonies mainly from Jewish Holocaust survivors, numerous documents from the Jewish Councils, and more than 40,000 photos about Jewish life and Jewish culture in Poland.

Person passionately gives us numerous interesting texts and books that can give us a better picture of the enormous tragedy that took place here in Warsaw. We are given access to moving testimonies from the ghetto residents and from the Polish residents themselves. They saw how the Germans started building walls around the ghetto on 16 November 1940. Then they removed the Jewish families from their houses and apartments and sent them to the neighbourhood that was closed off to the outside world. Soon transports of Jews from the surrounding towns and villages arrived, causing the ghetto to become overcrowded. Yet life apparently continued as normal. People with a lot of money could still go to restaurants, where they ate exquisite delicacies and drank wine, while an excellent, professional pianist provided background music. They went to evening concerts and literary meetings. At the same time the impoverished Jews were trying to sell things on the street which was full of beggars, old, sick, disabled Jews, as well as children with bulging eyes, dressed in stinking rags. They begged standing, sitting or lying down, sometimes with a newspaper as their only shelter. The Jewish police forcibly maintained order and the Jewish Council, led by Adam Czerniaków, tried fruitlessly to meet the many needs of the population. Food supplies were far too small; only smugglers succeeded in bringing food into the ghetto. They sold their goods to rich Jews and restaurants, and enriched themselves without scruples. The poor received nothing. Many people, including children, were starving and dying in the streets. 'The number of deaths from starvation and disease between the closing of the ghetto in November 1940 and the beginning of the deportations in July 1942 may have been as high as 100,000,' said Saul Friedländer.[85] The corpses were collected by a special unit every evening and thrown into mass graves.

High-ranking SS leaders came to the Czerniaków office on 22 July 1942. They had an important announcement, in fact an order, for the ghetto leadership. The well-known Jewish literary critic Marcel Reich-Ranicki took care of the minutes as head of translation in the Jewish Council. All Jews regardless of their age or gender would be evacuated to labour camps in the east. An exception was made for a number of groups, such as forced labourers, hospital staff, police officers, workers employed by German factories and members of the Jewish Council with their families. The Jewish police were instructed 'to bring 6,000 people every day to go "east", and if they didn't bring 6,000 than they had to bring their own relations and parents.'[86] When that failed, heavily-armed SS men randomly picked Jews and herded them to the station. At the same time, Czerniaków was trying, albeit unsuccessfully, to make exceptions, in particular for the orphans. He was even ordered to 'deliver' 10,000 Jews the next day. One day later he committed suicide. He probably realised that it was not about 'evacuation' or 'resettlement' in the east but a radical and complete extermination. However, many Jews continued to believe that they would be sent to a labour camp, as the German propaganda claimed, and came forward. Others were brutally arrested and put in jam-packed cattle wagons, at least 6,000 a day. From 23 July to 21 September 1942, approximately 300,000 Jews were taken to Treblinka in this way.

After that, the pace of the deportations slowed down, but that was short-lived. On 18 January 1943 something unprecedented happened. The Germans had started that day with a second wave of arrests. The nearly 50,000 Jews who had not yet been deported realised that they, too, had been sentenced to death. Jewish combat groups prepared themselves for resistance. They built underground bunkers, opened sewers, and hid. They started shooting at the Germans, causing the deportations to stop.

In a letter dated 16 February 1943 to *SS-Obergruppenführer* Krüger in Krakow, Himmler ordered the demolition of the Warsaw Ghetto. Led by *SS-Gruppenführer* Jürgen Stroop, the Germans sent reinforcements and entered the ghetto with heavy artillery on 19 April 1943. In the battle that ensued, gunfire, grenades and homemade molotov cocktails were used against the heavily-armed SS men. The resistance was so fierce that the Germans decided to burn the houses one after the other. Jews were jumping from the houses, killing themselves The others had to gradually withdraw. However, it took until 16 May 1943 for the uprising to be suppressed. More than 13,000 Jews died. The remaining 40,000 were transported to Majdanek and Treblinka. The entire ghetto was literally wiped off the map with only ruins remaining.

There is very little left of the ghetto. Only on a section of the Próżnastraat can we still see weathered buildings that were part of it. A small piece of wall is still standing on Złotek and Sienna Street. We visit the impressive granite memorial stone for the heroes of the uprising in the ghetto in 1943 and a little farther on the *Umschlagplatz*, where the Jews were loaded into the train wagons destined for Treblinka. The first names of 448 deportees are engraved on the wall. A marking on the ground indicates where the former ghetto wall used to be. Behind that wall 450,000 people lived on 2.4 per cent of the total surface area of Warsaw, squeezed in like animals. Most disappeared for good in the extermination camps. Others died of hunger, exhaustion, illness, murder ... . The rest perished heroically in the 1943 uprising in the ghetto. One year later, the Germans, tipped off by Polish citizens, discovered another underground bunker in Grójecka Street with forty hidden Jews. Amongst them was the eminent historian Emanuel Ringelblum. From the very beginnings of the ghetto, he had collected all kinds of documents, diaries, papers and artefacts and also made notes about life in, and the destruction of, the ghetto. Just before the final destruction, he hid his archives in three iron milk cans and a few metal boxes in the cellars of buildings in Warsaw. Ringelblum was shot dead, but in 1946 and later in 1950 a number of those cans and boxes were discovered. They contained detailed information about the deportations from the ghetto, the Jewish Council, the underground newspapers, the resistance and much more. He himself described how people in the streets of the ghetto died of hunger and how others were taken away. 'The "Jewish Question" will soon be resolved very quickly in Warsaw,' wrote Ringelblum.[87] One milk can has still not been found. Katarzyna Person helps to make the archives accessible; it is her life's work and we are grateful for her enormous dedication and help.

Not much was left after the war not only of the ghetto but also of the rest of Warsaw. After the Soviet troops advanced to the outskirts of the capital in the summer of 1944, an uprising by the Polish resistance group *Armia Krajowa* began on 1 August with nearly 25,000 armed men and the support of the civilian population. Some had counted on the Red Army coming to their aid, but Stalin stopped his troops until the Polish insurgents had been destroyed by the Germans. Others had wanted to use the uprising to prevent themselves from coming under Stalin's rule and believed that they could defeat the Germans on their own. They did manage to gain control over a few neighbourhoods, including the area of the former ghetto. Testimonials show that Polish soldiers discovered Jewish men and women who had kept themselves hidden since the destruction of the ghetto, and then shot them.[88] The Germans continued to bring in new troops, reducing the chance of Polish success by the day. The capitulation of the rebels followed on 2 October 1944. The Germans initiated the complete destruction of the remaining houses soon after that, especially historical buildings and monuments of historical significance. Almost all of Warsaw was destroyed. It wasn't until 17 January 1945 that the Red Army entered the desolate capital.

The next day we leave for Belgium. The Polish motorway runs seamlessly into Germany as if there had never been a border between the two countries. Everything is peaceful as if nothing had ever happened. After seventeen hours we are back in Antwerp. Ninety-two years ago, on 1 April 1929, Ide Leib Kartuz arrived here.

Part Two

Antwerp

Leaving Poland

At the end of March 1929 a train from Mysłowice, in southern Poland, arrived in Antwerp. It carried dozens of Polish Jews who wanted to emigrate to America or Canada. The Red Star Line in Antwerp was a particularly popular choice for this. The shipping companies placed advertisements in Yiddish in Polish newspapers to publicise the crossing. Jewish organisations portrayed a bright future in the West for the migrants. The shipping companies were well aware that the Jews wanted to flee Poland. The prevailing discrimination and the anti-Semitic outbursts increasingly made their lives miserable and the economic prospects were bleak. The advertisements were, of course, aimed at those who were financially sound, mainly rich Jews who had been able to obtain a visa. Those less well off could at most only afford the train ticket to cities such as Antwerp or Brussels from where they hoped to be able to make the crossing at a later date.

Antwerp was a magnet for Jews. Before the First World War Polish Jews had already settled there as labourers, shopkeepers, diamond workers or diamond traders. During that period the Jewish quarter was established in the streets around Central Station. However, the 1914-18 war caused many foreigners to flee the port city and the majority of diamond dealers settled in Amsterdam. The Netherlands was neutral during the war. After the war, some of Antwerp's diamond dealers did return[1] and the city on the river Scheldt therefore remained a centre for the diamond trade.

A new wave of migration started in the 1920s. Many Eastern European Jews, especially from Poland, came to Antwerp to try their luck. They sought stability, prosperity, and safety for themselves and their families as modest businessmen or craftsmen. They felt safe in hospitable, multicultural Antwerp and tried to gain a foot on the ladder in Belgian society by renting a place to live, setting up a business or working as pedlars. Their numbers increased rapidly. Historian Lieven Saerens writes that in the period between 1919 and 1930 around 20,000 Polish Jews came to Antwerp. Half of them stayed permanently, mainly in the city of Antwerp, in Berchem and in Borgerhout.[2]

Why did the Jews leave Poland? Anti-Semitism definitely played a major role. More than three million Jews had been living in Poland. The vast majority practised the Jewish faith. 'Many dressed differently from Christian Poles and had beards or sidelocks (*payot*), in line with the traditions of their religion. They formed a clearly recognisable national minority and were increasingly discriminated against by the anti-Semitic Polish military regime in the second half of the 1930s,' says historian Richard Evans.[3] Hatred towards the Jews was also continually inflamed in sermons from the pulpit by priests who constantly asserted that the Jews were the murderers of Christ and that their descendants should pay for this. The Church leadership supported them in this. 'Easter, when the priests portrayed the Jews as the murderers of God in their sermons, was a recurring excuse for anti-Semitic violence,' writes historian Jan Gross.[4] At the same time there were the absurd accusations of ritual murders by Jews of Christian children, the so-called 'blood libel'. According to the canard, Jews need blood from Christian boys to prepare *matzos* for the Passover feast, their ritual Easter meal. A ritual murder must be committed for that blood. These accusations date back to the twelfth century and were spread by Christians and used as propaganda for pogroms against the Jews. In addition, there was also economic anti-Semitism, prompted by the supposed wealth of the Jews. In the eyes of many Poles, they formed an elite who held the key positions in the country and stole their jobs. However, many Jews were small traders and simple craftsmen who tried to work their way up, while others lived in poverty and barely made ends meet.

Many Catholics, such as our guide Wojtek in Żarki, believe that Jews and Christians lived peacefully together before the Second World War, but the reality was different. Ever since the beginning of the twentieth century there have been tensions between Jewish and Christian Poles. Many Christians regarded the Jews as traitors who even sided with the enemy during the First World War.

In the first three months after that war, pogroms took place in many towns and villages. The hostility towards the Jews grew even stronger after Poland was forced to accept the Minority Treaty by the Allies on 28 July 1919 – on the same day as the signing of the Treaty of Versailles. This provided for equal rights for national and religious minorities. Many Christian residents considered it to be an unfair coercive measure imposed on them by outsiders with the result that it turned them even more against the Jews.[5]

The Polish government adopted the Sunday Rest Law at the end of 1919. This limited the working week to forty-eight hours. Its implementation meant an improvement for the Polish workers, but many Jews lost their jobs because it forced them to work on Saturdays. According to Jewish belief, working on the Sabbath, Saturday, is prohibited. In 1927 Poland passed a law that imposed a licensing system on the free practice of a craft. Although more than a third of Polish artisans were Jewish the law stipulated that the exams should only be conducted in Polish. Thousands of qualified Jewish artisans, especially the elderly who only spoke Yiddish, could not get a permit. Without a permit, they were not allowed to employ helpers, finishers and students. As a result, many Jewish families had almost no means of subsistence.[6] Jews who ignored the law were reported to the government by Polish artisans. In other sectors, too, such as industry and government, the Polish government pursued a policy of discrimination against the Jews. The deteriorating socio-economic situation in the country at the end of the 1920s fuelled growing anti-Semitism. It is a myth that all Jews were rich and dominated the Poles economically in an underhand way. The Polish-Dutch journalist of Jewish descent Milo Anstadt says:

> Centuries of economic exclusion had squeezed Polish Jews into a narrow band of employment. They were merchants, market people, pedlars, shopkeepers. Almost half a million Jews were tradesmen and that was almost a third of the Jewish labour force. Others were blacksmiths, coppersmiths, shoemakers and tailors. Some worked from home, struggling with the whole family from early morning till late at night for a dry piece of bread with a few slices of onion. There were bakers and grocers, butchers and those who, under rabbinical supervision, worked in the abattoirs. Many were factory workers in the textile industry of Lódz and Bialystok. ... There were also Jewish millionaires,

owners of hotels, cinemas, factories and even entire streets but the vast majority were just hardworking, poor, second-class proletariats.[7]

The Polish nationalist *Endecja* nurtured an increasingly hostile atmosphere. In several places this led to physical threats and violence. One of the slogans was 'Poland is only for the Poles'. Access to schools became increasingly difficult for the Jews and Jewish companies were put under more and more restrictions. The ultimate goal of the *Endecja* was to make the lives of the Jewish people so difficult that they would leave voluntarily. Party supporters regularly either blocked access to Jewish stores or smashed up the contents. Young Jews organised themselves into self-defence groups to protect themselves which led to even more fights and acts of violence.

Anti-Semitism not only existed in the countryside but also in the larger cities. That was certainly the case in areas where the church played an important role, such as in the Catholic stronghold of Czechtochowa. The most senior Catholic leaders, including Cardinal August Hlond and Archbishop Adam Stefan Sapieha, as well as most Polish priests embraced the anti-Semitic government policy. Under the influence of the extreme right *Endecja*, anti-Semitism became increasingly widespread.[8]

Many Polish Jews, usually young adults, wanted to try their luck somewhere else and get away from not only their xenophobic and anti-Semitic fellow citizens, but also the closed Jewish community with its stifling habits, rituals and lack of freedom. During the interbellum period, a split occurred in the Jewish community between those who wanted to continue following the age-old traditions and others who wanted to assimilate and embrace modernity. This trend was felt especially in that part of Poland previously under Russian law. Young people considered the traditions of their parents as medieval and wanted to live in the modern world.[9] In his diary, Isaac Deutscher, the son of an Orthodox Jew, noted: 'We grew up in the Jewish past. We experienced the eleventh, thirteenth and sixteenth centuries of Jewish history both in the houses next to us and under our own roof; and we wanted to escape and live in the twentieth century.'[10]

This created two worlds: one in which the elderly spoke only Yiddish or poor Polish and the other where their children spoke perfect Polish. Some young people even joined the new socialist and communist movements. Due to the poor economic conditions and anti-Jewish economic policy, it was almost impossible for young adults from the lowest social groups to become the breadwinners for their families. As a result, many of the adventurous and impulsive young people, who dreamed of a better future, ventured into the free and modern West to seek their fortune there. Ide Leib Kartuz was not only an accomplished tailor, married to a beautiful woman, but also an adventurer. There was nothing to prevent him from leaving for Antwerp.

Bulgaria

Someone we haven't met yet is Cathy, Ide's eldest granddaughter. She had been very involved in our search from the beginning but lives in Bulgaria, which has not always made communication easy. She had already sent us some photos and documents via Messenger; but so far, we had found most of the information in the Belgian State Archives or at the Kazerne Dossin. She also told us about a box with papers and newspaper clippings that was still somewhere in her basement. There was too much for it all to be photographed and moreover it was all in a pretty bad condition. She sent us the most important things via Messenger. One of those things was a postcard from a certain Paula Weintraub from Netanya, Israel.

> *Dear Kartuz,*
> *For you and Beni* [Benno Kartuz] *my best regards and a happy*
> *New Year. If you are willing to send me a reply, I will write back.*
> *P. Weintraub*

There was also a letter from Paula in the box. In it she called Ide 'Comrade' Kartuz.

Why did she call him Comrade Kartuz?

Perhaps there was much more to be found in Cathy's archive. It was difficult for her to judge which documents were important and which were not. We knew from experience that documents that appeared insignificant at first glance could mean a lot in a certain context. We decided to travel to Sofia. After all, Cathy was also an important witness herself and we didn't want to overlook any details. Cathy would perhaps remember things that others no longer did. A short time later we are on the plane, on our way to Sofia, the capital of Bulgaria.

Cathy lives in a village about a three-hour drive from Sofia. Because there are no street names, she asked us to call when we get there. 'Where are you? What do you see?' We see a square with a bench and a glass-recycling container. We have to turn around. Someone is waving at us about 200 metres away. We finally see her in real life.

We get a warm welcome from Cathy and her husband Willy. Their two golden retrievers also seem happy to see us. We talk about our research, our discoveries and our story. Willy disappears into the house for a moment and returns with a big box. It contains Ide's personal papers. Moisture and mould have had a pronounced effect on the documents over the years. Fortunately, the majority are still clearly legible. Many papers look familiar as we have already come across them in the National Archives. But there are also documents that we had never seen before. We found some index cards from the International Tracing Service in Bad Arolsen. We find one for Chaja Artman, one for the children, but also one in the name of Jacob Artman and one in the name of Fajgla Artman. It is the first time that we come across those names and we have no idea who they are. We take pictures of them, talk for a long time and return to Sofia.

We visit the large synagogue in Sofia, one of the oldest in Europe. In a side building we walk through the Jewish Historical Museum and read about the fate of the 50,000 Jews in Bulgaria during the Second World War. The country was an ally of Nazi Germany, but the Bulgarian Jews were not deported despite heavy pressure from the Nazis. It is not, however, entirely correct that, as in Denmark, the Nazis had no success in implementing their extermination policy.[11] King Boris III had previously sent to Treblinka 20,000 Jews from Thrace and Macedonia, territories annexed to Bulgaria after the Nazi conquest in 1941.[12] He also introduced several anti-Jewish laws in 1940 and 1941 which closely resembled the Nuremberg Race Laws in the Third Reich. However, with the resolve of Dimitar Peshev, the vice-president of the Bulgarian parliament, the Jews in the country were not sent to the extermination camps in Poland.[13]

We take a taxi to the airport but first stop at the statue that was erected in 2013 in honour of Peshev. Later that day we take the plane back to Brussels in search of more information about the life of Ide in Antwerp before the war.

Antwerp

In order to obtain a temporary residence permit for Belgium before the Second World War, the Polish Jews had to be able to prove that they had sufficient financial means or that they could earn money there. The Belgian state wanted to ensure that foreign nationals could take care of themselves. It was mandatory for anyone who wanted to come to Belgium to prove that someone there had a job for them or that they had a guarantor. The guarantor had to sign a document stating what kind of work the newcomer would be doing and how much he would be paid. The employer or guarantor had to specifically sign the following: 'I undertake to repatriate the above-mentioned to Poland at my own costs if he should become reliant on social welfare'. A tried and tested practice was that first one Polish family member would try to settle in Belgium, search for work and obtain a permanent residence permit. If he succeeded, he could then invite other family members by vouching for them or offering them a job.

One family who made active use of this practice were the children of Henoch Artman and Hadessa Apelowicz from Gidle. Ide Leib Kartuz had married Chaja, their eldest daughter in 1929. In the State Archives we discovered that Chaja's brother, Litman Artman, was the first to go to the West. He was born in Gidle and was a year younger than her. As early as 1914 he decided to move to the West to avoid serving in the Russian army. Polish Jews who had to fight for the tsar were used as cannon fodder. Whoever enlisted virtually signed his own death warrant. Although he moved from place to place aimlessly for some time, in 1922 he arrived in Liège. Without the necessary documents, he started working as a miner. His wages must have been particularly low. After six months he travelled on to Antwerp, where he became, successively, a butcher, a diamond cutter and even a coal shoveller in a silver factory. He lived in the heart of the Jewish Quarter. On 16 March 1926 he married Deborah Zucker, a Russian Jew. She was born in Antwerp. Together they had two children, Elaine and Mireille. On 11 December 1940 he and his two daughters entered their names in the Jewish Register. At that time he ran a tobacco shop in Antwerp.

The second Artman who came to Antwerp was Fajgla Artman, a younger sister of Chaja and Litman. In Częstochowa in Poland she worked as a shop girl but, thanks to an acquaintance of Litman,

64

she was able to work as a maid for the Jewish family Stybelman in Antwerp. She earned 200 francs a week there. She joined the family on 19 January 1925. When she met Abraham Dzierlatka a year later, her life changed. Abraham was born in 1904 and left Warsaw at the age of 19 to go to the West. On his arrival in Vienna he acquired a Belgian visa. We are not able to find out how he managed that, but in his application he wrote that he was unable to find a job as a diamond cutter in his own country but should be able to find a job in Antwerp. In 1925 he went to Antwerp, starting work almost immediately at a diamond processing company in the Jewish Quarter. He initially earned 140 francs a week. His file from the State Archives contains a document in which his employer wrote the following: 'I am very happy with his work and I would struggle to replace him.' He received a salary increase to 200 francs a week and thus succeeded in converting his temporary residence permit into permanent residence.

Abraham Dzierlatka and Fajgla Artman fell in love with each other and on 13 October 1928 they married and went to live together. In 1930 their first daughter, Lilliane, was born and, three years later, their second daughter, Laura. Fajgla helped Abraham in his diamond studio at 62 Vestingstraat, also in the Jewish Quarter. That way they could save some money. In 1936 they also helped Laja Dzierlatka, Abraham's sister, to come to Antwerp to marry a Jewish butcher. In the end she didn't marry him, but Laja nevertheless ended up in Belgium. She lived in Borgerhout and stated that she worked for free as a maid for her brother Abraham. The third Artman who came to Antwerp was Chaja, the oldest child in the family. She had married Ide Leib Kartuz on 23 March 1929 in Poland in accordance with the old Jewish customs. The relationship was unusual: she was nine years older than him. She, too, hoped for a better life in the West. On 1 April 1929, barely eight days after his wedding in Pławno, Ide arrived on his own in Belgium. It is unclear where he spent the first two days. It may have been with his brother-in-law Litman or with his sister-in-law Fajgla. On 3 April 1929 he rented a house in Berchem, near Antwerp. He made himself known to the Public Security Administration in the town hall where his personal details, including his profession, his Polish nationality and that he had leave to stay in Belgium indefinitely, were all noted. Ide put on his record that his reason for leaving Poland was 'the social and economic irregularities there'. He also mentioned that he had handed over his military pocket book with number 2787 on 7 November 1928 to Helior Rawski, captain in the Polish army. Surprisingly in the box 'Place and date of marriage' is written 'married in Gidle (P)'. Next to 'Wife' it says 'Artman Chaja, no children'. All later documents, however, always say 'unmarried'. Apparently, the marriage between Chaja and Ide in Poland was a religious marriage and not a civil one. This first official document about Ide Leib Kartuz on Belgian soil was signed by the Catholic mayor of Berchem.

From that moment Ide could move freely on Belgian territory. Immediately after his arrival in Antwerp he started work as a tailor. To that effect he had a professional card with number 3554. For the first few months he worked for himself, but later he worked as a 'home worker-tailor' for the large clothing company Beukelaers. Although he was already a master craftsman in tailoring by then, he continued learning the craft at Beukelaers. Fashion was probably different in Belgium or he may have only learned how to make Jewish clothing in Poland.

It was a year after his arrival before his wife Chaja finally came to Belgium. She entered the country on 18 April 1930. A rabbi from Antwerp confirmed that they were married and provided a sort of certificate. However, since this was not valid in law to allow Chaja to settle in Belgium, consideration had to be given to references from her brother Litman and her sister Fajgla. She immediately moved in with Ide, who had already moved to a house closer to the Jewish Quarter. The city's registration document stated that she was unmarried, but it had the following comment: 'Lives as common law partner with Kartuz Ide Leib, born in Pławno (Poland) on 18 September 1905, tailor, of Polish nationality.'[14]

Ide regularly travelled to Brussels during that period to meet friends and probably also to ask for their support. The economic situation worldwide, including in Belgium, was particularly grave as a result of the Wall Street crash on 24 October 1929. The crash was the fundamental cause of the crisis during the 1930s and led to the most severe economic recession of the last century. The economic turmoil also affected the Antwerp diamond sector. Of the more than 95 per cent of Antwerp diamond workers who were members of the General Diamond Workers' Association of Belgium, more than half lost their jobs in 1930. The number of unemployed diamond dealers rose even further in 1932 to more than 80 per cent. Many didn't have a cent to their name and tried to earn a living as pedlars. They were often regarded as hustlers or quacks who wanted to swindle people. They were popularly called 'chukchuks' (travelling salesman) by Flemish people. It was also often the only way for the totally destitute Eastern European Jewish newcomers, who were fleeing desperate poverty in their home country, to try and keep their heads above water. Jews from Germany who had fled for political reasons often suffered the same fate. The increase in the number of foreign pedlars was a thorn in the side of the 'homegrown' pedlars and caused tensions. In order to limit the number of street traders, the government introduced hefty taxes in the 1930s for obtaining an official pedlar card.

It was only from 1934 onwards that the diamond sector began to recover and provide more work for the Jews. Due to the crisis, which began at the end of 1929, Ide received hardly any orders as a tailor. He earned too little to pay for his rented home and support his family, and asked for financial support from other Polish immigrants in order to survive. A family in Schaarbeek near Brussels helped. Two months later they helped them rent a house at 7 Schupstraat, in the heart of the Jewish Quarter in Antwerp.

From 1934 Ide once more had Jewish customers. They asked him to make tailored suits for them. The diamond dealers in particular called on his skills since a large number of them also came from Poland. They all spoke Yiddish with each other. Ide earned just enough to take care of himself and his family.

We don't know much about his wife, Chaja Artman. She probably did the household chores and took care of the children. The only photo we have of her turned out to be of a beautiful woman with a fashionable haircut. She dressed in a modern way. There was no trace of an orthodox religious life in either her clothing or appearance. Ide and Chaja had two children. On 31 December 1931 Chaja gave birth to Charles-Victor, a strikingly non-Jewish name. We have unfortunately hardly any information about him. The only thing Benno can tell us about him is that he was intellectually very gifted. More than a year and a half later, on 18 June 1933, their daughter Simone was born. We can't find anything about her either.

Nowhere can we find anything about the children. Fortunately, the State Archives can tell us more about other members of the Artman family.

A few months after Chaja, her youngest brother Jacob Artman, and also the brother of Litman and Fajgla, arrived in Antwerp. On 14 May 1930 his brother-in-law Abraham Dzierlatka wrote that he wanted to employ Jacob as a workman at his home. He would pay 800 francs a month for that. He also promised to cover possible repatriation costs if Jacob became dependent on State benefits. Five days later he arrived by train at Antwerp Central Station without a visa. Ide and Chaja immediately offered him a place to live in their house. On 14 October 1930 Jacob wrote a letter to the governor with a view to obtaining a longer residence permit. He pointed out that he currently had a paid job as an apprentice hairdresser; he earned 250 francs a week. He also mentioned that he received support from his two brothers-in-law, Kartuz and Dzierlatka, and from his elder brother, Litman. He wanted to stay in Belgium, since the core members of his family lived in Antwerp and worked as a hairdresser in his own right, also in the Jewish Quarter. German-Jewish Paula Singer and her mother lived a few houses away. Paula worked as a furrier at the company Ftoimowitz. Jacob fell in love with her and they were married on 18 March 1941. In the summer of 1942 Jacob was summoned by the German occupier to work as a forced labourer. Together with 2,252 other forced labourers from Belgium, he had to help with the construction of the Atlantic Wall in northern France. He was part of the Organisation Todt, a government organisation that initially belonged to the German Ministry of Armaments and Ammunition.

Paula was arrested on 22 September 1942 during the fourth raid of Antwerp. She was taken to Auschwitz on 26 September with Konvooi XI. Two days later she was killed there. Jacob never arrived at the building site near the Atlantic Ocean. He was deported from Northern France to Auschwitz with Konvooi XVI. He arrived there on 3 November 1942 and his arm was tattooed with camp number 72261. A court ruling paper from 1953 stated that Jacob Artman died in 1945 during the death march from Auschwitz to Bergen-Belsen. According to testimonies of fellow prisoners, he simply fell to the ground from exhaustion and couldn't get up. He died while the column of prisoners marched on.

Family members from the Polish region of Pławno and Gidle came together in Antwerp on holidays and also at other times such as the Sabbath. Just before the German occupation in 1940 they had a celebratory meal together: Litman Artman, Deborah Zucker, their children Elaine and Mireille, Fajgla Artman, Abraham Dzierlatka, and their children Lilliane and Laura, Chaja Artman, Ide Leib Kartuz, and their children Charles-Victor and Simone, Jacob Artman and Paula Singer. Laja Dzierlatka, the younger sister of Abraham, was probably also there. She came from Poland in 1936 to work with her brother. It was a close-knit family that followed Jewish customs and traditions, but not strict religious rules. The children all played together; they were about the same age. The adults were having a good time eating and drinking, and enjoying a liberated carefree life without restrictions, helping each other out. In the summer months they would sometimes all go to Blankenberge. They enjoyed the sun, the sea and the beach, in the knowledge that they had a better life in Belgium than in Poland. Their future lay here.

It is surprising that all children in this family have non-Jewish names. They probably wanted to integrate and assimilate as quickly as possible. It must have been fun to be in their company on Friday nights and public holidays. They were independent, free and full of ambition. But at the same time a dark shadow was hanging over their gatherings. From newspapers, radio reports and, more importantly, conversations from new Polish refugees, they realised that the German invasion of their home country was a tragedy for their parents and grandparents, brothers and sisters and cousins who had stayed behind. Ide thought about his parents Moszek and Sura, his brothers Abram and Zyskind, his sister Chaja (who had the same first name as his wife), his half-brother Chaim and his half sister Ita, and his courageous cousin Sura. Chaja and the other Artmans must certainly have thought about their parents Hejnoch and Hadessa, their sisters Gitla and Mindla, and their youngest brother Abram who was also in Poland. They had no idea how they were doing, and even less what would happen to them later.

Anti-semitism

In addition to the depression of the 1930s, nationalism with its xenophobic and anti-semitic resentments crept back into society. Along with other European countries, and with Germany leading the way, new extreme right and nationalist parties emerged in Belgium. These were radically opposed to foreigners, in particular to Jewish people. In the German elections of 14 September 1930 the Nazi party won 107 seats, making it the second largest group in the Reichstag. In Flanders, Joris Van Severen founded the *Verbond van Dietsche Nationaal Solidaristen (Verdinaso)* (Union of Diets National Solidarists). The agenda of the party was fundamentally anti-democratic, anti-semitic and anti-Marxist. Two years later, on 8 October 1933, Staf de Clercq founded the *Vlaamsch Nationaal Verbond* (Flemish National Association) (VNV). His party fought for an independent Flanders and soon supported the anti-Jewish laws adopted in Germany. The Catholic student club Rex was also founded in the early 1930s. Its members sympathised with Italian and German fascism and in 1936 Rex transformed into a political party. On the other side of the political spectrum, communist parties grew in popularity, which in turn inspired many people. Like many other Polish Jews, Ide became a supporter of communism in those years. While the aversion of Flemish nationalists and Catholics to both Judaism and Bolshevism played a role in this, the developments in Nazi Germany in particular pushed him to the extreme left.

After sweeping election victories in September 1930 and July 1932, the *Nationalsozialistische Deutsche Arbeiterpartei* (NSDAP) became the largest party in the German parliament with 230 seats. In the Reichstag elections of 6 November 1932, it lost thirty-four of its seats. The *Kommunistische Partei Deutschlands* (KPD) gained eleven seats. This result alarmed the conservative forces. Although the Nazis were still the largest party, nobody wanted Hitler as chancellor, which resulted in a lot of unrest within the ranks of the Nazi party. Hitler faced fierce opposition from Gregor Strasser who wanted to follow a rather left-wing course. It was only through the scheming of, among others, the former Chancellor Franz von Papen, that after much procrastination, German President Hindenburg appointed Hitler Chancellor of Germany on 30 January 1933. Papen assured the president that the Nazi party would pose no danger because they only had two ministers in the new government.[15]

However, things turned out differently. The first victims were the communists. Hitler had them prosecuted and locked up in KZ Nohra near Weimar, the first concentration camp opened on 3 March. KZ Dachau near Munich was completed on 20 March in the presence of Heinrich Himmler and the following day KZ Oranienburg near Berlin and KZ Colditz in Saxony.[16] There was nothing secretive about them and they were reported on by the Nazi controlled press. People were well aware

70

that in these particular prisons inmates were treated badly and no one wanted to end up in them. The Nazis said that if you had done nothing wrong then you had nothing to fear. Right?

The first action against the Jews took place not long after on 1 April. The Nazis called for a boycott of Jewish businesses. Members of the *Sturmabteilung* (SA) stood guard in front of the doors of Jewish stores to deter potential German buyers.[17] Six days later, on 7 April, the 'Wiederherstellung der Berufsbeamten' Act was introduced. Jews were excluded from government posts. A few days later, the government passed further laws to exclude Jews from all legal and medical positions. The number of Jewish school children per school was limited by law. 'Non-Aryan' professors, judges, lawyers and other civil servants were skillfully purged. There was no longer a rule of law. On 25 April, the *Gesetz gegen die Überfüllung deutscher Schulen und Hochschulen*, which de facto prevented Jewish children from attending German schools, was implemented, albeit quite chaotically. On 29 April 1933 the Nazi press published a black list of authors whose books could no longer appear in public libraries. On 10 May students, librarians, professors, members of *Stahlhelm*, the SA and the *Hitlerjugend* gathered at the Opernplatz in front of the Berlin State Opera. They brought more than 12,000 books from 150 unwanted authors for a huge book burning.

Most foreign media disapproved of the Nazi measures. They therefore did not understand why the Vatican entered into a concordat with the Third Reich on 20 July, thus recognising the Nazi regime. The Secretary of State for the Vatican, Eugenio Pacelli, the later Pope Pius XII, signed the agreement in the presence of Hitler's representatives. Protestant and Evangelical churches also remained silent and even approved of most of the measures. As a result, criticism from the clergy was no longer an issue and the Nazis did as they pleased, in particular in their conduct towards the Jews.

The events in Germany triggered a new immigration wave to the west and to Antwerp. There, the attitude towards the predominantly Jewish foreigners changed with a growing hostility, especially within the emerging extreme right-wing, nationalist factions and parties. In the publication *Hier Dinaso!* from the Verdinaso there were increasingly harsh allegations made against the Jews. All Jews should be expelled from Dietsland (the entire Dutch-speaking area). In the 1934-1935 copy the publication described the Jews as 'foreign elements' who exploited other peoples and caused 'racial degeneration'. The Vlaamsch Nationaal Verbond (VNV) stated that it would fight 'the franskiljon and Jewish parasites'.[18] The fascist movement National Legion, which mirrored the black militia of Benito Mussolini, also published powerfully anti-semitic, anti-Communist and anti-democratic texts during that period. Jews were presented as a danger to society. From that moment on, small-scale riots against Jews and Jewish institutions took place repeatedly.

The VNV and Rex, as well as the Communists, were very successful in the 1936 elections to the detriment of the traditional parties. That led to even stronger anti-Jewish rhetoric and riots. These actions became increasingly racist in character just like in Nazi Germany. At the beginning of 1937 Antwerp lawyer René Lambrechts launched the anti-semitic publication *Volksverwering* (Popular Defence). In it he argued for the total eradication of Jews from society. The paper printed the anti-semitic *Protocols of the Elders of Zion* and saw the Jews as a danger 'to race and soil'.[19] 'Enough protection of the Jews! Jobs for our own people first!' was the message. Research by historian Lieven Saerens shows that in addition to the New Order supporters, the Catholic press and the middle-class organisations were also hostile towards Jews in society.[20] They were not in real danger during that period but the atmosphere was turning sombre.

From 1935 anti-semitic politics in Nazi Germany became ever more extreme. On 15 September 1935 the Reichstag passed the Nuremberg Race Laws, thereby robbing the Jews of all their civil rights. These laws were aimed at protecting the purity of the German blood and prohibited any Reich citizen from having a relationship or intercourse with someone who was not a Reich citizen. To determine definitively whether someone was a Reich citizen or not, the race laws looked into the backgrounds of the grandparents. The laws defined a German as someone who had four German grandparents. Someone with one or two German grandparents was a *Mischlinge*, Quarter-Jew or Half-Jew. And someone with only one or no German grandparents at all was a Three-Quarter Jew or a full-blooded Jew and therefore not a Reich citizen or German citizen. Quarter-Jews, Half-Jews and Three-Quarter Jews who practised their faith were considered to be full-blooded Jews. The new law caused an outrage and received a lot of international attention. The number of laws and measures against the Jews continued to increase over the next few years. By 1938 more than 150,000 Jews had fled from Germany.

The situation became very critical after the Austrian Anschluss to the Third Reich on 13 March 1938. Men in SA and SS uniforms entered Jewish shops in Vienna and took money and other valuables. Crowds shouted 'Away with the Jews' and 'Death to Judaism'. Jews had to clean the streets with their toothbrushes under the humiliating eye of Austrian men and women. The onlookers laughed at them. *The New York Times* published the following on 23 March 1938 on these anti-semitic excesses:

> In a fortnight the Jews have been brought under an infinitely severer regime that was reached in Germany after a year. That is why the daily list of suicides is so great, for the Jews are exposed to arrest, plunder, deprivation of their opportunity for a livelihood, and mob fury.[21]

The Catholic Church supported the Anschluss and called on believers to vote 'yes' in the plebiscite on the annexation of Austria to Nazi Germany. More than 99 per cent of Austrians voted in favour. Tens of thousands of Viennese Jews were imprisoned around this time simply because they were Jews.

Although this news also stirred emotions abroad, Jews on the run received little help. This was evident, for example, during the Evian Conference from 6 to 15 July 1938. On the initiative of US President Franklin Roosevelt, thirty-two countries had gathered in Evian-les-Bains, France. They had to decide on the fate of the Jews in the German Reich. The possibility of admitting them as refugees in other countries was explored. The conference ended in total failure and is one of the darkest pages in history. Most countries refused to accept vulnerable Jewish refugees. The United States and the United Kingdom did not want to change their quota systems and wouldn't allow more Jews into their countries. Most American newspapers were pushing for continued US isolationist policies. The *Christian Science Monitor* rejected any changes to immigration laws and wrote that the best protest was 'praying'.[22] Australia refused to accept more Jews 'since we don't have a real race problem yet, we don't feel like importing one'.[23] France claimed the country had already admitted enough Jews into their territory. Belgium followed France's reasoning and even tightened its conditions after the conference. From 30 September 1938 all Jewish immigrants who wanted to enter the country without permission were systematically sent back. Four South American countries, Argentina, Chile, Uruguay and Mexico, passed new laws that reduced the number of Jews that were allowed in the country.[24] Only a few smaller states, such as the Dominican Republic, made generous promises at the Evian conference, but the overall outcome was nothing short of sad.

Hitler and Goebbels scoffed at the countries that outspokenly condemned Germany's anti-semitic politics, but refused to accept more Jews themselves. The *Völkischer Beobachter* of Vienna wrote: 'We cannot take seriously President Roosevelt's appeal to the nations of the world [Evian] as long as the United States maintains racial quotas for immigrants.'[25] According to the Nazi press, the conference proved the validity of their policies towards the Jews. The Nazis also systematically tightened the conditions for Jews seeking to flee the country. When Hitler came to power, the Jews who wanted to leave Germany were allowed to take with them a maximum of 25,000 Reichsmark. That later dropped to 10,000 Reichsmark. However, an October 1934 law ruled that each emigrant was only allowed to take 10 Reichsmark.[26] It was cynical that the few countries that were still willing to admit refugees made it a condition that they should have sufficient funds to survive. Ludwig Wittgenstein, one of the most prominent philosophers of his day, was in Cambridge at the time. His family belonged to the higher and wealthier class within the Jewish community in Vienna. Ludwig had to use all the family capital to get his family members to safety. However, most Jews did not have the means to do this and could only attempt to cross the border illegally to Switzerland, France, the Netherlands or Belgium. From there, however, they were often sent back.

Meanwhile, there was a dramatic increase in the number of anti-Jewish measures taken by the Third Reich which resulted in overt violence. The German and Austrian populations directly witnessed the anti-semitic wave of violence and terror during and after the infamous *Kristallnacht* on 9-10 November 1938, which was instigated by Goebbels. It was a so-called expression of 'spontaneous' public anger after a Jew shot dead a German diplomat in Paris. Synagogues and Jewish houses of worship were set on fire, thousands of shops and businesses were destroyed, houses, schools and cemeteries were destroyed. About 240 Jews were exterminated. Passers-by in Berlin saw how members of the *Hitlerjugend* beat Jews unconscious with lead pipes while women stood applauding and even lifted their children up so they could have a better view of the violence.[27] In Frankfurt am Main, arrested Jews were met at the station by a mob that yelled at them and attacked them with clubs and sticks.[28] A few days later the Gestapo and the SS arrested more than 25,000 Jews, who disappeared in the concentration camps of Dachau, Buchenwald and Sachsenhausen. .

Fear

Many Jews in Antwerp felt powerless to do anything against these developments. In 1937 Ide moved to a rental house at 26 Vestingstraat, near Central Station and the Portuguese synagogue in the Jewish quarter. The police station in the Sixth District was located 50 metres away. It was a lively area with restaurants, cafes, dance halls and brothels. Next to Ide's house was the tailor I. Binkowicz Tailleur pour Hommes, and opposite was a Hollandsch Restaurant. At number 93 there was the Grand Restaurant Léon Ringer with a banquet hall for weddings and other ceremonies. At number 3 you had an Alsace Traditional House. In the adjacent streets were diamond shops, shops with kosher products and craft shops. A little further south there were dilapidated rental houses, Jewish shops and small businesses. In some streets 'almost half of the residents were from Poland' said historian Herman Van Goethem.[29] Ide was still employed as a tailor, but also had his own studio at home. There he made bespoke tailored suits for Jewish diamond dealers. Each customer had to come to his studio at least twice. The first time to take the measurements, a little later for the final fitting.

During this time tensions were increasing in Antwerp. The Anschluss of Austria by the Third Reich on 13 March 1938 and *Kristallnacht* on 9 November 1938 sparked a new influx of Jewish refugees from Nazi Germany, particularly Jews from Poland, where anti-semitism had flared up. Many Flemish people were unhappy about this migration. Extreme right-wing groups in particular were always vilifying the Jews. Ide and his family must have seen this at first hand. People called out 'Heil Hitler' from their cars and threw fire crackers at groups of Jews.[30] Rex, the National Legion and Popular Defence organised many meetings where the 'Jewish problem' was the main focus of discussions. The national government as well as the Antwerp city council were under increasing pressure to curb the influx of foreigners. Many migrants were accused of disrupting the local small- and medium-sized businesses, engaging in unfair competitive practices and, in general, overrunning the country. It's a little known fact that at the Flemish Conference of the Antwerp Bar on 26 May 1939 the decision was made to exclude any Jewish colleagues. This decision was in line with anti-semitic measures taken against Jewish lawyers which had been in place for much longer in Nazi Germany. It proves that racism was gaining ground in Antwerp.

The story of the *Saint-Louis*, a ship full of Jewish refugees who were trying to escape from Germany for a future elsewhere in 1939 highlights the reluctance to allow in more Jews. On 13 May the *Saint-Louis* left Hamburg for Cuba with 937 Jewish refugees, including 200 children. Each passenger had a valid visa for a temporary stay in that country. They paid about $150 per person for it. It was in fact one of the last refugee ships to depart from Nazi Germany. Shortly after the ship left, Cuban President Federico Laredo Brú, under pressure from anti-semitic groups, signed a decree declaring visas and landing certificates invalid. On 27 May 1939, the *Saint-Louis* entered Havana harbour. She would stay there for days. The police guarded the ship to make it impossible for the passengers to disembark. The Cuban government decided that only twenty-nine passengers were allowed to enter the country because their entry visas were valid. The other passengers were not allowed entry and the ship had to leave Cuban territorial waters. The ship headed for Florida and negotiations began with the United States government. The government emphasised that the quota for foreign nationals entering the United States had been reached and that the boat refugees would be denied access to the country. They made a dramatic appeal to President Roosevelt, but he did not respond. Moreover, the US government sent a Coast Guard vessel to ensure that no passengers would jump off the ship and reach the mainland by swimming. Four days later, there was an official announcement that US authorities were denying them access to the territory. The captain subsequently tried to dock in Canada, but refugees were not welcome there either. After forty days of drifting in the ocean, they eventually returned to the European mainland and moored in Antwerp. The refugees were labelled vagrants by the newspapers and, because they were not welcome here either, arguments started about whether to repatriate them. Right-wing extremist groups demonstrated against them. The fact that there was hardly any compassion for these poor people illustrates the change in mentality.[31] In the end, the British government decided to accommodate 288 of the Jewish passengers, the Netherlands took in 181 passengers, France 224 and Belgium, despite fierce protest, 214. Their safety was only temporary, however; 264 of these Jews were to be arrested, deported and murdered in the extermination camps in Poland after the German occupation of Belgium, the Netherlands and France.

The atmosphere in the Jewish quarter in Antwerp became even worse at the end of August 1939 when openly anti-Jewish riots broke out in the station area, barely a few hundred metres from Ide's house. On 26 Saturday a group of about a hundred demonstrators, men and women, marched through the neighbourhood. They chanted slogans like 'Get rid of the Jews' and 'Out with the Jews'. A shop window was shattered and there was unrest all night in the surrounding area. On the first floor of the Jewish synagogue, a window was smashed with a stone. Young people in the station area also behaved provocatively. The agitators were usually far-right nationalists who admired Hitler and his handling of the Jews in Germany.

During this time Ide was also having dealings with the courts. In May 1938 someone reported to the police that his home was actually a hidden workshop. When the police raided his house they found that he did have some sort of sewing workshop there. According to the police report, other people had been present to help him make clothes. They had asked him about his workshop certificate but he had not been able to present one. The police report stated that as a 'tailor employer' he had violated the law of 15 June 1896 by not displaying a 'workplace certificate'.[32] A few months later he was sentenced by the Court of First Instance to a fine of 140 francs or seven days in prison, with a year probation. Ide paid the fine and stopped taking on staff – usually poor Jewish wretches who did odd jobs for a small amount of money or food.

Much more serious was a complaint filed against him in 1940 for usury. The police arrested him for this. He was released two days later.[33] He was also convicted by the court for this. 'Kartuz was engaged in the sale of ground cocoa husks from July to September. This merchandise that was almost worthless before 10 May 1940 was traded at very high prices.' the April 1942 ruling said.[34] For this he was fined 700 francs or a month in prison. The two convictions would later come back to haunt him.

Anti-Jewish decrees

In May 1940 German troops invaded Luxembourg, The Netherlands, Belgium and France. In Belgium, which capitulated on 28 May 1940, 62-year-old General Alexander von Falkenhausen was appointed as military governor. He had units of the Wehrmacht, the *Feldgendarmerie* and the *Sicherheitspolizei* (SIPO), which included the Gestapo, at his disposal and was also able to call on organisations that collaborated with Nazi Germany, such as the Flemish Guard, Rex and the VNV; later this also included *DeVlag* (The Flag) which was amalgamated into the SS in May 1941. War mayors were appointed in many cities and municipalities. Usually these were supporters of the New Order, collaborators who worked with the occupiers. For the latter, Antwerp was one of the most important cities in Belgium. The Catholic politician Leo Delwaide was acting mayor of Antwerp from May 1940 until 12 December 1940 when his position as mayor was made permanent. During that time the Germans integrated the municipalities of Berchem, Borgerhout, Deurne, Hoboken, Merksem, Mortsel, Wilrijk and a part of Ekeren to form Greater Antwerp.[35]

In the months that followed Mayor Delwaide did what the occupiers expected of him and played an instrumental role in the application of the anti-Jewish laws. From October 1940 to September 1942 the German occupiers issued seventeen decrees aimed at identifying, registering and systematically banning Jews from public and economic life. On 28 October 1940 a decree was issued which required Jews over the age of 15 to register themselves with the municipality in a Jewish register before 30 October. About 42,000 Jews gave their names and addresses.[36] Ide was registered there, in document No. 3837 on 16 December 1940 as were Charles-Victor and Simone. At the top of the card are his name, first name and profession (tailor), followed by his birthplace, Pławno, and his date of birth, 18 September 1905. Underneath he recorded the names, official information and religion of his children. Each of them is marked 'Jew'. Remarkably, he doesn't mention his wife Chaja. In the field 'civil status' it says 'unmarried'. At the very bottom is his address, 26 Vestingstraat in Antwerp. Chaja was registered separately 'without occupation' at the same address. She was mentioned on the same card as her brothers Litman, 'maître d', and Jacob, 'hair stylist'. This personal data about Ide and the other family members was important information for the Germans to have. The Artman-Kartuz family could be easily located using all their addresses.

> Since their registration the Belgian Administration knows the whereabouts of the Jews. The Belgian Administration knows where they live, the Belgian Administration follows them when they move, the Belgian Administration urges them to comply with the other anti-Jewish decrees. The Belgian Administration passes systematically all information on to the occupier, writes historian Herman Van Goethem.[37] The Jews were trapped.

Other stipulations in the decree of 28 October 1940 included a ban on the ownership of businesses and an obligation to indicate which restaurants and off-licence buildings were Jewish. The latter meant that all Jewish cafes, restaurants and hotels had to display a sign with the following heading: *Jüdisches Unternehmen, Joodse Onderneming, Entreprise Juive*. The signs were checked by members of the New Order who notified the local police when there wasn't one or if it was not sufficiently visible. With this law the Germans and their anti-semitic collaborators publicly stigmatised the Jewish population for the first time.

Before 1940 Ide enjoyed life in Belgium. He was a craftsman and worked hard. After eleven years he had built a life here. But suddenly they were outsiders, marked, stigmatised and excluded. His brother-in-law Jacob lost many clients as a hairdresser in the Jewish neighbourhood. Many Flemish people started to avoid Jewish businesses, which led to a loss of income and increasing isolation within society.

Another discriminatory measure concerned working for the government.

> Jews are no longer allowed to hold public offices and, indeed, may no longer hold office with public administrations or associations, foundations and companies, where the State, a province, a municipality or another public-law entity is involved. They may also no longer work as a lawyer, a member of teaching staff at schools and colleges of any kind, nor as a manager, director or editor with the press and radio broadcasting companies.[38]

Although there was a great deal of opposition to these Nazi decrees, the occupiers were still able to impose their will. Mayor Delwaide started by firing the ten Jews who were employed by the city.

The hatred of Jews in Belgium proliferated. This led to an outbreak of violence in Antwerp in April 1941 after the film *Der ewige Jude* (*The Eternal Jew*) was broadcast. In 1939 two propaganda films were commissioned by Joseph Goebbels to stir up anti-semitic sentiment among the German population: *Jud Süss* (*Süss the Jew*) and *Der ewige Jude*. The first one portrayed the Jews in a particularly negative light and was based on a historical novel. The storyline was littered with anti-semitic views and sentiment. The Jews in the film were caricatured and depicted with big hooked noses and dirty clothes. More than 20 million Germans watched it. For the second, which was more of a documentary, Goebbels sent crews to Łódz on 11 October 1939 to film Jews in daily life. The film showed Jewish religious ceremonies, ritual slaughters and bartering. Most of the recordings were shot with actors under duress and with sickly looking Jews. The film had no other purpose but to present them as unreliable, unhealthy and dangerous *Untermenschen*. According to the film, they reproduced like rats that spread diseases. Goebbels personally went to Łódz to visit the Jewish neighbourhoods and wrote in his diary that they had to be dealt with urgently, otherwise 'Europe would succumb to the Jewish disease'. The completely impoverished Jews in Warsaw, Krakow and Lublin were also featured. Their purpose was to reinforce the image of the degenerate Semites. The result was a documentary about a people made to look like animals in the form of hordes of rats and bloody, ritual slaughters, all reinforced by fictitious quotes from the *Talmud*, by Hitler's infamous prediction of January 1939 about the destruction of the Jewish race in Europe and by portraying healthy Aryan youth marching at the end as a symbol of the future, unspoiled German *Volksgemeinschaft* (people's community). The film premiered on 29 November 1940 at the Ufa-Palast am Zoo in Berlin. From December it was broadcast throughout the German Empire but it was less popular than *Jud Süss*. Nevertheless, it had a massive influence on a lot of people and in particular on the members of the Hitler Youth and SS members who had watched the film before everyone else in order to strengthen their ideological views and harden them. Ordinary spectators were greatly shocked after the performance. In some cinemas people walked out feeling sick, complaining about the

'Jewish filth'. In other cinemas the audience spontaneously applauded Hitler's statement about the destruction of the Jewish race. Almost all of them were convinced that the world would be better off without the Jews.

In 1941 the film was released in a Dutch and French-language version. In the early afternoon of Easter Monday 14 April 1941, it was screened in the Antwerp Cinema Rex on De Keyserslei, not far from Ide's rental house. Members of Volksverwering, the Black Brigade – a militia of the VNV – and members of DeVlag, some of whom had sticks and iron bars with them, urged the hundreds of visitors afterwards to teach the Jews a lesson. The agitated crowd stepped to the Jewish Quarter and smashed the windows of houses inhabited by Jews. Then part of the group went on to destroy the contents of the synagogue and set it on fire. They did the same to another synagogue and the rabbi's house, as well as smashing shop windows, damaging belongings and looting.[39]

Eyewitness Ephraim Schmidt described how the far-right nationalists smashed the synagogue's entrance gate, gathered the prayer boards and set them on fire along with the sacred scrolls. Members of DeVlag posed in front of the fire with their flag which was inscribed with *Juda Verrecke* and *Ras en Bodem* (Blood and Soil). The police didn't interfere and at first did not even allow the fire brigade to put out the fire. To avoid more unrest the police decided to impose a curfew from 10 o'clock in the evening. Two days later the curfew was lifted, except for the Jews. From that moment on they had to stay indoors from 6:00 pm. Later on they were no longer allowed in the Antwerp parks. Over the following days several more incidents took place in the Jewish Quarter during which windows were frequently smashed, doors were kicked in or defaced. On shop windows the text 'No Jews here' appeared and the collaborating, German-led press shifted responsibility for the riots onto the Jews in scathing articles. The events have gone down in history as the *Antwerp Kristallnacht*. They clearly showed that the Jews were no longer safe and were becoming more and more isolated.

On 31 May 1941 a new decree stipulated that, in addition to the catering establishments, all other Jewish businesses must have a trilingual sign. The Jews also had to declare all their assets and real estate. These included houses, apartments, commercial dwellings, undeveloped land and second homes. They were also required to deposit their assets in a designated bank and were not allowed to open an account in any other bank.[40]

Jews were forced to hand in their radio sets before 30 June 1941 to the local *Kommandantur* and this had particularly far-reaching results. In return they were given a receipt. To the outside world the German occupiers presented this as a necessary measure to ensure security and to prevent Allied information being heard and circulated by the 'enemy'. This had an enormous impact on the Jews because they were now cut off from one of the most important news sources and leisure pastimes of that period. From July 1941 they were no longer allowed to keep carrier pigeons for the same reason.

As was the case in other countries, from the summer of 1941 Jews were also forced to have a 'Jew' stamp on their identity card. This was a consequence of the Anschluss in 1938, when many Jews tried to flee Austria and Germany to, for example, Switzerland. Since they weren't welcome there, the Swiss government therefore asked the Nazis to mark the passports of Jews with a two-centimetre-high letter 'J'. This was agreed in a protocol between Bern and Berlin at the end of 1938. The *Judenpass* was born. It helped the Swiss immigration authorities to reject and send back tens of thousands of Jews desperate to escape the Germans. Many of them would later die in the concentration camps. The German occupiers thought this was an excellent means of identifying the Jews and, on 29 July 1941 a circular was sent by the Ministry of Interior to all municipalities: 'This means of identification must be inserted by you above the photo of the person concerned, in red ink, by means of a rubber stamp, in block letters of about 1.5 cm.'[41] Its implementation was in the hands of the local authorities. In practice it meant a second kind of Jew count. Each municipality also had to provide the *Sicherheitspolizei* with a copy of the full list of names in the Jewish Register and indicate who had already been registered. This way the occupiers gained an overview of any new Jews or those who had not previously registered.

But their freedom of movement was to be restricted even more. The decree of 29 August 1941 stipulated that the Jews could no longer go abroad and that they were no longer allowed to leave their homes between eight o'clock in the evening and seven o'clock in the morning. They had to settle in Brussels, Liège, Charleroi or Antwerp. Other cities were excluded as the occupiers not only wanted to isolate the Jews but, above all, concentrate them so that they could get a tighter grip on them. On 25 November 1941 a Jewish Council, the Association of Jews in

Belgium, was established on the orders of the German occupiers. Its main objective was supposedly to promote the emigration of the Jews. But soon it acted as an organisation that participated in the identification, discrimination, arrest and deportation of the Jews from various Belgian cities. A few days later, on 1 December 1941, a law came into effect which stipulated that Jewish children were no longer allowed to go to non-Jewish schools. The Jewish Association had to organise its own education.

In 1942 the situation deteriorated further. On 6 March a new law was established which involved compulsory employment for all inhabitants of Belgium. Five days later, on 11 March 1942, a similar measure was passed which was aimed specifically at the Jews, who were now at the mercy of the occupiers.[42] An example of this was seen over the following months when more than 2,000 Jews were brought to the north of France for Organisation Todt to help with the Atlantikwall, a defence line with barbed wire, bunkers and other coastal reinforcements which was built as a defence against a possible invasion by the British and Americans. Most of them were deported to Auschwitz.

These measures also affected the Artman-Kartuz family. Jacob Artman, Ide's brother-in-law, was transported from the north of France to Auschwitz. No one was aware of what had happened to him at the time. At the end of March and early April 1942, a third kind of Jewish count took place. The Jewish Association compiled cards with the family composition of the Jews. As a result, the children were now also known and the Nazis had a complete insight into the exact number of Jews, their origins, their parents and grandparents, their marital status, their faith, their profession and, most importantly, the address where they resided.

The last crucial step in the final approach to the 'Jewish problem' was the decree of 27 May 1942 which said that every Jew from the age of 6 had to wear a Star of David in public. The six-pointed star was made from yellow fabric, outlined in thick black lines and was the size of the palm of a hand. On it was a black letter 'J'. The mark of shame had to be sewn on the garment according to strict rules; at the height of the left breast.[43] The Jews had to pick up the felt star from the municipal council. Officials then put a stamp of the Star of David next to the name of the relevant Jew in the Jewish Register. Natan Ramet, who grew up in Antwerp and later survived Auschwitz, recalled this event as follows:

Father had to pick up those stars from city hall for the whole family. And he had to pay for them; 1 franc for three stars. That felt really humiliating for me. I had already been permanently marked as a Jew, there was a stamp on my passport 'Jew', and now the star! No, we weren't locked in a ghetto, but you could call Antwerp a virtual ghetto at that time.[44]

Ide likewise must have collected three stars, one for himself and two for the children. His wife Chaja probably picked it up separately because she was unmarried under Belgian law. Usually the women took care of sewing the stars onto the clothes, but as a tailor Ide would undoubtedly have done this himself and he must also have had a lot of requests from his customers to sew them on a jacket or tailored suit since this would have been a regular occurrence. After all, the star had to be sewn regularly on to other garments.

In the meantime the occupiers continued to restrict the freedom of movement and professional activities of the Jews. From 1 June 1942 Jews were excluded from all medical professions. Jewish doctors, dentists, midwives, paramedics and other nurses had to mark their practice clearly with a Star of David and were only allowed to treat Jewish patients. From 13 July 1942 Jews were no longer allowed to sit in the front part of urban trams, they were no longer welcome in cinemas, cafes, restaurants, theatres, public swimming pools or at public demonstrations. Later they even had to hand over their bikes. Everything had been made ready for the systematic deportation of the Jews. The names and addresses were to hand. All that had to be done was lure them to the Dossin barracks in Mechelen and transport them to the east.

The search

To begin with it looks like it might be difficult for us to find out exactly how the family members reacted to the increasing lack of freedom, the oppression and the violence. Ide had never really talked about it with his son Benno. Benno, for his part, had never dared to ask about it. Instead of focusing principally on the Kartuz family, we also try to find out more about the Artmans. We discover at the Belgian State Archives that not everyone had died during the war, something we have suspected for a long time. Litman Artman and his sister Fajgla Artman apparently managed to flee or go into hiding. But where are their children and are they still alive? According to their birth dates they would now be at least 87 to 110 years old. Basing our search on the name Artman proves almost futile; there are many thousands of Artmans in the world and we have no clear starting point. Our search methods are many and varied, including Facebook. However, we realise that we are trying to find information about women who may have married and taken their husbands' surnames, which we don't know. For this reason, we focus our research on Abraham Dzierlatka, Lilliane and Laura's father. That name is much less common. His file shows that he fled to the United States in 1940. That is an important starting point. After extensive Googling we find a reference to him in New York.

The discovery gives us hope. All day we are making and taking calls; at work, on the train, during dinner. After all, there is a chance that Dzierlatka's children, Lilliane and Laura, are still alive and that they knew Ide and his children Charles-Victor and Simone Kartuz. Maybe they can tell us more about the conditions before the war. Perhaps they can tell us about how they lived together as a large Jewish family and about how they all ate *matsebrei* (*matzah brei*) together.

We're asking our friend Michael Danziger for help. He calls himself 'a creep' because he is so good at tracking down Jews, anywhere in the world. He has helped us before and maybe now his search talents will come in handy again. The Holocaust is ingrained in him. His parents were refugees themselves and lost many family members in the extermination camps. Less than twenty-four hours after our request he sends us an e-mail with information about Lilliane Dzierlatka. She is married to Nathan Shuman and has taken his name. That makes it harder to find her. But Michael finds an article via Google about the children of the diamond industry in Cuba and from this he is able to find the family. Apparently, she has a son, Kip Shuman, a lawyer in San Francisco. Through his office's website we find his phone number and call him. His mother Lilliane, who knew Ide and who could have told us so much about her family before the war, died a month earlier at the age of 89. That's a serious blow for us, too; we are a few weeks late and assume that we will now never speak to a witness again.

Lilliane

Although Kip Shuman is still in mourning, he offers to join our search and help us with our story. He sends us a piece of text that his mother Lilliane dictated before her death. Finally, a unique and first-hand testimony from an Artman. With this text and the archive file on Abraham Dzierlatka we have an insight into the life of Lilliane and her family members before and during the war.

Lilliane described how her father had come to Antwerp from Warsaw in 1925 and found work there as a diamond setter. They lived on the second floor of an apartment in the centre of town. Her mother Faigla was a housewife and she had a younger sister, Laura. Together with the other Artmans they went on holiday to the coast in Blankenberge, where the children would play on the beach. Lilliane had a busy but pleasant social life. Only her grandparents were missing. They were still living in Warsaw and later ended up in the ghetto. Lilliane wrote that she did not understand why her parents had not brought them to Belgium. Her happy life came to an end on Saturday 10 May 1940. The invasion of the Germans sent shock waves through the Jewish community. Her father Abraham decided to leave Belgium. Lilliane and Laura each put their most important possessions in a small bag which they took with them. Their father carried two suitcases. Out of necessity, they had to leave the rest behind in their apartment. Along with thousands of other refugees they took a train to France. En route her mother Fajgla miscarried. Her three uncles' families had also joined them: Ide Leib Kartuz, Litman Artman and Jacob Artman. After three months they decided to return to Antwerp while her parents wanted to carry on to Bordeaux in the unoccupied part of France. From there they hoped to make the crossing to America but Fajgla became increasingly ill from the miscarriage and had to be admitted to hospital. She had a high fever and was delirious. Lilliane and Laura were hospitalised with blood poisoning and leg infections. Meanwhile the Germans advanced. The Luftwaffe bombed Bordeaux while they were in the hospital. Their father Abraham came to visit them every evening. One day he told Lilliane and Laura that they wouldn't see him for a while. He told them to stay strong and take care of their mother. They didn't see him again until after the war, five years later.

Abraham managed to find a job as a stoker on the SS *Edith*, a steamship that would sail to the United States. He left without his sick wife and children and arrived in Virginia on 7 July 1940. He immediately tried to obtain a residence permit so he could then get permission for his family to join him. Abraham failed because the US applied strict immigration rules. He was supposed to leave the country but ignored the ruling. In a document from 1942 addressed to the Immigration and Naturalization Service in Philadelphia, his lawyer, Jacob Singer, made a plea for him to be allowed to remain in the US.[45] He argued that as a diamond setter he could financially support himself and his family and therefore did not need the help of the government. He even declared himself willing to enlist in the US Navy. If he was not granted permission to stay in the US, he asked immigration authorities to give him permission to go to Cuba. Abraham Dzierlatka's initial plan to have his wife and children join him quickly was unsuccessful because he himself was refused settlement. From this moment he went into hiding.

America no longer allowed entry for refugees, forcing his wife and children who were searching for a safe place to live to stay in Bordeaux. Fajgla sold her jewels to survive. After a few months she moved to Marseilles, where she left her daughters in a refugee camp for children. Lilliane and Laura had to harvest figs, while their mother Fajgla went to the consulates of France, Spain and Portugal to try to get the necessary papers to be able to travel to the United States. She wasn't successful. In April 1941 Fajgla and her daughters decided to return to Belgium. She paid a smuggler who took them to Belgium. They went into hiding in their former apartment for a month. Fajgla tried to convince her sister Chaja and her brothers Litman and Jacob to flee, but they refused. As the Anti-Jewish Laws became stricter, she returned to Bordeaux with Lilliane and Laura and from there to Lisbon, where they joined more than a hundred other Jewish refugees, without the necessary visas, on board the SS *Serpa Pinto*. On 24 January 1942 she sailed from Lisbon to the United States via Casablanca. The 850-passenger ship docked in Havana, capital of Cuba, on 16 February 1942. Fajgla and her daughters were allowed to disembark but were locked up in a detention camp. However, they were released because Fajgla was a good diamond setter. At that time dictator Batista had dreams of a diamond industry in his country and needed professionals for it. She, together with hundreds of other Jewish refugees, was therefore able to work in the diamond sector for over three years. Lilliane and Laura went to a local school. Fajgla

Artman's story was later picked up and turned into the documentary *Cuba's Forgotten Jewels, A Haven in Havana.* The then Cuban government accepted a total of more than 6,000 Jewish diamond workers and their relatives from Belgium and other countries. Lilliane wrote in her testimony that that period in Cuba was the happiest of her life.

Meanwhile, Abraham was working illegally in the diamond sector in New York City. Through his Jewish lawyer he submitted new applications for a residence permit. On 23 June 1943 his application was denied again by the Immigration Department and he was ordered to leave the country again. On 8 February 1944 his application was rejected for the third time. On 29 March 1944 his lawyer sent an emotional letter to immigration:

> This man escaped tyranny and oppression and arrived here where freedom, equality and justice prevail, and in a country in which all persons regardless of race, colour and creed may live in peace, honour and dignity. This man was threatened with extermination if he had not escaped as he did and was doomed for destruction. By executive order of His Excellency, Franklin Delano Roosevelt, recently, a refugee board was created to take action for the rescue of as many people as possible of the persecuted minorities. I trust that your facilities can be employed to aid this man and his family in their present dilemma, as in my judgment, this case is a tragic one as many others are.[46]

He wrote that his client was stateless and would be perfectly capable of building his own life as a diamond worker in the US and be an excellent citizen of the country. He was even willing to enlist in the US Army. On 14 November 1944 the Immigration Department revoked Dzierlatka's order for deportation. They would continue to consider his request for residency.[47] He finally got the green light in 1945. A friend gave him an article about Jewish refugees in Cuba. From one of the photos he recognised his wife Fajgla and his daughters Lilliane and Laura. On 11 November 1945 his wife and children travelled to Miami, where they finally met again after five years. The family moved to New York, where the children went to school and learned English, their fourth language.

In her testimony Lilliane wrote that she found out that her father had been seeing other women. That came as a great shock to her because her mother had never spoken ill of him and loved him dearly. Lilliane met a beautiful young man at Hunter College in New York City, Shuman. They married and moved to California. She lived there until her death on 30 March 2019. They had one son: Kip Shuman.

Mimi

According to our research, there is another family that survived the Holocaust. Litman Artman managed to go into hiding with his family and our latest records show that he moved to the United States with his wife and two daughters. With the help of Michael Danziger we find Mireille Artman on Facebook under the name Mireille Brodsky, the name of her ex-husband. Hopeful, we try to contact her but, because we don't get through to her immediately, we contact her son-in-law, David Finkelstein. Thanks to him we finally find Mimi, who is able to tell us something about Ide's life before the war.

Mireille or 'Mimi', the last Artman, is 89 years old and lives in a service apartment in Sarasota, Florida. We ask her if she knew Ide, Chaja and their children Charles-Victor and Simone. Her answer is promising and could mean a breakthrough in our investigation. She writes to us that Charles-Victor and Simone were her favourite cousins and that she knew them well. She adds that she and her sister Elaine survived the war by going into hiding in Brussels. We can't pass up this opportunity. Mimi is our key witness. She is the only one who can help us answer some crucial questions. Two weeks and six hours later we're flying to Miami.

The border police are understaffed when we arrive after an unexpected six-hour delay. Moreover, entering the US since the 9/11 attacks is no easy feat. We wait in line for more than two hours. Fingerprints of all ten fingers are taken, as are two pictures of our faces, and we are asked if we have anything to declare. We have an apple and dutifully declare it. We are told to stand to one side, our luggage is screened and then we are directed to another airport security checkpoint. A police officer points out to us that we mustn't eat the apple or it will cost us $500 to $800. Once we've passed security, we pick up our rental car and have a boring drive through the night in the Everglades. Four hundred kilometres farther west lies our destination, Sarasota, a town on the Gulf of Mexico. We're exhausted but luckily we are able to sleep for about five hours. We have an appointment with Mimi the following day.

When we meet Mimi the next day, she greets us cheerfully and warmly. She is very happy to meet new family after all these years. She's not alone. Her daughter Suzan, her son-in-law David Finkelstein, and Kip Shuman, who took the plane from Los Angeles, are also present. It's an emotional moment for everyone. Mimi talks non-stop in English, French and even some Dutch about the extraordinary course of her life. She also wrote it down for us in an eight-page testimony.

She was born in Antwerp in 1932, the eldest daughter of Litman Artman and Deborah Zucker. Her parents had come to Belgium from Poland in the early 1920s. As a child she experienced the period before the war as a happy time being surrounded by aunts, uncles and cousins. She lived with her parents and older sister Elaine at 7 Schupstraat on the ground floor. Her uncle Ide, whom she called Yidle, and her aunt Chaja, whom she called Ushkele, lived with the children on the top floor. She often played with Charles-Victor and Simone and went to school with them in Antwerp. They enjoyed good times and had little trouble with rising anti-semitism in the city before the war. However, she heard from an uncle that he was smuggling desperate Jews from Germany to Belgium. Mimi didn't remember exactly who that was but as a child she understood that Belgium was a better and safer place to live.

Everything changed after the Germans invaded Belgium in May 1940. Many thousands of Belgians, Jews and non-Jews, fled to France. Mimi remembers her father carrying her on his neck because she was sick and also carrying two suitcases. She felt sorry for him. Her mother and her sister Elaine followed. They got on a full train. Above their heads they heard the German planes. Close to the French border her family got off, but the train continued with the other families still on it. Because Mimi had terrible earache, she couldn't continue the journey. The family went looking for help and stopped at a farm. The farmer's wife gave Mimi her own child's bed because she was so sick. There was no doctor or hospital but there was a platoon of British soldiers nearby. The army doctor was kind enough to examine the girl. He diagnosed meningitis and gave her penicillin, a drug Dr. Alexander Fleming had invented only one year earlier. She was probably one of the first civilians to receive the drug as it was only released to the public from

January 1941. Mimi survived and continued her journey with her family to France where they joined the rest of the family and where they found shelter in a school. Everyone, Abraham Dzierlatka and Fajgla Artman, Litman, Ide Leib Kartuz and Chaja Artman, Jacob Artman and Paula Singer and all the children, welcomed them. They didn't have many worries. The summer was beautiful. They played hide-and-seek at the nearby cemetery and played on the small farm. But it wasn't a situation that could last.

The Germans were advancing and the families discussed what to do. Abraham wanted to flee to Bordeaux and from there take his chance to make the journey to the US. The other families decided to return home. It was the end of August and the schools were due to start again soon. Their lives and work were in Belgium. The money ran out and many just wanted to pick up their daily life again at home. Mimi, her sister Elaine, her cousins Charles-Victor and Simone all went back to school. In the first few months of the war they still felt free, but the Nazis were tightening the noose for the Jews. Due to the many anti-Jewish decrees they were not allowed to go out after 6:00 pm, they were denied entrance to cinemas and parks and they had to hand in their radios. For many it became really difficult when the Nazis banned them from doing certain jobs or owning a business. From May 1942 they had to wear the Star of David. Mimi recalled that at that moment the situation changed. The non-Jewish children walked along one footpath to school, the Jewish children with their Star of David on their coats on the other side.

Another witness

After our trip to Florida and our meeting with Mimi we contact several newspapers. Mimi's story is unique and it's almost a miracle that she lived to tell the tale. *Gazet van Antwerpen* is immediately interested in what we have discovered and sends Patrick Vincent, a journalist, to interview us. We show him the different places where the Kartuz, Dzierlatka and Artman families lived in Antwerp. When we are standing in front of the house at 169 Kroonstraat he suggests ringing the bell. Of course no one in the family lives there anymore, but a visit to the house where Jacob Artman and Paula Singer married is very special. Nowadays it houses an association that deals with youth activities.

We ring the bell and hear a croaky voice. Patrick explains via the intercom why we're here. A few seconds later the door buzzes and we go up the stairs. The office space is divided up and there are people working. For a brief moment they wonder why we are here but our story soon gets their attention.

'It's said the building was owned by painter Luc Tuymans or at the very least that he had a studio here,' someone says. That's a nice detail, but we are of course here for the historical significance of this building. We are all silent, emotionally overcome to be in the house where almost the whole family gathered for the last time, seventy-seven years after the deportations. After our visit we tell Patrick in detail about our research which has been going on for over a year and a half. He listens carefully but it must undoubtedly have been quite a challenge for him to be able to summarise the story of this large family in a captivating article. The next day our detailed story is in the papers with the headline: 'It wasn't until after his death that I learned he had survived Auschwitz.' There are pictures of our journey, of Mimi and, of course, of Ide who posed with his wife and children, the photo Kip found in his mother's archive – the one where we first saw Charles-Victor and Simone.

We get a lot of feedback on the article. One morning we get a phone call from Claude Marinower, the Alderman for Economic Affairs in Antwerp. He tells us the unbelievable story of an elderly woman who addressed him at the newsagent's. The lady told him that her husband had lived next door to 'the Kartuz' before the war. Our interest is once again aroused immediately because, with the exception of Mimi, this is the only direct witness who knew Ide before the war. Claude sends us his phone number and we call him right away. He tells us that as a young boy he lived next door to the Kartuz family and that he had many Jewish friends. He becomes emotional. Almost everyone he knew then, when he was young, was deported and murdered in camps. We ask if we can meet him and record his story.

That same weekend, with a large bunch of flowers, we pay a visit to the husband and wife. We are grateful to Arlette and Henri De Deken for inviting us. Henri's story is crucial to our reconstruction of Ide's life (Henri always uses his nickname Jules) and may give us answers to the key questions about his life before the war.

I remember often having to turn on the electricity on Fridays because it was sabbath. Kartuz himself didn't really

92

follow this rule but many other Jews from the neighborhood did. As 13-year-old young lads, we were constantly going into each other's houses. Jews or non-Jews, none of that mattered to us. We all spoke Dutch with each other. There was no animosity at all, even though we were traditionally Catholic and they were Jewish. I do remember that around 1942 one of my friends was wearing a 'Star of David' on his clothes. Even though we were both at different schools we had to go the same way. That's why we walked down the street together. I thought the star was strange but I had no idea what it meant. The Jewish children told us they had to wear it.

Henri witnessed that the synagogue was plundered completely by the Germans. 'The doors were open and we played there with our scooters. I also saw the Antwerp police going on a rampage. I do remember people being picked up in trucks.'

Henri remembers Chaja's departure.

I don't remember seeing Jules (Ide) before he left, but Chaja came to see us at our house before she left. She said the Germans would be coming to fetch them. Chaja had no idea where she was going. Kartuz himself must have known that something bad was about to happen because at some point he asked my mother if she could look after his tailor's table. That was one of those tables tailors used to sit on during their work. The table remained in our house for the rest of the war, after which we returned it to him. There were even diamond dealers who would conceal their diamonds in the cellar walls of their houses. Everyone tried to hide their belongings. Many of those buildings were demolished in the 1970s. The construction workers must have had some good pickings back then.

Henri also recalls other deportations:

A lot of my Jewish friends left, but I had no idea where they were going. When we were young it looked as if they had simply moved out. My parents must have been aware of a lot more, because my father Jos has a certificate from the Jewish Community in which he is recognised for his heroic acts for the Jewish community. My mother and father also helped people to escape from Antwerp to Brussels where the situation for the Jews was less precarious. My parents risked their lives doing this. Litman Artman has never forgotten that and that's why he testified for my father. It's also why my father got that certificate, says Henri.

Henri also knew the Kartuz children. He even has a picture of his brother Raymond De Deken, who won a fancy-dress competition with Simone at the Ancienne Belgique in Antwerp. 'You can keep it. Send it to Mimi in Florida. It's a precious memento.'

After the war they still saw Ide regularly although he never spoke about his children Charles-Victor and Simone. Everyone knew what had happened to them though. 'After the war it was too painful for a lot of people to recount those stories.' Arlette and Henri De Deken married in 1960 and it was Ide who made a wedding suit for Henri. Unfortunately, they don't have the actual wedding suit anymore but they do of course have a picture of it. Henri is still very fond of that suit. 'You won't find in the shops today a suit that fits so perfectly. The one Kartuz made was perfect. He made sure his customers looked great and he always looked dapper as well,' concludes Henri. Kartuz lives on in his memory as the master tailor of Antwerp.

Employment in the east

Mid-July 1942 Maurice Benedict, a director of the Jewish Association, was called to the *Sicherheitsdienst* in Brussels where he was told that the Jews would be sent for employment in the east to replace the German manpower which had been deployed to the army.[48] The Jewish Association was responsible for the organisation and prepared the selection cards of 10,000 Jews. The Germans promised that families would not be split up and that Jews with Belgian nationality would not be affected. Later they would break that promise. In July 1942 the selected Jews received an *Arbeitseinsatzbefehl*. The summons letter stated a specific day and time the person concerned had to register at the Dossin barracks in Mechelen. They were instructed to bring the following things: (1) food for 15 days, but only non-perishable edibles such as tinned food, dried vegetables and flour. (2) A pair of heavy duty work shoes, 2 pairs of stockings, 2 shirts, 2 pairs of underpants, 2 sheets, a bowl, a cup, a spoon and a pullover. (3) Clothing coupons, ration books, their identity cards and other documents. They also had to follow the guidelines of the Jewish Association. They were forbidden from raising any objections with anyone but the assembly centre. Finally, there was the threat of deportation to a concentration camp in Germany and the sequestration of their property for those who failed to report.

About 4,000 Jews complied with this summons. The first of these arrived at the Dossin barracks on 27 July 1942. Convoy I left Mechelen as planned on 4 August 1942 with 1,000 Jews for an unknown destination in the east. This was a particular cause for concern. People soon realised that it wasn't ordinary employment. Women, the elderly and small children had to accept the order and they, too, were to be deported. This was something completely different from the previous calls for 'compulsory employment'. These had been restricted to adult men and, as a result, insufficient numbers of Jews were presenting themselves voluntarily in Mechelen and so the transports were therefore being delayed. Nevertheless, the German High Command decided that the deportation of Belgian Jews had to continue at all costs.

During the night of 15/16 August the Nazis carried out a raid. Flemish collaborators together with the Antwerp police men arrested the Jews by force and under the threat of death took them to Mechelen. The SS had lists of addresses detailing where all the Jews lived. They also knew the exact composition of the families.

Emile Vos, an Antwerp Jew, was one of those dragged from his home. He stated:

> There was nothing for me to suspect in the evening that the next morning at 4:30 am someone would knock at my door. It wasn't in a civilized way; the police hammered on the door. They gave us 20 minutes to pack everything and go with them. That's how we were taken to Mechelen. In Mechelen we had to jump out of the van quickly and

then get the kids out. Anyone who had any dealings with them knows that everything had to be done *schnell, schnell, schnell, loss, loss, loss, loss.* So we rushed to get out of that van as quickly as possible and then line up on two sides. That was my first introduction to the Germans. There they stood: my wife and her three children and I immediately wanted to be with them. I thought, that is where I belong, and then one of those Germans grabbed me by the neck and swung me over to the other side.

Vos was deported to Auschwitz-Birkenau on 1 September 1942 in Convoy VII along with 999 other Jews. He never saw his wife and three sons again. He himself survived several concentration camps.

The Jews were still in danger, even after the largescale raids underpinned by the Antwerp police in August and September 1942. Many went into hiding with the help of the resistance, some in the city, others in the countryside. Flemish Jew-hunters and other collaborators received tip offs and drew up lists of designated houses where Jews in hiding were arrested and taken away in trucks or in other methods of transport.

Hiding

When the first rumours circulated about forced labour for the Jews, Litman Artman decided to go into hiding with his family; Jacob Artman and Ide Leib Kartuz didn't. Father Litman entrusted his daughters Mimi and Elaine to a Catholic couple in St Gillis near Brussels. This didn't end well. The wife made too many appearances with the children in the street, taking them to the cinema and ice cream parlours; the children should have been at school, so it attracted attention. They therefore found a new hiding place with another, more discreet, French-speaking couple in Uccle near Brussels. The girls stayed in the attic there from October 1942 until the liberation in September 1944. The house at no. 25 August Dansestraat was right next to a school. The couple, Cora and Leon Clement, were called 'marraine' and 'parrain' by the children. The first thing they learned was how to hide quickly if there was an unexpected visitor. Mimi was very small and had to hide in a laundry

96

basket in the kitchen cupboard, under the dirty laundry. Elaine had to hide in the basement behind a coal bin. During the day Mimi was taught by her sister who was three and a half years older. Their mother had told them to do this. The last thing that Elaine learned in school were fractions. Mimi therefore learned nothing but fractions for three years. They also played cards and read books such as Antoine de Saint-Exupéry's *The Little Prince*.

The highlight of the day, Mimi said, was watching with binoculars other children in the school playground. Sometimes they were allowed outside when it was dark, and occasionally they could go for a walk on the street with *marraine*, without a Star of David on their clothes of course. When someone asked who they were, Marraine said they were nieces from Bruges who had come to visit.

During this time, their parents had moved to a street next to Central Station in Antwerp, where they hid on the top floor. Mother Deborah sold some of her jewellery to pay the rent and for their food. The Germans carried out raids regularly in that neighbourhood but they didn't find them because the Jewish Register had them at a different address. One day when their building was searched they were alerted by Leopold, the caretaker who was a close friend. He locked their apartment from the outside while Litman and his wife climbed a ladder onto the roof of the building and then pulled up the ladder. The members of the Gestapo had not found them and had left but Litman realised that the neighbourhood was becoming too dangerous. In the end the Clements agreed to hide the parents in their attic in Uccle as well. Before going into hiding Deborah took risks and would travel to Antwerp with *marraine*, without a Star of David, to sell her remaining jewels there; having no ration books they had to buy everything on the black market. On one of those dangerous journeys their train stopped in Mechelen and the Germans came on board to arrest Jews. She distanced herself from *marraine* and sat down at the end of the carriage. Just before the Nazis got to her, they turned and left. They were never discovered in Uccle, although on one day this was almost not the case. A neighbour saw *marraine* go home with a lot of food, which was suspicious because officially they were just two people. She informed on them to the occupier but *parrain* Leon's contacts let him know immediately. They smuggled the girls to one of *marraine*'s cousins. Mimi's parents went into hiding at another address. The Gestapo searched the house, but did not find them at 25 August

Dansestraat. Three days after the search, Elaine, Mimi, and later on their parents, returned to the attic to hide again.

On 3 September 1944 the allied forces liberated Brussels. Yet the danger had not gone away. The Nazi propaganda machine continued to insist that Germany would prevail because it had brand-new weapons with enormous destructive power. Propaganda Minister Goebbels called them *Vergeldungswaffe* (retaliatory weapons), hence the abbreviation V-. They had a range of 240 to 400 kilometres. From October the Germans fired V-1 and V-2 missiles at Belgian cities; especially the Antwerp region and Brussels which were badly damaged.

Mimi and her family were still living with the Clement family in Uccle at the time. On 1 February 1945 at 9:45 pm, a V-1 struck a building just behind the house of *marraine* and *parrain*. Stones went flying through the air, windows came away from their frames and a cloud of dust spread everywhere. Elaine's face was bleeding excessively and she screamed that she was blind. Deborah was injured in the neck but Litman and Mimi were unharmed. Deborah rushed down and found *marraine* seriously injured on the floor. She quickly ran out and tried to find American or British soldiers. They came to the rescue and saved her. Eleven people were killed and forty-eight injured that night. Once again, Mimi had a narrow escape.

The house was partly destroyed but the family continued to live in Brussels. Litman commuted to Antwerp every day and worked there as a diamond dealer. Yet they kept in touch with the Clement family almost daily. Mimi studied later in Brussels and visited *marraine* and *parrain* regularly. In 1949 the family sailed on the steamship *New Amsterdam* to New York. They had almost no family left in Belgium and the bond with Ide was not that strong. Deborah had family in New York. Only Elaine stayed behind and got a job as an air hostess with Sabena, which kept her in Belgium. Mimi worked for a company in Massachusetts and married Brodsky. They had a daughter Suzan and a son Richard. Her sister Elaine died in 1991, her father Litman died in 1992. He was 95 years old.

Mimi remembers her Aunt Chaja very well. 'She was loving and hugged us like no one else could.' Chaja's children, Charles-Victor and Simone, were her favourite cousins. She was a little more critical about Ide. He wasn't considered to be a full member of the loving Artman family because he didn't want to marry Chaja. That's why her brothers disapproved of him. We have no idea why he didn't want to officially marry her. Maybe he valued his freedom, maybe he thought marriage was just an administrative matter. We'll never know. Ide is not often pictured in the many pre-war photographs that we see thanks to Kip Shuman. Apparently, Ide was often on his own. The others were always there, at parties, at the seaside or in Antwerp. After the war Mimi was not allowed to see Ide straightaway. He looked like a skeleton and her parents wanted to protect her from such a cruel image. Mimi saw her uncle once more. That was in 1948 with his second, much younger and very good looking wife, Joséphine. After that never again. Mimi doesn't speak badly of him but clearly thinks that he was a bit of a maverick. Ide was special.

Ide

In a questionnaire after the war from the Consultative Committee for Political Prisoners Ide stated that he belonged to the Independence Front (*Onafhankelijkheidsfront*) from July 1941 until his arrest on 22 June 1942. This resistance movement was formed in March 1941 by the Belgian Kommunist Party and became the most important one in the country. In fact it was the umbrella organisation for several groups with different political ideologies: the Belgian Army of Partisans, militant trade unions, the Youth Freedom Front, the Patriotic Militia and also the Jewish Defence Committee. One of its main activities was to keep hidden and 'get to safety thousands of Jews, including more than 2,000 children'.[49] Another task of the Independence Front was to circulate illegal publications. An example is the liberal magazine *De Vrijheid* (*The Freedom*), which reached a circulation of 500 copies from December 1940 and focused on opposition to the freedom-robbing measures of the Nazis. Several men from the resistance who contributed to the publication were arrested during the course of 1942 and ended up in concentration camps. In addition, there were several other clandestine papers which fought Nazism and promoted communist ideals instead. One remarkable clandestine paper was *Het Vrije Woord* (*The Free Word*), produced by the resistance movement Vrank and Vrij (Straight and Free). Its circulation reached several thousand copies and it was compiled by Jews and non-Jews and appeared as early as 1940.

The authors, like Ide, were of Polish Jewish origin and published articles specifically against the persecution of the Jews. Towards the end of 1941 the publication began calling on Jews to go into hiding.

> Try to find a safe place in a non-Jewish home, where you can stay illegally from the moment your safety is jeopardised. ... It is high time that you finally learn for yourself the necessary lessons from the fate of the Jews in the Third Reich and Poland! Don't wait till it's too late![50]

Equally important was *België Vrij (Free Belgium)*, the militant publication of the Antwerp Independence Front, which advocated both the independence of Belgium and the recapture of the democratic freedoms as well as the rights of the Jews.

Ide was recruited into the resistance by Jewish trader Joseph Feld. His job was to distribute clandestine papers, put up manifestos and allocate financial resources. One of the papers he secretly posted through people's letterboxes was the militant publication *België Vrij*. It contained liberal, patriotic, communist and Jewish opinions and was under the supervision of the Independence Front.

The writing, printing and distribution of such clandestine articles was not without danger. Usually the papers were put through the letterboxes of houses and apartments at night. But, as a Jew, Ide was not allowed to go out after 6 o'clock in the evening. If the police or a German *Feldgendarm* or patrol had found him and asked for his passport, they would have seen the stamp 'J' and would have arrested him immediately. Ide was small, nimble and agile. He would go to another neighbourhood before curfew and quickly distribute the forbidden publications. He found shelter with another resistance member and did not return home until daylight. One of Ide's other tasks at the Independence Front was the distribution of money. He received large sums of money that he passed on in tranches to the underground press. They used it to buy paper and ink, but part of the money was also for the many destitute Jews who had no income and did not receive any state support. Some of them were Jews in hiding who refused to follow the calls from the occupier to present themselves for 'voluntary employment'. This was, of course, a dangerous predicament. While other resistance men often knew only one or two accomplices, thus keeping to a minimum the risk of a crackdown on the illegal network by the Germans and their Flemish collaborators, Ide knew plenty of them because of his role as money distributor.

During this time the police office in the sixth district of Antwerp, which was located in Vestingstraat where Ide also lived, took on more and more committed Flemish-nationalist German-minded policemen, the so-called 'blacks'. They dealt more and more harshly with the Jews in the district, which also endangered Ide. Because of the clandestine press the Independence Front was both a thorn in the side of the Antwerp police as well as the German occupiers. In addition the resistance regularly attached posters to windows and doors calling for opposition to government orders. It is quite possible that the Gestapo or Flemish collaborators were watching Ide because of his resistance activities.

Razzia

On 22 July 1942 the first major arrests of Jews were made in Antwerp and Brussels, carried out by *Feldgendarmen*. Flemish SS men also played a role in this. That same day, together with the Germans, they arrested Jewish commuters on the train going to and returning from Brussels–Antwerp.

A number of young female detainees had to do the administration for the Dossin barracks. At that time it was dealing with the establishment and opening of the camp from where the Jews would be deported to Auschwitz. The Germans detained Jews not only directly from the trains but also from the streets surrounding Antwerp station. Ide was arrested on the footpath near his house in Vestingstraat and a number were arrested in other side streets. According to Ide, the resistance was the principal reason. In a *pro justitia* from the police of the sixth district, Kartuz stated on 8 February 1949:

> I was arrested on 22 July 1942 in Antwerp on the public road Vestingstraat. This was done by *Feldgendarmen*, who handed me over to Gestapo members in civilian dress. The latter were Belgian. I was transported by train to Mechelen station where we were loaded on trucks and taken to Fort Breendonk.[51]

In a report by the Deputy Police Commissioner of the Antwerp Police of 26 November 1949, Ide explains why he was arrested. 'I had been a part of the resistance movement O.F. ... since 1941. In my opinion the people who detained me were aware of my membership of the resistance, although I was never directly questioned about this.'[52] The police stated that his arrest and subsequent deportation happened for reasons of race and therefore 'it is reasonable to assume that the person concerned was arrested because he was a Jew'.[53]

Whatever the reason, Ide was arrested on 22 July 1942 together with at least 163 other Jewish men and women and taken to Fort Breendonk.[54] Breendonk was a Flemish *Auffanglager*, not a concentration camp, but the conditions for the prisoners hardly differed. Camp commander *SS-Untersturmführer* Philipp Schmitt was particularly cruel. He didn't carry out the killings, but he made his officers torture and kill many prisoners. From 15 July 1942 Schmitt was also put in charge of the Dossin barracks. During this period the camp was transformed and prepared as a transit camp to the east. A central registration office was set up in the long room on the ground floor in the left wing of the barracks.[55] Tables, chairs and typewriters were brought in. Other wings were converted into workshops, dormitories, an infirmary, decontamination rooms, showers, latrines, cells and a kitchen. Several women who were arrested at the same time as Ide and mastered the German language or knew dactylography, were enlisted as administrative employees.[56]

Meanwhile, Ide had to conform to the hard regime in Breendonk. Like the other prisoners he was at the mercy of the guards, who included Flemish SS men who manhandled them in a particularly brutal manner. Life in the camp hardened him. He behaved as unobtrusively as possible to avoid being humiliated, hit and other consequences. For him it was – somewhat cynically – a 'training ground' for what was still to come. Furthermore, in addition to Yiddish, Polish, French and Dutch, he also spoke German. That, too, would help him later.[57]

One day the Germans forced him to write a letter to his wife and ask her to come 'voluntarily' with the children to the Dossin barracks. If she didn't, he wrote, it would have serious consequences for him. In this devious way the occupier was able to arrest as many Jews as possible. Ide stayed in Breendonk for thirty-two days and was transferred to Mechelen on 23 August 1942. He was only there for two days during which time he saw his wife and children again. It was a terrible farewell for him, he declared after the war. In the Dossin barracks, the registration office was now working at full speed, as described by researcher Laurence Schram: 'The *Aufnahme* (registration) staff work day and night: finishing lists for deportation, handing out identity plates, carrying out searches, finishing documents for when victims give up their belongings ... .'[58]

On 4 August, the first deportation train departed with 998 people, including fifty-one children. New deportations, each involving about 1,000 people, followed on 11, 15 and 18 August. The first transports consisted of Jews who had voluntarily responded to the call from the Jewish Association or had been arrested for violating one of the anti-Jewish decrees. After that it was more difficult, because the Jews no longer presented themselves voluntarily. In this, too, German soldiers, Flemish collaborators and the police force were involved. They said the detainees were refusing to work. They arrested a total of 845 people. The youngest person 'who refused to work' was under five years old. All were taken by trucks to the Dossin barracks. The news of the raid quickly spread amongst the Jewish community in Belgium and caused many to hide. By then it was too late for Ide who was in Breendonk from where he was transported to Mechelen. On 25 August he and 995 other detainees had to line up in the courtyard of the barracks. In rows of ten, groups of fifty to eighty people boarded the train carriages that were waiting there. The men had to sit separately from their families in a different wagon. Ide, Chaja, Charles-Victor and Simone left Mechelen with the fifth convoy. Their destination was 1,200 kilometres farther east, a camp they had never heard of before: Auschwitz.

Part Three

Auschwitz

Camp history

Almost all Jews who were deported from Belgium ended up in the Auschwitz-Birkenau concentration and extermination camp. The Polish city of Oświęcim is at the confluence of the rivers Wisła and Soła and for this reason has been strategically important since the beginning of the twentieth century. In 1916 a military camp was built there. The city has long been home to large groups of Jews. They accounted for about half of the total population.[1] When the war began on 1 September 1939, Oświęcim was immediately bombed. Barely three days later the Wehrmacht entered. After Poland was defeated the Germans started looking for suitable barracks to house the prisoners. They were drawn towards Oświęcim, which they gave the German name of Auschwitz. The city station was easily accessible from all directions. There were good train connections to Krakow in the east and to Katowice in the west and from there farther west via the important railway line to Breslau, on to Berlin and Hamburg. The SS men drove out the Polish residents from the most beautiful blocks around the station and along the rivers; the SS officers and their families then moved in.[2] On 4 May 1940 Rudolf Höss was appointed commander of the nearby camp. At that time it consisted of twenty-two brick barracks. Four of them were two-storey. In the middle was a large exercise square that had previously been used by the Polish cavalry. Under Höss's command the entire camp was fenced off with barbed wire and at the entrance a cast-iron gate was put up with the inscription *Arbeit Macht Frei*. The barracks were divided into workshops and sleeping areas.

The first prisoners were thirty German criminals. They arrived on 20 May 1940 from the concentration camp in Sachsenhausen. They were housed in Block 1 and numbered from 1 to 30. Later on they would become the *kapos*, notorious and feared for their enormous cruelty.

The block was used simultaneously as an annex for the kitchen and as a clothing warehouse (*Kleiderkammer*) and a shoemaking and sewing workshop.[3] On 14 June 1940 a first transport of 728 Polish prisoners arrived. They were locked up in blocks 2 and 3. The following transports from Warsaw with more than 2,000 Polish prisoners ended up in blocks 4 to 8 . The Poles remained the largest group until the middle of 1942.

SS-Obergruppenführer Oswald Pohl, who on behalf of the SS was responsible for the inspection and the management of the concentration camps but also the deployment of prisoners for forced labour, issued an order that the capacity of Auschwitz should be substantially increased. The prisoners therefore built eight new blocks on the exercise square and floors were added to the existing, ground-floor barracks. The intention was to create a transit camp for Polish prisoners of war. On the corners of the camp high guard towers were erected and the double fence was electrified. The prisoners also built a kitchen, made stables of the former workshops and transformed the old Polish army ammunition depot, which was located to the left of the entrance outside the camp, into a crematorium. At the end of July 1940 the company Topf und Söhne installed two ready-to-use incinerator rooms. They had a throughput capacity of seventy bodies a day. In the course of 1941 the same company added two double muffle furnaces with a total cremation capacity of about 400 corpses per day.[4] Many of the dead came from the infamous Block 11. It was isolated from the other blocks. On each floor there was a cell for about a hundred prisoners. Downstairs were some small cells in which the victims were only able to stand upright. Sometimes prisoners were starved. In this block prisoners were tortured and then shot dead in the space between Block 10 and Block 11. The bodies then had to be transported to the crematorium on the other side of the camp. However, this method was not workable. The Germans realised that they needed a system whereby the murder sites were out of sight of the victims but in the immediate vicinity of the various crematoria. Only in this way would they be able to efficiently and methodically kill and cremate the large numbers of prisoners without too much shouting and opposition.

In the meantime Auschwitz' *Stammlager* was expanded further. By the end of 1941 it already had 18,000 prisoners. During 1943 that number rose to 30,000.[5] The chemical company IG Farben was looking for a suitable location for the construction of a factory for the production of synthetic rubber and fuel. When Himmler visited the company at the beginning of March 1941 he decided to support the project. The location for this future Buna factory was located in Monowitz, about seven kilometres from the main camp. Auschwitz would provide the necessary forced labourers. IG Farben agreed to pay 3 Reichsmark per day for an unskilled worker. For skilled workers the amount was 4 Reichsmark per day. At the end of 1942 3,500 prisoners were employed there; by the summer of 1944 the number reached more than 11,000. Later, when more camps had been added, they operated under the name Auschwitz III-Monowitz.

Operation BARBAROSSA began on 22 June 1941. Nazi Germany attacked the Soviet Union and initially achieved great success. In a few weeks the Germans had captured hundreds of thousands of Russian soldiers. They held them in makeshift camps and starved them. In the autumn of 1941 the Nazi leaders decided to expand Auschwitz to 200,000 prisoners. Ten thousand Russian prisoners of war were sent to the camp and deployed to build the sub-camp three kilometres away in Brzezinka, which in German translated into Birkenau. This camp was huge. On an area of 100 hectares they built more than 300 brick and wooden barracks, industrial kitchens, latrines and warehouses. The area was double fenced with sixteen kilometres of electrified barbed wire.[6] The working life conditions were terrible and the SS men treated the forced labourers particularly brutally. The 945 Russians who were still alive after five months in Auschwitz I had to go to Birkenau. With new incoming transports their numbers were continually being replenished. Himmler had also instructed Höss to allocate and reserve space in a number of barracks in the main camp for Jewish women where they would carry out forced labour. From March onwards several women's transports arrived from Ravensbrück. But Jewesses also arrived from Slovakia, Romania, Hungary and Upper Silesia. They ended up in blocks 1 to 10. At the end of April 1942, 6,700 women were crammed together in the crowded barracks. Some had no beds and slept on the floor.[7]

Höss wrote in his memoirs that the living conditions in the women's camp were even worse than in the men's camp.

> They were far more tightly packed in and the sanitary and hygienic conditions were notably inferior. Furthermore the disastrous overcrowding and its consequences, which existed from the very beginning, prevented any proper order being

established in the women's camp. When the women had reached the bottom, they would let themselves go completely. They would then stumble over like ghosts, without any will of their own, and had to be pushed everywhere by the others, until the day came when they quietly passed away. These stumbling corpses were a terrible sight.[8]

The women were there until August 1942, after which the survivors were transferred to the women's camp in Birkenau. The first ten blocks were now empty. In the meantime the camp continued to expand. In the period from 1942 to 1944, a network of more than forty sub-camps was established in the wider area of Oświęcim and it grew into the largest concentration and extermination camp in the Third Reich.

Zyklon B

During this time the Germans continued to look for a means for the large-scale eradication of prisoners. The killings by gunshot were a psychological burden on the SS men. In other extermination centres carbon monoxide was used but that too had many disadvantages. For this reason they started looking for a more efficient method of getting rid of the prisoners. At the end of August 1941 *SS-Lagerführer* Karl Fritzsch experimented in Block 11 with the disinfectant *Zyklon Blausäure* (Zyklon B). The hydrogen cyanide or prussic acid had first been used to disinfect the barracks of the Polish prisoners but it also turned out to be an efficient means of killing people.[9] Because at first it didn't work well, the dose was increased and 'good results' were achieved.

Camp commander Höss described a new experiment with the gas as follows:

> The gassing was carried out in the detention cells of Block 11. Protected by a gas mask, I watched the killing myself. In the crowded cells death came instantaneously the moment the Zyklon B was thrown in. A short, almost smothered cry, and it was all over. During this first experience of gassing people, I did not fully realise what was happening, perhaps because I was too impressed by the whole procedure.[10]

However, he was clearly not distracted by the procedure for a long time because, on 3 September 1941, 600 Russian prisoners were murdered with the deadly gas in the morgue next to the crematorium. Höss wrote:

> I have a clearer recollection of the gassing of nine hundred Russians which took place shortly afterwards in the old crematorium, since the use of Block 11 for this purpose caused too much trouble. While the transport was detraining, holes were pierced in the earth and concrete ceiling of the mortuary. The Russians were ordered to undress in an anteroom; then they quietly entered the mortuary, for they have been told they were to be deloused. The whole transport exactly filled the mortuary to capacity. The doors were then sealed and the gas shook down through the holes in the roof. I do not know how long this killing took. For a little while a humming sound could be heard. When the powder was thrown in, there were cries of 'Gas!', then a great bellowing, and the trapped prisoners hurled themselves against both the doors. But the doors held. They were opened several hours later, so that the place might be aired. It was then that I saw, for the first time, gassed bodies in the mass. It made me feel uncomfortable and I shuddered, although I had imagined that death gassing would be worse than it was. ... I must admit that this gassing set my mind at rest, for the mass extermination of the Jews was to start soon.[11]

From that moment onwards the system of mass gassing was used more frequently. The morgue in the main camp was converted into a permanent gas chamber which remained in operation until well into 1942. In total, at least 10,000 people, mostly Jews, Poles and Russian prisoners of war, were exterminated here.[12] The Jew Filip Müller, who came to Auschwitz with one of the first transports from Slovakia, had to work with the *Sonderkommando* of the crematorium in the main camp from April 1942. In the crematorium, next to the converted morgue, there were two ovens on the left and four ovens on the right. According to his testimony, each oven had a capacity to incinerate three corpses at the same time.[13] Outside the building an SS officer would address the Jews. He told them they had to work in the camp. But first they had to disinfect themselves by taking a shower, supposedly in their own best interest, after which they would get a bowl of soup. Once they were in the gas chamber, guards locked the door and SS men with a gas mask on poured the Zyklon B through the holes in the ceiling. When the gassings took place the prisoners who worked in the camp were not allowed to leave their barracks. To drown out the screaming and yelling, motorcycles were left running but people inside the gas chamber could still be heard on the outside. The prisoners knew all too well that an extermination session was taking place.[14]

From the spring of 1942 the Germans also used two converted farms near Birkenau, the Red House and the White House. Due to the increasing influx of prisoners, more and more people were being gassed there, in particular Jews and sick people from the camp. The first house had a capacity of about 800 people, the second about 1,200. After the gassing the *Sondercommandos* were deployed to throw the corpses into mass graves and sprinkle them with lime. In September 1942 it was decided that the bodies had to be exhumed for cremation. *Sonderkommandos*, which consisted of mostly Jewish prisoners, were told by their guards to do this with their bare hands. It must have been a terrible job. Erko Hejblum, one of the *Sonderkommando* survivors described it thus: 'We waded in a mix of mud and decaying bodies. We would have needed gas masks. The corpses seemed to rise to the top – it was if the earth itself was turning them back.'[15] Others talked about the diabolic fate of the working Jews who had to haul the decomposing corpses full of maggots out of the pits, move them and then burn them.[16] In his autobiography, camp commander Höss wrote about this:

> During the summer of 1942 the bodies were still being placed in the mass graves. Toward the end of the summer, however, we started to burn them; at first on wood pyres bearing some 2,000 corpses, and later in pits together with bodies previously buried. In the early days oil refuse was poured on the bodies, but later methanol was used. Bodies were burnt in pits, day and night, continuously. By the end of November all the mass graves had been emptied. The number of corpses in the mass graves amounted to 107,000.[17]

On 26 March 1942 the first two transports arrived. A first train brought 999 Jewish women in enclosed cattle wagons. They came from the concentration camp in Ravensbrück and upon arriving they were tattooed with the numbers 1 to 999 on their left arm. Among these women were some who were later appointed as the first female *kapos*.[18] *Kapos* were prisoners who had to supervise fellow prisoners for which they were given certain privileges. Two hours later a second train carrying 999 Jewish women arrived from Slovakia. They were given the numbers 1000 to 1998. Two days later a further 798 Jewish women arrived from Slovakia and on 30 March another full train from Drancy, France, arrived with Jewish men.[19] They were all kept alive, at least temporarily. Selections on the basis of competence and economic use began on a regular basis from 4 July 1942.[20] From the summer of 1942 onwards, large transports from Austria, Slovakia, Poland, The Netherlands, France and Belgium arrived. The selections happened immediately upon arriving at the camp. Those who were 'useful' ended up in Auschwitz I or in Auschwitz III-Monowitz. In particular, locksmiths, carpenters, bricklayers, builders and tailors had at that time and in the short-term a better chance of survival.[21] The 'useless', including the sick, disabled, elderly and women and children, were sent to Birkenau and gassed.

In order to kill and burn even larger numbers of Jews, the Germans in Birkenau built the gas chambers and crematoria II, III, IV and V from March 1943 until June 1943. Supplies for their construction were received from the company Topf und Söhne. According to the sinister calculations of the engineers who built them, they had a capacity of 4,756 corpses per day.[22] With these installations the extermination camp was running at full speed. Before their extermination the victims arrived in a kind of changing area. Along the side were benches and numbered coat hangers. They were supposedly having to shower in the room next door but in reality it was the first step to the gas chambers. To facilitate the arrival of new transports for extermination the SS men followed strict guidelines. Höss described this as follows:

> It was most important that the whole business of arriving and undressing should take place in an atmosphere of the greatest possible calm. People reluctant to take off their clothes had to be helped by those of their companions who had already undressed, or by men of the Special Detachment [*Sonderkommando*]. The refractory ones were calmed down and encouraged to undress. The prisoners of the Special

Detachment also saw to it that the process of undressing was carried out quickly, so that the victims would have little time to wonder what was happening.[23]

The naked women kept their children by their side and stepped into the gas chamber. They believed they were going to be disinfected. According to Höss, this usually happened quickly and calmly, with one or two exceptions.

> It sometimes happened that, as the men of the Special Detachment left the gas-chamber, the women would suddenly realise what was happening, and would call down every imaginable curse upon our heads. I remember, too, a woman who tried to throw her children out of the gas-chamber, just as the door was closing. Weeping she called out: 'At least let my precious children live.'[24]

It didn't always go the way Höss would like us to believe. A lot of prisoners started crying and screaming. They were brutally pushed and beaten into the gas chambers until no one else could fit in. When the doors behind them closed the Zyklon B was poured in via the roof. The air in the room was warm due to the body heat of the victims. As soon as the pellets came into contact with it, they turned into a deadly gas. People close to the holes in the roof suffocated quickly. The others screamed and pounded on the doors. Some tried to get some fresh air by crawling on top of others. After about twenty minutes everyone was dead, the ventilation turned on and, after a short wait, the doors were opened. In Birkenau a total of about 2,000 Jews worked in the *Sonderkommandos*. They had to haul the corpses out of the gas chambers, cut off the women's hair, rip off prosthetics, pull out the gold teeth. A small elevator was used to transport the bodies to the furnaces where they were burned two or three at a time. The soiled gas chambers were then cleaned out for another load. Other working Jews were responsible for collecting the clothes, suitcases and other abandoned items. They took them to the large sorting warehouse Kanada, named after the 'rich' country of Canada. The remains of human bones were crushed with a special *Knochenmühle* (bone grinder) and the ashes were poured into the nearby Wisła and Soła rivers. Local residents could smell the stench from the cremations in the furnaces kilometres away. 'This extermination had to be carried out in secret. But the terrible and sickening stench of uninterrupted burnings of corpses permeated everywhere in the area. All the people who lived nearby knew that there were exterminations in Auschwitz,' said camp commander Höss.[25] It was impossible to keep the crimes secret.[26]

Convoy V

On 25 August 1942 the fifth convoy left the Kazerne Dossin barracks in Mechelen in Belgium for Auschwitz. Ide left very little information about this hellish train journey to the east that lasted several days. In the State Archives we found a short questionnaire which he completed in 1951. It describes the circumstances of his arrest and deportation. In it he states that he sat in a third-class passenger train with sealed windows for three days. The occupiers used third-class carriages in the first months of the deportations from Belgium, The Netherlands and France. This contrasted sharply with the transports from the east which usually took place in freight trains. After the twentieth convoy on 19 April 1943, freight trains with locked doors were used for deportations from Belgium.

The travel conditions in the fifth convoy were fairly good compared to the transports that followed later. Ide stated that there were no guards in the carriage, that the wagon offered enough space for the deportees and that there was a separate room to relieve themselves. Asked what the food arrangements were like, Ide replied that he had brought a 'parcel from home' but no drinks. 'We had nothing to drink. German women offered us water despite it not being allowed by the supervisors.' He doesn't mention his wife and children, but a deportation list from the Kazerne Dossin does show that they were in the same transport in a different wagon. Ide also says very little about his first days in Auschwitz. He briefly talks about two selection processes that were carried out immediately on arrival at the camp. The first was for those 'who were unable to go on foot' and who were therefore transported by truck. The second was based on 'age and signs of ageing', and also 'on occupation'. He did not provide more information in writing. However, after the war he stated in various documents that his wife and children were gassed immediately upon arrival and that he worked there as a tailor.

Handteekening van den vreemdeling,

Right: Signature of
the foreigner, *Ide Leib
Kartuz*, on his arrival
in Antwerp in 1929.
(© Belgium State
Archives)

Below: The house
where Ide Leib
Kartuz was born,
27a Młynarskastreet
in Pławno (Poland).
(© Private collection
David Van Turnhout)

Train with German soldiers heading for Poland in September 1939. (© Yad Vashem Photo Archive)

An Einsatzkommando commanded by Arthur Nebe kills 476 Jews. (© United States Holocaust Memorial Museum)

Above and below: Mass murder of Jewish women, children and babies from the Mizocz ghetto (Ukraine) by an Einsatzkommando on 14 October 1942. Anyone alive, got a neck shot. (© United States Holocaust Memorial Museum)

The burning of corpses at Hadamar's euthanasia centre. (© Dioezesanarchiv Limburg (DAL), Papers or Father Hans Becker)

The SS-staff in Bełżec with amongst others Lorenz Hackenholt, Ernst Zieke, Karl Gringers and Heinrich Barbl, who were previously active in the T4 Program. (© United States Holocaust Memorial Museum)

Right: Deportation of Jews to the Treblinka extermination camp. (© Hubert Pfoch – Treblinka Museum)

Below: The remains of the Jewish cemetery in Plawno. (© Private collection)

Above: Procession of young Polish nationalists in 1934. (© Narodowe Archiwum Cyfrowe)

Left: Ide with Chaja and the children in 1936. We only found this photo at the end of our research. (© Kip Shuman private collection)

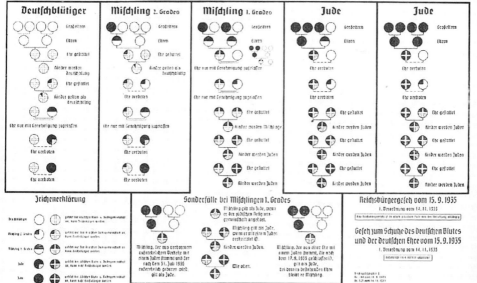

Above: Classification into Germans and Jews according to the Nuremberg Race Laws of 15 September 1935.

Right: Three Jewish girls with the Star of David in Brussels: Mathilde Bein, Sarah Skala and Nicha Kichka. (© Kazerne Dossin – Maximilien Skala Fund, Mechelen)

Above: The SS Serpa Pinto which saved thousands of Jewish refugees from the Holocaust. (© United States Holocaust Memorial Museum)

Left: Mimi Artman-Brodsky, 89, in Sarasota (Florida). (© Kip Shuman private collection)

Inner yard of the Kazerne Dossin barracks in Mechelen. Spread out on the floor are the possessions of the Jews. (© Kazerne Dossin)

DAS KONZENTRATIONSLAGER AUSCHWITZ I ("STAMMLAGER")
HÄFTLINGS-LAGERBEREICH - AUSBAUSTAND AUGUST 1944

	0	50	100	200 m

a – Schutzhaftlagerführung
b – Lagertor
c – Blockführerstube
d – SS-Krankenrevier
e – Verwaltung
f – Lagerkommandantur
g – Krematorium 1 und Gaskammer
h – Politische Abteilung (Gestapo)
i – Kfz-Abstellplatz
j – Hauptwache

k – Wohnhaus des KL-Kommandanten
l – Magazin (ehem. Theater)
m – Exekutionsstätte (Kiesgrube)
n – Wäscherei für die SS
o – Postbaracke
p – Häftlingsküche
q – Häftlingsschreibstube im Block 24
r – Sammelgalgen
s – Häftlingskrankenbau (HKB)
t – HKB/Tötung von Häftlingen mit
    Phenolinjektionen

u – Block 11 ("Todesblock") Strafbunker
    Lagergefängnis
v – im Hof Erschießungswand/Galgen
w – Block 10 - Versuchsstation für
    "medizinische" Forschungen
x – Waschbaracke
y – Sichtschutzwand
z – Nebengleis für Häftlingstransporte
◼ – Wachturm
✳ – Stacheldrahtzaun, doppelt um das
    Häftlingslager, elektrisch geladen

Map of Stammlager Auschwitz I. Circled is Block 1 where Kartuz was imprisoned.
(© Wikiwand.com)

Two symbolic train wagons on the site of the original Judenrampe in Auschwitz. (© Auschwitz-Birkenau Memorial Museum)

Collection of sewing machines from the various clothing workshops in Auschwitz-Birkenau. (© Photo St. Mucha 1945)

Prisoners at work in the tailoring workshop of the Ravensbrück women's concentration camp. (© Mahn- und Gedenkstätte Ravenbrück)

Block 1 in Stammlager Auschwitz (left in the picture), where the tailors' Kommando worked. Between Block 1 and Block 2 was a lower wooden building that contained the old laundry. The photo dates from after the war in 1945. (© Auschwitz-Birkenau Memorial and Museum)

Maryan Gnyp who arrived at the camp four days after Ide. (© Auschwitz-Birkenau Memorial and Museum)

Female prisoners in the Kanada Kommando sort the stolen items of the gassed Jews. (© United States Holocaust Memorial Museum)

Jewish prisoners disinfect the attire of the newly arrived and gassed Jews. (© Auschwitz-Birkenau Memorial and Museum)

Dr. Wladislaw Dering, who successfully treated Ide Kartuz against phlegmon. (© Auschwitz-Birkenau Memorial and Museum)

SS officers and SS-Helferinnen enjoy the Solahütte in June 1944. (© United States Holocaust Memorial Museum)

Arrival of Hungarian Jews in Auschwitz-Birkenau in May 1944. (© United States Holocaust Memorial Museum, courtesy of Yad Vashem)

Gateway to the KL Mauthausen in 1940. (© Bundesarchiv)

Bodies of prisoners in the Gunskirchen concentration camp. (© KL Gedenkstatte Mauthausen)

Joséphine Vervloet with Ide Leib Kartuz in 1946. (© Private Collection Cathy Eyletters)

Eichmann during his trial in Jerusalem on 4 May 1961. (© Israël National Photo Collection)

Swastikas on Jewish graves and the text "Wir Sind Zurück" on a wall in Oosterhout, the Netherlands. (© ANP)

To gain a better insight into Ide's deportation to Auschwitz-Birkenau, we visited Laurence Schram, a historian and senior researcher at the Memorial, Museum and Documentation Centre on Holocaust and Human Rights in Mechelen. She elaborately describes how the different convoys were organised, their dead and their survivors. Schram has her office in the original barracks where the victims of the persecution of the Jews in Belgium are commemorated. Next to it train tracks can still be seen. On these tracks, wagons carried the dehumanised prisoners like cattle to the East. Schram shows us the *Mechelen-Auschwitz 1942-1944* book series in which she describes the history of the transit camp. She opens the book on page 250 and points to the description of the fifth convoy. The fifth transport contained 996 people, 486 of whom were men and 510 were women.[27] Half of them had complied with a summons order from the Association of Jews of Belgium. On behalf of the SS they encouraged Jews to voluntarily report to the Mechelen assembly camp. From there they would go to Germany or another country for forced labour. The summoned Jews had to bring food for fourteen days – only food that does not spoil – a pair of sturdy work shoes, two pairs of socks, two shirts, two underpants, a work suit or work dress, two woollen blankets, two bed covers, a food bowl, a drinking cup, a spoon and a pullover, food and clothing coupons, an identity card and other papers. The first Jews registered at the Kazerne Dossin on 27 July 1942. In the weeks that followed 3,000 voluntary workers registered. Distrust increased though and many Jews went into hiding. About half of convoy V consisted of Jews who, like Ide, were arrested during raids in Antwerp and Brussels from 22 July 1942 onwards. The train arrived in Auschwitz on 27 August 1942. Seventy-eight per cent of the passengers were immediately gassed, including Ide's wife and two children. In the following weeks and months another 188 victims of convoy V died. In the end, only twenty-seven men survived the camp, including Ide. We can only keep guessing what his journey to the camp was like and how he spent his first few days there.

Hoping to find testimonials about the transport, we go over the names of the other survivors with Laurence Schram. After some searching, we strike it lucky: Simon Majzels, the son of a Jewish tailor from Warsaw who had fled to Belgium and was deported as a 17-year-old with convoy V. Next to his name is written his profession: 'tailor'. We are very happy when we find a short testimony by him on the website of the USA Holocaust Memorial Museum in Washington. In it he talks about his arrest and deportation. The testimony of Simon Majzels dates from 1997 and was recorded by the Musée de l'Holocaust Montréal in Canada. To obtain the full testimony, however, we need permission from a direct relative of his. By googling the name Majzels, we arrive at Robert Majzels, a 70-year-old Jewish writer, poet and professor at the University of Calgary in Canada. His year of birth, 1950, corresponds with our estimate that a possible child of Simon who survived the camp must have been born relatively shortly after the war.

We send him an e-mail and wait in excitement. After two days, we finally get an answer. Robert Majzels is indeed Simon's son. He has never heard of Ide Leib Kartuz. Via e-mail, he grants us permission to request the testimony of his father.

101 tailors

Having paid for the copy and shipping costs, one week later we receive a DVD with the full testimony of Simon Majzels. More than half a century after his liberation, he testified about his youth in pre-war Antwerp, where he arrived with his parents in 1925. His father worked there as a tailor, his mother as a housewife. They had a good life until the Germans occupied Belgium. In 1941 young Simon was no longer allowed to go to school; later he had to wear a Star of David and be home before curfew. Just like Ide, he was active in the communist resistance. He helped out with the underground press, distributed flyers and sabotaged German trucks by sprinkling sugar in the petrol tanks. During the first raid in Antwerp on 22 July 1942, German *Feldgendarmen,* men in black clothing, picked him off the street and led him to the Kazerne Dossin in Mechelen. He stayed there for over a month with his parents. On 25 August 1942, however, they were brutally separated and about a thousand Jews boarded a passenger train that took them to an unknown destination. They did not receive any food or drink; only those who had volunteered to work in the east brought food and drink. They shared it with the others.

> After a journey of a few days and nights, we arrived in Auschwitz in the afternoon. German SS men beat up

everyone. '*Raus, raus, raus,*' they shouted. The elderly and women with babies had to go and stand on the left at the instruction of the infamous army doctor and *SS-Hauptsturmführer* Josef Mengele and were sent straight to the gas chambers. A group of 101 men was led to the main camp under the guidance of SS soldiers. I had to work in a furniture factory, said Majzels.

Majzels' testimony gives us a first-hand picture of what Ide must have experienced when he arrived at the camp. But there are mistakes in his story. For example, he says that on arrival he was subjected to a selection by Mengele. It is a statement of someone whose memories are clouded by subsequent knowledge. Mengele was indeed active in Auschwitz, but only from 30 May 1943, and therefore not when the Belgian Jews arrived on 27 August 1942. The selection was probably done by another SS doctor.

For greater certainty we try to find another survivor from the list. With the help of our researcher, Wendy De Poorter, we come upon a testimony from David Mandelbaum. He was born on 31 August 1922 in Oberhausen, Germany. In the 1990s he gave a testimony for the Belgian Auschwitz Foundation. Her offices and archives are in Brussels and we make an appointment to watch the video. On the screen we see an old man with big black sunglasses. He is blind. In a very serene way, he talks about convoy V and his ordeal on the way to and in Auschwitz. It was the first time he had talked about this. His father left Poland in 1917 because he did not want to serve as a Jew in the army and went to Germany with his wife to start a bakery. In 1924 the family moved with 2-year-old David first to Brussels. David left school at the age of 14 and learned the craft of tailoring. His father and mother had communist sympathies. They were horrified to hear the news about *Kristallnacht* in Germany in 1938. A refugee from Germany, who had been in a concentration camp as a communist, visited them and recounted his terrible experiences to the family. The stories encouraged young Mandelbaum to join the Independent Front in 1940, after the Germans invaded Belgium.

But in the summer of 1942 things went wrong. Members of the Gestapo arrested resistance fighter Mandelbaum. He was ill treated by his interrogators in the Gestapo building on Avenue Louise in Brussels. Afterwards they took him to Kazerne Dossin in Mechelen. There he saw the third and fourth convoys leave for the East. On 25 August 1942 it was his turn to join convoy V along with 995 other Jews. Mandelbaum remembered many details about the journey in the third-class carriage. The train first stopped in Leuven. Some people got out to buy some food and drink at the station buffet. Everyone simply returned to the train. 'I could have escaped,' says Mandelbaum, but neither he nor the others did.[28] The next day the train stopped again near a village. Again, some were allowed to disembark, but as soon as they heard the train whistle, they all returned voluntarily. The carriages were packed with men and women of all ages. There were also a lot of children. 'They were anxious,' says Mandelbaum, but they had a kind of expectation that they would work in the east. Nobody knew what was about to happen, but everyone must have had an image in their minds of life there. The children must have asked their mother where they were going. What are we going to do, mommy? Will we be going to school there?

These were questions Chaja could not answer because she herself did not know what happened in the 'labour camps'. Maybe she replied that the children would go to school when she went to work. Maybe she thought she could be with the children every night after work. Maybe, like Ide and so many others on that train, she still had blind hope that it would be better than expected.

Two days later they stopped in Auschwitz. Mandelbaum:

> The train pulled in very slowly between two and three in the afternoon. The weather was nice and we saw people in striped prisoner uniforms. When the train stopped, we all had to get out quickly. They shouted: 'Fast, fast, leave your luggage in the carriage'. When everyone had got off the train, the *triage* of people started. They asked us what profession we had. I said I was a tailor and they put me to one side. The others were put on a truck and taken away; I don't know where. When we were 100 tailors, they divided us up into rows. The person who carried out the selection came from Brussels and was also a tailor. That made us 101. Then we walked to Auschwitz.

Like Majzels, Mandelbaum speaks about that group of 101 selected people in his testimony but he explicitly states that they were all tailors.

'I was one of a hundred tailors hand-picked to work but the others were taken away and gassed. We walked to Auschwitz, the main camp, and the rest to Birkenau, the gas chambers.' The testimonies of Mandelbaum and Majzels and Ide's written answers correspond on specific points. The train ride in a third-class carriage, the lack of drink and food, the arrival in Auschwitz, the immediate selections and, especially, the composition of a unit of 101 people. An additional and very important confirmation of that number can also be found in the reference work *Kalendarz wydarzeń W KL Auschwitz* by the Polish researcher Danuta Czech. She made an overview of what happened day after day in Auschwitz. Dated 27 August 1942, she says: 'After the selection, 101 prisoners were sent to the camp. They were given camp numbers 61938 through 62038.'[29]

It is strange that so many tailors were on that train. That is why we ask Laurence Schram for the complete list of Jewish deportees in convoy V. The Germans kept a careful record of everything and next to each name they wrote the date of birth, the place of birth and, in a final column, the occupation of those involved. On the list we find fifty-six tailors (*Schneider*), seventeen leatherworkers (*Lederschneider*), thirteen furriers (*Pelzarbeiter*), eleven skinners (*Kürschner*), ten shoemakers (*Schuhmacher*), five hat and bonnet makers (*Hut & Mützenmacher*), two shirt makers (*Hemdenschneider*), two glove makers (*Handschuhmacher*) and a raincoat maker (*Regenmäntelarbeiter*). A total of 117 men who were involved with tailoring in one way or another. Apparently sixteen of them were not selected and were immediately removed. Perhaps because they were sick, weak or simply too old. In addition to the 101 men, 114 women were also found suitable by the SS to work in the concentration camp or in one of the sister camps. And amongst this group, too, there are a striking number of tailors, furriers, seamstresses and needlewomen, a total of eighty-three of 114 women. Ultimately, of the 215 people who passed the selections, only twenty-seven men will survive the camp. Not a single woman survived the horror.

Judenrampe

It is late when we arrive in Auschwitz after a long drive. Our hotel Olecki is located directly opposite the *Stammlager*, the Auschwitz

I base camp. From the window in our rooms we have a direct view over the gigantic, empty car park. It is already dark but we decide to take a look anyway. The place has an air of menace and mystery. Nobody visits Auschwitz in the dark. We wander around the car park and see a giant sign above a kiosk saying: 'Snacks'. 'That would not have been here at the time,' we both point out. A bit further on we arrive at a steel wire fence. We see the entrance, but can only get a glimpse of the buildings and the camp itself.

It is foggy in Auschwitz when we get up the next morning. We cross the street and look for the guide we have agreed to meet at 9 o'clock. Yesterday's desolate car park has turned into a sea of buses and tourists. In the spacious entrance hall large groups of people of different nationalities come and go. Dutch, Spaniards, French, Americans, Japanese, Chinese and many others. We also recognise many Israelis with their blue and white flags. There are many young people as well as senior citizens, supported by volunteers, sometimes in wheelchairs. They have all come to see hell on earth. Most of them spend the night in trendy Krakow, where there are plenty of hotels and restaurants. Dozens of guides come and go to find their group. In the hall are old posters with aerial photos of the camp, close-ups of barbed wire and other montages that are meant to reflect the horror of the place. To the right of one such poster we see a counter with another 'Snacks' sign. While we are waiting at the entrance, we hear Sunday church bells ringing in the distance. Sunday or not, it is always extremely busy in Auschwitz. We join the crowd which moves very slowly because, in a similar way to airport checks-ins, every visitor has to walk through a metal detector that is strictly monitored by a private security team. Keys, jewellery, cell phones, belts and money must be placed in a separate container and then, one by one, we shuffle through the gate with the alarm system. We see groups leaving in the direction of the widely known entrance gate. With headphones and the amplified voice of a guide, the crowd shuffles into the *Stammlager* underneath the words *Arbeit Macht Frei*. Our Polish guide, Dorota Kuczyńska, speaks excellent French and gives us a private tour. She tells us that she wants to show us something special and takes us back to the car park. 'It is wrong to go straight into the camp,' she says, 'we must start at the place where the Jews arrived by train.' We get into her car and drive around the camp in a big circle. We arrive at a remote place with some detached houses. Apart from that there is nobody here, no tourists at all. A train track with two old freight wagons appears out of the fog. 'This is the *Judenrampe*.'

'Because of photos and films, many people think that all Jews entered Auschwitz via the well-known train gate in the second camp, Auschwitz-Birkenau. But that's not right. That was only later in 1944. From the summer of 1942, hundreds of thousands of Jews from all over Europe arrived at this Judenrampe,' says Dorota. Victor Vrba, who managed to escape from the camp in 1944, wrote about this in his book *I escaped from Auschwitz*: 'A huge, bare platform that lay between Birkenau and the mother camp and to which transports rolled from all parts of Europe, bringing Jews who still believed in labour camps.'[30] Vrba saw 300 transports arrive there over eight months. Today there is hardly anything left of the platform, but in the past, there was a vast railway yard with the name *Bahnhof West*. 'It was built at the same time as Birkenau,' says Dorota. In his book *Auschwitz, De Judenrampe*, the Dutch writer, artist and grandson of an Auschwitz-survivor, Hans Citroen, describes this dilapidated station. 'The Jewish platform [was] a 500-metre-long wooden platform built at the beginning of 1942, with tracks on both sides along which in 1942/1943 transit tracks for the supply and disposal [of Jews] were subsequently built as well as sidings for the storage of unused wagons.'[31] With the help of military aerial photos of the site and eye witness reports, Citroen establishes that the *Rampe* was 35-metres wide with tracks on both sides. The original tracks were enlarged to eighteen separate tracks to accommodate not only the incoming transports with prisoners but also the equipment and soldiers. Every day one or more trains arrived here; sometimes they were 1,000 metres long. Most wagons contained human cargo. As there were sometimes so many arrivals, trains often had to wait for hours and even days. The crowded, confined conditions in which the Jews found themselves must have been unbearable on very hot or cold days. 'On the sidings long rows of freight wagons with thousands of people packed like sardines often stood there for days on end without food, drinks or sanitary facilities. They cried out for water.'[32]

Eventually the wagons were opened. 'Here the deportees had to get out into a world completely unknown to them. But the spotlights

and yelling guards with dogs must have immediately scared them,'
according to Dorota.

> The doors flung open, and SS men and some inmates in
> striped uniforms hurried the Jews off the trains. To speed
> things up, they screamed and pushed those who hesitated.
> There were kicks and blows, though the guards rarely went
> further. Restraint was more likely to guarantee order and
> compliance, since it helped to deceive the victims about
> their fate.[33]

The Jews had to get onto the wooden platform as quickly as possible
and stand in rows next to the railway track. Immediately afterwards
selections started. Trucks waited near the stopping place. The bodies of
the people who had not survived the train journey were loaded in the
first trucks. The remaining trucks were for the disabled and the senior
citizens.[34] Women with babies and children were also removed with the
trucks. The other selected Jews had to line up, were no longer allowed
to speak and had to leave for the main camp on foot. A gravel road
that led to Birkenau was approximately one kilometre long. A different
road of about a kilometre and a half led to the main camp in Auschwitz.
The original place of arrival no longer exists. Instead a rather symbolic
monument has been erected. 'The current *Judenrampe* with the two
freight wagons was built in 2005 as a reminder of the place where
more than 600,000 Jews arrived until 1944,' says Dorota. From the
spring of 1944 the train tracks were extended inside the Birkenau camp
to 100 metres from the gas chambers and crematoria. That image in
particular is what most people associate with Auschwitz. Another half
million Jews arrived through this gate from April 1944, mainly victims
of the Hungarian Holocaust.

We look bewildered at the tracks and the two wagons. This is the
place where Ide got off the train on 27 August 1942, where his life took a
dramatic turn and where his wife and children would disappear from his
life forever. We can only guess how Chaja, Charles-Victor and Simone
felt when they were shouted at to get off the train. They must certainly
have been extremely anxious and confused. Would they have cried? Did
they see their dad? We can only hope that they did not suffer too much.
That they didn't get too many beatings and that they were allowed to

stay together. That the warm hugs of mother Chaja was the last thing the children were allowed to feel when they were crammed into the gas chambers with hundreds of other naked people.

'The symbolic wagons on the *Judenrampe* have no windows. Could it have been third-class carriages with at least two access doors?' 'Yes, that is quite possible,' says Dorota. From wealthy countries such as Belgium, France and the Netherlands, they arrived with such carriages in 1942. At the front of the Judenrampe we see the gravel road. This road now starts next to a villa with a garden with toys for children. Along this road Chaja left with the children, by truck or on foot, towards the gas chambers. According to Dorota, the gassing took place the same day in the Little Red House on the outside of Birkenau. The farm was about two and a half kilometres from the Judenrampe and was built from red bricks. The building had four rooms. In March 1942 prisoners of war knocked down the interior walls, bricked up the windows and converted the rooms into two gas chambers, each with a hermetically sealed door.[35] At the top there was a hatch through which an SS soldier could sprinkle the Zyklon B and then close it with a lid. Each room had a maximum capacity of 400 people. This allowed the Nazis to gas 800 prisoners in one go. Subsequently, members of the *Sonderkommando* opened the rooms and dragged the dead bodies out. They took the corpses to mass graves on the edge of a nearby forest via a narrow track and with carts. From August the corpses were also burned. Today there is nothing left of the Little Red House. The building has been demolished. On a small fenced piece of pasture stand three black tombstones to commemorate this terrible place and the mass murders that took place here seventy-nine years ago.

While his wife and children were being deported, Ide was selected to work. He lined up with a hundred others in a row next to the *Judenrampe*. When asked whether this could have been a Kommando (work unit) for tailors, Dorota answered in the affirmative. 'That Kommando went on foot to the main camp under SS surveillance. The road to it runs in the opposite direction from the gravel road to Birkenau.' Thus, the testimony of Majzels and Mandelbaum about the selection of 101 tailors appears to be correct. The subsequent events after the arrival also gradually become clear. Mandelbaum explains in his testimony that he marched with the group under the surveillance of SS soldiers for about a mile and a half further to the *Stammlager*

Auschwitz. Then they arrived at a gate with the cast-iron text *Arbeit Macht Frei*, a statement that camp commander Höss had chosen himself. The paths and blocks were neat. 'I thought: how beautiful is that. We walked along a wide avenue with flowers on the side. Then along a building without floors with a chimney. I wondered what that was. But then I saw at least seven dead bodies on the side of the road.'[36] Only then did he realise that they had ended up in a horrific concentration camp. Ide must also have realised this when he marched into the camp with the other selected tailors.

Mandelbaum continues that at the end of the avenue with the beautiful flowers they had to walk to the right, between two buildings and completely undress. Then four prisoners pushed a cart with clothes towards them. Some items of clothing were bloodstained. The prisoners did not talk to the newcomers. The latter were also not allowed to talk to them. The newcomers did not fully understand what was about to happen to them. 'First, they completely shaved us, everywhere. Then, they made us take a cold shower without soap, without a towel. We walked past prisoners holding a water container that smelled of petroleum. They rubbed us under the arms and between the legs to disinfect us.'

Majzels also talks about having to take off all their clothes and getting shaved everywhere. 'They shaved us with one knife for the 101 remaining people. It was done in a very brutal way. That knife quickly became blunt, you can imagine what the fiftieth or sixtieth must have felt. Then they sprayed us with a disinfection product.'[37]

Mandelbaum continues talking about being tattooed with their serial number, a time-consuming activity that lasted until the evening. On his left arm he got camp number 61997 with an inverted triangle underneath, as a symbol for 'Jew'. Ide must have stood slightly in front of him, because he was tattooed with camp number 61979. Majzels stood twelve places behind Kartuz and six places in front of Mandelbaum. He was given camp number 61991. After being administered with their animal tattoo, the prisoners were given a pair of trousers and a jacket with blue-grey stripes, but also some sort of primitive clogs. These could only be tied to the feet with a piece of string. 'We received a uniform that was covered in clotted dry blood. Completely covered. The cap was also stiff with blood,' Majzels testifies. Apparently, he was quickly separated from the other tailors.

122

He had declared that profession, but that was wrong. The Germans sent him to Block 18, where he stayed with 200 people in one room and had to work as a carpenter. The others, including Kartuz and Mandelbaum had to go to Block 1. Mandelbaum confirms the latter in his testimony and that is of great importance for our further research. 'We were located in Block 1, a building with one floor. They led us to a room with three level bunk beds. I was allowed to choose a bed and climbed on the top one. We still didn't get any food or drink. The lights went out. The fleas jumped on us,' says Mandelbaum.[38]

Block 1

We are standing with our guide Dorota in front of Block 1 in the main camp of Auschwitz, but the building is closed. Until 2015 there were archives here from the city of Oświęcim, but these have since been moved to a building outside the camp. Now it is empty and may not be visited for security reasons. We can look through the windows and see approximately the same layout as found in most other blocks. Those also have a lower floor, an upper floor and an attic space under the roof. In addition to the group of 101 tailors, there were probably more prisoners living in Block 1. Mentioning the first day after his arrival, Mandelbaum testifies:

> The next day [28 August 1942] at five o'clock in the morning we had to attend a roll call after which we had to go and work in the tailors' Kommando. We went to the village of Auschwitz, and after 3 to 4 kilometres we arrived at a hangar that was furnished as a workshop. Here we had to repair SS uniforms.

Purchasing clothes, making and repairing uniforms, suits, shoes, belts, gloves and other items of clothing were important activities in Auschwitz. To get an idea of the various units and buildings involved, we have an appointment with Krzysztof Antończyk, head of the digital archive at the Auschwitz-Birkenau Memorial Museum. His office is located in the former Block 24, near the entrance gate to the main camp. It feels particularly strange to find our way to an operational office in between the barracks. The building has a bell and various nameplates. Shortly after we press the button with his name, we are buzzed in. We push the door open. For the people who work there, the building may feel very normal, but for us it is as if we are entering a sort of sanctuary, like archaeologists discovering an old site. It is surreal to walk around in a place with so much history.

Krzysztof radiates tranquility. After a short introduction he retrieves a staff map. It shows the area around the camp, with details and names of all buildings. On the right is the *Stammlager Auschwitz* in Oświęcim, on the left are the barracks and grounds of the *Vernichtungslager Birkenau* in Brezinka. Between them is the *Judenrampe*, which according to the plan was almost a kilometre long. Antończyk points his finger at the *Schutzhaftlager* E sub-camp. It was about three hundred metres outside the main camp and consisted of twenty buildings. According to him there was a *Schneiderei* in one of those buildings.

There is a photo of an attic space in this sub-camp. It shows dozens of sewing machines that are placed together, like in a storage room. According to controversial French Holocaust denier Jean-Claude Pressac, these were machines brought by the deported Jewish seamstresses to work with in Auschwitz. According to him, that was proof that the women were actually doing well. In this way he tried to minimize the atrocities in the camp. But that is a lie. The countless photos of deported and later gassed Jewish women do not show one woman carrying a sewing machine on her back or in her hands. The only thing they were allowed to bring was a suitcase with some clothes and food. The sewing machines were anyway far too heavy to be carried. They were Singer with a cast-iron pedestal and a large flywheel, which had to be operated manually. It is much more likely that the Germans had seized these sewing machines from one of the many Jewish tailors and sewing workshops in the ghettos. Especially in Lódz, many Jews worked in the clothing industry. The photograph, which dates from 1945, shows the sewing machines that were brought together from the various tailors in the attic of building E after the war. They formed a lot for a public sale.

Mandelbaum was clearly not talking about this sub-camp as he was talking about a hangar a few kilometres away from the main camp. Antończyk pauses. He then points at building G. This is located in an industrial zone, at the top right of the map, in the south of Oświęcim.

The building served as a tannery and later became a *Bekleidungswerkstätte* (clothing workshop) under the name *Lederfabrik*. It consisted of various departments such as a tailor shop, a shoe-maker, a workshop for leather goods, a forge, and so on. Not only were the Jews' suitcases brought here for processing, but also their clothing, shoes and even their hair. After the war the Soviets found 7,000 kilograms of human hair from around 140,000 women. From 1942 between 500 and 800 prisoners worked in this building. This is probably the workshop that Mandelbaum talked about. In this production unit, clothes were made and repaired on a large scale, mostly for the SS guards, but also for their relatives. This unit was headed by professional criminal Erich Grönke (camp number 11), one of the first thirty prisoners. Most of them were criminals who were transferred from Sachsenhausen to Auschwitz in 1940 where they were in charge of the various work units in which the Polish and Jewish prisoners had to work. After the war Grönke was tried for the murder of at least 212 prisoners.

The fact that camp prisoners were at work in the *Lederfabrik* is evidenced by, among other things, the testimony of the Polish prisoner Władysław Czajkowski (camp number 9239), who was an early prisoner in Auschwitz.

> In 1941 I worked in the *Bekleidungswerkstatte Kommando*, starting in the tannery. There were also departments for shoemakers, tailors, and other fields related to clothing. Over the course of 1942 I transported goods from *the Kanada* warehouses that were located next to the railway line. They consisted of suitcases, clothes, shoes and other belongings from the gassed Jews.[39]

Upon arrival at the *Judenrampe*, the Jews had to leave all their belongings beside the train. These were then collected and transferred to the *Lederfabrik* and other tailors' departments as well as to Block 1 in the main camp of Auschwitz. There were also tailors in Birkenau. In the BIIB sector there were not only the hangars where clothing from the gassed Jews was sorted and stored by the *Kanada Kommando*, but also a large *Schneiderei* (tailoring) with female Jewish tailors. Almost all the tailors had to repair the zebra clothes of the prisoners, and some also the uniforms of the SS guards.

Ravensbrück

The blue-grey striped prison uniform was introduced in all concentration camps from 1936 onwards. The first uni-colour prison outfits were produced by the notorious company Lodenfrey.[40] Later, the Gesellschaft fur Textil-und-Lederverwertung mbH (Enterprise for Textiles and Leather Recycling Ltd), abbreviated Texled, produced the typical striped jackets, trousers and hats. This company was founded on 21 June 1940 by SS-*Brigadeführer* August Frank and *Generalleutnant* of the Waffen-SS Georg Lorner. The latter had been head of the economic and administrative department of the SS since April 1939, which was responsible for the supply of clothing to the prisoners in the concentration camps. Texled's commercial management was in the hands of SS-*Führer* Fritz Lechler; technical management was in the hands of SS-*Führer* and former tailor Felix Krug.[41] The company's main production units and workshops were first located in Dachau. SS-*Obergruppenführer* Oswald Pohl had them transferred to the Ravensbrück women's concentration camp because, in his opinion, tailoring was 'a woman's job'. Texled took over the *Bekleidingslager* (tailoring). Female prisoners in Ravensbrück were treated as slave labourers and had to make the prisoner outfits and uniforms for the Waffen-SS at a very high rate. On the industrial estate around Ravensbrück there were several tailor workshops, a weaver and a shoemaker workshop. The female workers had high-quality sewing machines and other equipment. 'The equipping of the workshops was carried out in line with the most modern practices,' says Lechler. He bought the latest appliances such as the most modern and fastest *Pfaff-und-Dürkopp* sewing machines. He also provided buttonhole machines, cutting machines, ironing machines, picoting machines, two-needle column machines and flat knitting machines, each with its own engine.[42]

Krug, for his part, was responsible for the training of the female workers and imposed their daily quotas. The supervisors in Ravensbrück were master-tailor Friedrich Opitz, who previously worked in the tailor workshop in Dachau, and SS-*Unterscharführer* Gustav Binder. Workers who did not meet the quotas were beaten and sometimes killed by them. One prisoner described their situation as follows: 'We suffered a life of fear from morning to night.'[43] The large sewing workshop was one of the most feared places to work. British journalist Sarah Helm wrote the following in a study about the camp: 'The noise from the machines was deafening and the air always thick with dust. Stretching down the room were conveyor belts, with lines of women sitting alongside at sewing machines, making uniforms for the Waffen-SS as well as clothes for the camp prisoners.'[44] The work in the tailor workshop must have been hell. The prisoner Alfredine Nenninger-Wawcziniak testified after the war that the tailor workshop operated like a modern large company.

> There were day and night shifts with 600 detainees in each. In a large hall, there were 13 rows, each with 26 machines next to the fitting tables, operating like conveyor belts. In addition, there were special button hole machines, which made a lot of noise. Apart from the noise of the machines and the suffocating air, you could hear from all sides the screams of the SS men and the female guards and witness the most indescribable floggings and beatings.[45]

Yet many female prisoners preferred this work to that in an external Kommando, where the chances of survival were much slimmer. Moreover, women who met the quotas were given extra rations. Their productivity was therefore high.

We receive help from Professor Bärbel Schmidt of Carl von Ossietzky University in Oldenburg with our research into the place where and the circumstances of how the prisoners' clothing was made. She sends us a thick bundle of documents by post with a lot of information on this subject, including copies of the original orders of the SS in Raven brück. In 1940 and 1941 600 female inmates in Ravensbrück produced 73,000 shirts, 28,500 trousers, 25,000 jackets and 20,000 cloaks. In 1943, 798,210 garments, 706,307 pieces of underwear and 415,000 pairs of gloves for male prisoners were made, and 81,842 garments and 70,922 pieces of underwear for female prisoners.[46] The number of female slave labourers increased from 600 in October 1940 to 5,000 in September 1942. Initially the forced labourers mainly made and restored the striped clothing for the prisoners, but from 1943 they also produced large quantities of uniforms for the Waffen-SS. In the winter of 1942, when the German soldiers suffered extreme cold on the Russian front, warm clothes, which were often trimmed with fur, were made in the workshops as well as hats, boots and gloves.[47] For that purpose the workers were given clothes stolen from the Jews.

Communist Maria Wiedmaier, who survived the camp, testified after the war:

> We had a lot of companies in Ravensbrück, mainly textile factories with almost 4,000 female forced labourers. In the years 1940 to 1942 prison clothing exclusively was produced for all concentration camps, penitentiary facilities etc. From the beginning of 1943, the production and repair of uniforms began. First it was camouflage jackets, which were made by the thousands. When they started taking fur from the Jews, a new branch of production appeared. The fur had to be sewn into the flying jackets of pilots. The best fur, such as ermine, mink and astrachan, also taken from the Jews, was used for the clothes of SS officers' wives.[48]

Thus the SS, which managed all the concentration camps, had a huge and inexpensive labour reserve in Ravensbrück. The women worked in shifts, usually eleven hours a day, under extreme conditions.[49] However, due to abuse and malnutrition, the women tailors did not always manage to meet the production targets, which led to them being punished by the guards or replaced. Texled was one of the few profitable SS companies. This was only able to happen through a combination of management, modern equipment and cheap slave labour.[50]

The head offices of the various concentration camps were not really responsible for ordering and paying for the prisoners' uniforms. Until 1938 they had to address their questions about this to the Inspectorate of Concentration Camps under the direction of *SS-Oberführer* Theodor Eicke.[51] He was a commandant of the first concentration camp in Dachau and founder of the *SS-Totenkopfverbände*. These special SS units were responsible for guarding the concentration camps. In 1934 Eicke was appointed as inspector of concentration camps and commandant of the SS guards. From 1939 to 1942 the number of concentration camps increased and the number of prisoners quadrupled from 25,000 to 100,000.[52] This led to a re-organisation and the creation of the *SS-Wirtschafts-Verwaltungshauptamt* (Economic and administrative main office), led by Oswald Pohl. From March 1942 the various camps had to address questions about clothing to the chief of the Economic Bureau of the SS, office BII. That office examined the orders of each head office and decided which and how many garments the prisoners received in a particular concentration camp and bought them from Texled, who then sent the clothes from Ravensbrück by train to the various concentration camps. Many documents about the production and distribution of camp clothing were lost when the Nazis burned down Texled's headquarters at the end of the war. Nevertheless, there is sufficient evidence about what happened in Ravensbrück and how the SS used the prisoners' clothing for their own gain during the war.

From 1942 onwards the Nazis began gassing large numbers of people. The SS had their clothes collected, sorted and bundled. They were sent back to Germany by freight trains for *Winterhilfswerk des Deutschen Volkes* (Winter Aid for the German People), in other words for the benefit of the local population, given that many German families were homeless because of the Allied bombings and were being given houses as well as other possessions that the murdered Jews used to own, including clothes.

Prisoners who were not gassed but selected to work for the war economy wore the characteristic blue-grey striped prisoner attire, at least until stocks were exhausted. The uniform was meant to distinguish the detainees from civilians and thus make escape more difficult. In each concentration camp were one or more *SS-Bekleidungskammern* (SS clothing stores), which were responsible for distributing the clothes. The prisoners' winter clothes were made from an artificial wool, the summer clothes from a similar linen. This clothing was completely inadequate, especially during the harsh Polish winters, where temperatures could drop to minus-20-degrees Celsius. The prison uniforms were hardly ever washed or replaced. Only privileged prisoners could sometimes get clean or new zebra clothes.

The women originally wore a striped cotton dress, a vest, knickers, an underskirt and long stockings. They were later given a blue-grey striped coat which resembled the one for the male prisoners. The camp commandant decided which prisoners were given which clothing and when.[53] Due to lack of resources during the war years, the Germans failed to make enough striped prisoners' clothing. When that happened the detained tailors had to sew coloured badges or strips of striped fabric on ordinary civilian clothing.

Block 1 (bis)

After working in the *Lederfabrik* for a few weeks, Mandelbaum, Ide Kartuz and the other tailors of Convoy V had to work in their own Block 1. 'In Block 1 there were only beds at first, but afterwards also machines,' says Mandelbaum.[54] The prisoners no longer had to go to the *Lederfabrik* every day, but remained active in the main camp, equipped with the necessary tools. Block 1 thus developed into a repair site and manufacturing unit of every sort of clothing, even shoes. The tailors had to work on sewing machines which were probably brought over from building E.

Ide and the other tailors were particularly useful in Auschwitz, where thousands of SS men, who always had to look smart, worked as guards. Their uniforms had to be repaired or altered regularly. This happened in the *Lederfabrik* outside the camp, but also in the *Bekleidungskammer*, in Block 27 of the main camp. This clothing department, which was part of the camp administration section, was responsible for the delivery of the underwear, clothing and shoes of both detainees and SS men. The Germans were able to have their garments altered for size, hand them over for repair and swap dirty clothes. The garments that had to be modified, exchanged or were damaged were outsourced to the various clothing workshops.

Due to the sharp increase in the number of Jews, it was at one point no longer possible to deliver the striped uniforms for all the prisoners. From that time onwards, the clothes of the Jews who had been murdered in the gas chambers were used and a badge was sewn on them, often a blue-grey striped piece of fabric and a number.

Jewish prisoners were also put to work in the *Bekleidungskammer*, such as the Polish Jew Meyer Hack (camp number 73488), who testified about this.[55] Tailors were in demand, but that didn't mean that having this occupation in Auschwitz was without danger. Some, as was the case with those selected to work in other Kommandos, died during the first days or weeks after arriving at the camp. The prisoners were still at the mercy of the whims of SS guards and *kapos* who would beat someone to death without cause. The fact that prisoners survived was often because of their knowledge of German or because they had certain qualities that were useful to the Nazis. This was true for Ide. Besides Polish, French and Dutch, he also spoke German. Moreover, he was a craftsman. Tailoring held no secrets for him. He was useful, physically fit and he understood the art of survival.

We ask Antończyk for more information about the tailors in and around Auschwitz-Birkenau, but he cannot help us with that. He calls his colleague Szymon Kowalski, deputy head of the archive of the Auschwitz-Birkenau State Museum, who works in the same building. He is immediately willing to see us. Kowalski speaks excellent English and listens carefully to our questions about Ide's arrival in Auschwitz, the selection of the 101 tailors, the *kapo* of this unit, and the infamous Block 1. He types in Ide's camp number on his computer and immediately finds his *Häftlingekarte* (inmate card), number 61979. It not only shows his name and pre-war address, but also the names of his wife and parents. Next to *Rasse* (Race) it says 'Jüd' and the card mentions schooling up to *3 Kl. poln. Volksschule*. Kowalski explains that he probably went to school until he was 14 years old. He spoke Polish, French, Flemish and German, it says, although he also knew Yiddish, but presumably he withheld that information.

The card also contains information about his appearance. He measured 1 metre 55, had a 'normal nose', dark blond hair, a stocky shape, a normal mouth, no beard, an oval face, oval ears, grey eyes, and three missing teeth.

The archivist takes us to a reading room with two steel cabinets. In those cabinets the museum holds more than 150 volumes with thousands of testimonies from prisoners who survived the camp. Because the museum is going to close, we only have an hour and a half to do searches today. We start immediately and enter the keyword 'Kartuz' on the computer. No useful information comes up. We then try the keyword 'Schneiderei' (tailoring) and get seven results. We dive into the volumes and open the books on the pages where that word appears. But all documents are written in Polish. We ask Kowalski if we can take photos of the documents for our own use. He nods, but emphasises that we are only allowed to use documents that we have officially requested for publication. He gives us a form which we can use for these requests and leaves the room. We start immediately. We find a system whereby one of us searches for the document numbers and the other digs through the files in the cabinet. One book after another follows at a phenomenal pace. It seems as if we have never done anything else. In the meantime, we hope someone can translate our findings, because most of the testimonials are in Polish. Within an hour and a half, the job is done and we walk freely, with very valuable information, out of the gate with the words *Arbeit Macht Frei.*

A few months later, just after the *International Holocaust Remembrance Day* on 27 January 2019, we find ourselves again at Hotel Olecki in Oświęcim in Poland. The camp and the surrounding area are covered with snow and it is very cold. We can imagine what it must have been like for the prisoners, skinny and scantily dressed. Some kept themselves warm with paper or cardboard from a cement bag under their prison uniform, but, if they caught you, you were beaten.

In the hotel we meet German architect Peter Siebers who, together with Gideon Greif, published the monumental book *Todesfabrik Auschwitz: Das Konzentrations-und Vernichtungslager Auschwitz 1940-1945*.[56] Peter worked for fifteen years on the many detailed plans of the buildings, barracks, crematoria and gas chambers. The book is the best antidote for negationists and other Holocaust deniers. Moreover, he also knows the history of the development and expansion of Auschwitz-Birkenau and Buna-Monowitz very well, and explains how it evolved over the years from an old Polish military base to the most famous concentration and extermination camp in the world. On a few sheets of paper he draws with firm hand and precision how Block 1 and Block 2 were connected to an intermediate building, the old laundry. It is late when we say goodbye.

At the entrance to the camp we meet Kamila Sokalska, a Polish student who works in one of the museum's bookshops. Because we were looking for someone who lived nearby and could translate documents for us, we asked her if she could help. In the end she agreed and, together with us, dug out the archives again. We do not want to overlook any information.

Kamila will translate for us for the next three days. We are once again welcomed by the helpful and experienced archivist Kowalski and now look much more thoroughly for testimonies about the tailors' Kommando. Kamila goes over the Polish statements and points out what could be important. It is a success. We find five testimonials from former prisoners who speak specifically about the tailors' Kommando in Block 1.

The building was located in a corner of the camp and was separated from the *Kommandantur* (headquarters) by high and double barbed wire. It was only a few dozen metres from the villa of camp commander Rudolf Höss.

The first testimony is from the Polish Jew Marian Gnyp from Random with camp number 62692. He arrived in Auschwitz on 1 September 1942, four days after Ide. There are three camp photos of him. At first Gnyp was in a different tough outdoor work unit where people had to work with gravel and cement in rain and wind. He fell ill, ended up in hospital, and realised that to survive he had to find other, less demanding work. During a roll call, Gnyp stood next to a prisoner who said he would help him.

> One day they asked for tailors. A Jewish man who stood beside me and was a tailor, raised his hand and hissed at me that I had to do the same. He would help me if we were selected because I had almost no experience with tailoring. I did have a brother who was a tailor, and as a child I had been watching his work. Anyway, we were both admitted to the *Schneiderei Kommando*. It was in the fall of 1942. I don't remember the exact date. As a result, I moved from Block 7a to Block 1a [the first floor of Block 1], where all the imprisoned tailors were. The sewing room itself was in the attic of Block 1. Around twenty sewing machines were installed there. Nothing was made in the workshop; only camp clothing was repaired. The tailors were almost all Jews of different nationalities.[57]

Gnyp was unable to keep up with the pace at first, but luckily the sub-kapo let him stay. That way he got the hang of the work. In his testimony it says however that he was sometimes beaten violently.

But he made another interesting statement. 'In February 1943, SS soldiers took ten young tailors to Block 30 in Birkenau where they had to undress and be exposed to X-rays. They were then returned to Block 1 in the main camp.' Apparently Gnyp was one of them. Ide has not mentioned this. He was indeed a lot older than the other prisoners. But Mandelbaum did talk about such selections for experiments on humans. Gnyp survived the camp and the medical experiment, but was no longer able to have children.

The second witness who talked about the tailors in Block 1 is Polish Stanisław Dorosiewicz from Warsaw, with camp number 18379. He ended up in the tailors' Kommando in November 1942.

> In November 1942 I was in the *Kommando Häflingsschneiderei* on the first floor of Block 1. The Kapo was Ignac Szołtsyk, a German from Bytom in Silesia.

133

He had a red triangle. Head of the tailors was Netzlar
Tadeusz from Włochy near Warsaw. He gave me a job in
this Kommando.[58]

Szołtsyk was an ethnic German who lived abroad, a miner who was
convicted of treason in 1936 for his communist sympathies. He was
imprisoned in Sachsenhausen concentration camp and deported from
there to Auschwitz. He had camp number 25351. Dorosiewicz worked
in the Kommando until April 1943.

I was now a tailor and repaired and sewed prisoners'
clothing. We also ripped up the civilian clothing that
remained after the prisoners were gassed. The clothing
often contained large quantities of valuable items such as
bank notes and jewellery. I personally handed these over to
camp leader Hans Aumeier. In exchange for the gold and
the valuables that we gave to him exclusively, we received
sugar, bread and margarine. The Kommando was under the
supervision of the head of the *Effektenkammer* [this was
a sort of warehouse housed in Block 26 where the most
important possessions of the gassed prisoners were kept].[59]

Aumeier was the second in rank after camp commander Rudolf Höss.
From January 1942 he worked in Auschwitz. We google Aumeier's
name and discover that, on 18 August 1943, he was found guilty by the
SS leaders of stealing gold from Holocaust victims. He was exposed and
transferred to the Baltic states. After the war he was sentenced to death
for mass murder and hanged by the Polish Supreme Court during the
Auschwitz trial in Krakow.

The testimonies of Gnyp and Dorosiewicz give us a better picture of
the layout of the tailors' block. The tailors slept in bunk beds on the first
floor and worked in the attic with their machines. Maybe there were no
longer a hundred of them. According to Gnyp there were only about
twenty machines. In addition to the presence of other prisoners, there
must also have been a certain turnover of people who were transferred to
other sub-camps or work units, such as the leather factory and clothing
store. Others, on the other hand, were physically no longer able to keep
going or became ill and died. Others were simply killed by the SS.

New prisoners were regularly added to the tailors' Kommando – newcomers such as Gnyp, for example, or older prisoners such as Dorosiewicz. Both were 'lucky' enough to end up in the tailors' Kommando. Their testimonies indicate that it was better in this work unit than in others. After all, the prisoners worked inside, protected from the cold and the heat. They could hide extra clothes for themselves or trade them with other prisoners for food or other necessities. The testimonials show that they could even do business with some SS guards. Particularly interesting is Dorosiewick's testimony about the behaviour of some SS men towards the Kommando in Block 1. 'The Kommando was only allowed to repair the prisoners' clothing. SS men were not allowed to come here according to the camp rules. Still, they often came here illegally to have uniforms and civilian clothes made for themselves and their family.'[60]

According to three different, independent testimonials, Ide even had to make lingerie for the wife or mistress of an SS officer.

> He had never done this before. He got some fabric and had to make a bra with it, without having seen the woman or having taken her measurements. He was afraid he would be punished if it didn't fit. ... He got some extra bread for that, broke it in two and kept a piece for the next day, because it was never certain that people would get bread the next day, he told his son Benno.[61] He once told his granddaughter Nadine, 'I was lucky that I was a tailor. I had to repair officers' uniforms and even had to make a bra. Then I got some extra bread that I shared with fellow prisoners who really needed it.'[62]

Greta De Voeght (the mother of David Van Turnhout) also mentioned the fact that garments were made for German officers. In one of Ide's conversations with her, he told her, 'The Germans asked if I could also make shoes. I could not, but I said yes. In the end I made shoes and they were satisfied. I sometimes got an extra piece of bread for that. I shared that with camp mates who needed it.'

Even though we have found a few witnesses, it has been extremely difficult to find people with whom Ide has talked about his work in Auschwitz. But during a conversation with his granddaughter Nadine, we find out some information that might lead us to a new witness.

Ellen, Nadine's mother and Ide's daughter, had a younger friend. He was usually there when the whole family got together. Although Nadine was still small, she remembers the man very well. Luc Leemans was a true punk in the 1980s and had a shop in Antwerp. Ellen helped out at the store. But he was also very interested in Ide's story. 'I often heard him talk about the war with bompa,' Nadine said. This grabs our attention right away. Luc Leemans is our new key witness. We need to find him as soon as possible. Because the man still had a shop in Antwerp after his punk period, we find more information about him via Google. After a few days, an e-mail appears in our mailbox: 'I don't really see how I can help you but I don't mind meeting up. I live in Spain and will be in Belgium in two weeks' time. I will keep you posted. Greetings, Luc.'

After a nail-biting two weeks we meet Luc and his wife Conny in an Antwerp café. His friendship with Ide was a little strange, he says. He was a punk at the time. He walked around with a mohawk and gaudy bracelets with big pins on. Although Ide was always smartly dressed and meticulously groomed, he never made an issue out of that. Luc imitated him: 'Is gooeeed, is goeeeed. You must just be whoever you want to be.' Apparently, the little Jewish man spoke with an accent. It must have looked funny, like a scene from *The Young Ones*. A big punk with all the accessories, next to a 5-foot man in a suit frying eggs in his kitchen. Luc often went to Ide's to have lunch with him. He would close his shop and because the conversations were so intense, the store was sometimes closed for two hours. Ide told him that he was constantly living in fear in Auschwitz, fear of being killed, fear that the tailors' Kommando would be shut down. And that he put paper under his clothes to keep warm. That's how he tried to survive.

Luc remembers some significant details from his conversations with Ide.

> When a new transport of Jews arrived in Auschwitz, such as Czechs and Hungarians, he and the others crawled into the roof trusses to escape their lice and fleas. It was like a kind of Rumpelstiltskin. Ha yes! That's right. I also had that image of Rumpelstiltskin when he was sewing in a cross-legged position at his tailor's table. It was a strange sight, especially since he was so small.

We're glad he remembers something, but it's not the whole story. After some questions about the tailor workshop, Luc suddenly remembers an important detail that confirms what we had found out earlier: 'He once had to make a bra for the girlfriend of an SS man! He'd never done it before. He was given the fabric to use, but Ide was afraid he wouldn't succeed in doing it and that he'd get into trouble. In the end, he did succeed.'[63]

Racketeering

It is surprising that the SS guards, and probably also their officers, placed orders with the tailors of Block 1, especially since they had the clothing workshop in the *Lederfabrik*. There they could simply order such items and comply with the rules. However, there they had to pay for the mending of a suit, a shirt, shoes or something for their wives and children. In the archive we looked at files that show that they had to make an official request for new and additional clothing, after which production could begin. There were four forms for this. The first form was a question 'To the administration of KL Auschwitz'. On it the order was written down: a suit, a cloak, a shirt, a dress, children's clothing, shoes ... . The second form was an official order form for the relevant workshop. The third mentioned the material and where it came from. For example, on one such form 'rolls of silk' is written for making a cloak and a woman's jacket. The fourth form was the invoice. A suit cost 25 RM (*Reichsmark*), an alteration 10 RM, a cloak 25 RM, the woman's jacket 16 RM, and a dress 8 RM.

Bending the camp rules, for example by ordering a suit or something else directly from the work unit, probably cost them only some bread and sausage. This did not happen directly in consultation with the tailor involved, but via the *kapo* who then took his share of the food and passed on the rest to whoever made the item. Such facts highlight the important position of the *kapo* and the vulnerability of the tailors. Anyone who could make a good suit or dress benefited from the goodwill of the kapos, as long as the commissioning SS was satisfied. The others risked a transfer to another block and, in the worst case, to an outside *Kommando*. The chances of survival were much lower there.

Not only did the SS soldiers who ordered something against the rules run the risk of being sanctioned, but also the *kapo* who was involved. There was the possibility that that *kapo* in turn was protected by a higher-ranking SS. It proves that 'racketeering' was endemic in the camp. Everyone worked for their own benefit, which led to a lot of corruption.

'Racketeering' was common practice in all concentration camps. Prisoners and guards tried to turn the situation to their advantage, often at the expense of others. Stealing, smuggling, extortion, making contacts, acquiring favours ... . Those prisoners who were best suited to 'racketeering' were more likely to survive. Guards on the other hand were able to make a good profit from it. It was a continuous search for things with sufficient value to trade or sell. For example, banknotes and jewellery from the clothing of every new load of prisoners were often traded. It was customary for the Jews to have their valuable jewels, banknotes, money rolls, and gold sewn into their clothing with a view to their deportation. It was the only option for them to bring in valuables for use when needed. It shows how unaware they were of their fate. They had no idea they would be asked to undress and would be gassed. Even those who were not gassed had to give up their clothes and wear a striped prison uniform.

The clothing from those who were gassed in Birkenau ended up in the *Kanada Kommando*. There, female Jewish prisoners had to search the luggage for money, jewellery and other valuables. They collected everything into sealed boxes that were sent by train to Germany, up to twenty wagons every day.[64] But also the clothing itself, along with all other personal belongings, was sorted, stored, packed and transported by train to Berlin for the badly affected German population. The Polish-British-Jewish Kitty Hart-Moxon worked in the *Kanada Kommando* from April to November 1944 and testified:

> The suitcases were collected from the platform and placed in large heaps. We girls were divided into various groups. I was on the night shift in the eight months I was there and my first job was searching the men's jackets. So, I was put in front of a large pile of men's coats that I had to search, I had to put them all on a trestle table and feel if there was anything in the pockets. Very often we also had to unstitch the hems and when we found something, we had to take

it out. Very often at the end of the shift we had a bucket full of jewels or banknotes or whatever was hidden in those jackets.[65]

Despite severe sanctions, quite a few SS men and even female prisoners managed to keep valuables for themselves. After the war survivors of this *Kommando* testified about the number of risks they took to steal money and jewellery, and then to exchange them in the camp for food, alcohol, cigarettes and shoes. Some even differed in appearance to the others because they looked well fed. In turn, they were extorted by individual SS guards. The entire camp was steeped in a culture of theft and corruption. After an internal investigation, even camp commander Rudolf Höss was reprimanded and moved for corruption at the end of December 1943.

From July 1942 large numbers of Jews arrived on the *Judenrampe*. They had to leave their bags there. To re-assure the deportees, they had to write their names on them. The Auschwitz museum keeps an inventory of the suitcases that were recovered. The majority, however, were processed for their leather or other raw materials. Most of the prisoners were deported to Birkenau, but some were selected for the work units in the *Stammlager* or another sub-camp of Auschwitz. Their clothing was taken away, after which they had to put on the prison uniform. Part of this removed clothing ended up in Block 1.

The latter appears from the testimony of the third witness, the Polish-Jewish survivor Antoni Słapiński (camp number 93750) from Tarnów near Krakow. He joined the 100 other tailors of the *Kommando* in Block 1 on 25 January 1943. He also came from another work unit.

> Thanks to the help of a friend, I was transferred from the *post parcel point to the inmate tailoring*. The Kommando worked on the first floor of Block 1 opposite Block 12 and also lived on this floor. We sewed socks. From civilian clothing, which was delivered to Block 1 from the warehouses with the belongings of the people who were gassed, we cut out rectangular holes in which we then sewed pieces of camp uniforms. The civilian clothing was often torn and the lining removed. It was just a thorough search of the clothing to see if it contained banknotes, securities or other valuable items.

In the inmate tailoring, besides the kapo, an SS officer also supervised our work. We had to give him everything we found. And there was a lot hidden in the clothes. After checking the clothes and sewing in camp signs, everything was loaded into bundles in trucks. That was then driven to the prisoners' clothing room in the Birkenau camp. Here the clothing was given to the prisoners. Apparently, this clothing was also supplied to other concentration camps in the Third Reich. ... About 100 prisoners worked in the Schneiderei.[66]

The fourth witness, Adam Jerzy Brandhuber (camp number 87112), was a non-Jewish painter from Krakow who worked in the clothing store *Kommando*. In his statement after the war he refers indirectly and very briefly to Block 1. He saw the striped clothing of his murdered fellow prisoners. 'In Block 1 where the tailors were, there were pieces of fabric with camp numbers and triangles. The tailors worked upstairs.'[67] Brandhuber himself also had to use such pieces of fabric to put them on the clothing of other prisoners, hence his reference to Block 1. No matter how brief his testimony is, it is yet further proof that the tailors' Kommando worked there upstairs.

We know with certainty that the Jews in Block 1 lived on the first floor and worked in the attic. But what happened on the ground floor? There is a fifth testimony about this, from the German political prisoner Kurt Scholz (camp number 92367). He, too, mentions valuable things about the newly-arrived Jews and other prisoners. After working in an outdoor work unit, he ended up in the *Alte Wäscherei* (old laundry) that was located between Block 1 and Block 2. It was a wooden building that was set up between the two stone barracks for washing prison clothes. There were about twenty-five to thirty prisoners working there who had to boil, scrub, rinse and dry the striped prisoner clothes in hot water. Scholz testifies:

> In Block 1 there was a decontamination room. Whoever worked there was given milk. Block 1 also had drying rooms, where we dried the clothes. Upstairs there was the Kommando of the tailors led by kapo Ignac. There they searched for valuable items (jewellery and diamonds) in the

clothing of the newly arrived prisoners (civilian clothes). Those items were exchanged for bread and sausage, for example. Once we got a whole sausage. We cut it open and baked it with potatoes. It was a wonderful feast. The laundry existed until October 1944. Then it closed. There was a new laundry in the *Lederfabrik* (leather factory).[68]

Here, too, valuables were kept behind by the tailors and their *kapo* to trade for food, drink and cigarettes, and perhaps also for bribery or getting a favour, although the prisoners were of course always treading on dangerous ground with the guards.

The testimonials give us a more complete picture of Block 1. Clothing was washed in the wooden building between the first two blocks, then disinfected in the first room of Block 1 and dried in the second room on the ground floor. Then Ide and the other prisoners repaired the camp clothes upstairs and in the attic after which they went back into circulation. In between or after their day's work, the tailors carried out special orders from SS guards and even SS officers, for which they received extra food, alcohol, cigarettes and other benefits.

Daily life

Like the other prisoners, Ide had to get up at 6:30 am in the winter and as early as 4:30 am in the summer. They had to make their beds extremely quickly.[69] *'Raus, raus. Aufstehen!'* ('Out out. Stand up!'). The most senior prisoners in the block then drove them out, often using force. No matter what the weather they had to wash themselves. They could also use the latrines but they had to be very quick. The signal would then sound for the roll call. The prisoners had to stand in formation in rows of ten. The little ones, like Ide, at the front, the taller ones behind. A raucous voice blared over the square, *'Mützen ab!'* With their right hand the prisoners then snatched off their hat down to their right thigh in one synchronised movement. They had to stand still and upright, head up and look straight in front of them. Other prisoners in stripes with a green triangle on their chest, the mark of the professional criminals, then began to count them and passed the numbers on to the SS guards. If the number wasn't right, they had to remain motionless and the counting would start again until everything was correct and someone shouted '*Mützen auf*!' Then they had to put their hats back on their bare heads and firmly slap their right hand down on their thigh. Everyone waited for the liberating command '*Rührt Euch!*' ('At ease!').[70]

Sometimes the roll call was over quickly but sometimes it lasted for a very long time. This depended on the mood of the SS men or the times such as when a prisoner was missing because he may have died or possibly fled. After the count the prisoners went to their workshops in the various blocks or with the external work units to work areas outside the camp. In the morning, the prisoners were given half a litre of 'coffee'. In reality, it was no more than boiled water with some coffee substitute or a brew of tea. At lunchtime they were given three-quarters of a litre of turnip or cabbage soup, which was completely tasteless. Very exceptionally there was a minimal amount of meat in it. Many ingredients in the soup came from the rucksacks that the deportees were asked to leave with their luggage. Other objects were also found there, such as lighters or pencils. Around 7 o'clock in the evening everyone came back to the camp and the evening roll call took place. That, too, sometimes took an endless amount of time. Then it was queueing for dinner. This consisted of about 300 grams of black bread with a small piece of sausage, some margarine or a little cheese. The daily ration was not sufficient in relation to the amount of heavy labour that the prisoners had to do. Many died of exhaustion and malnutrition. After dinner, the prisoners had some 'free' time, when they would rush to the latrines and their barracks. At 9 o'clock the order was given, 'Lights out', unless the roll call lasted longer. The lights were extinguished, in so far as there were lights. Some *Kommandos* worked seven days a week, others had a Sunday off every two weeks to clean their block, wash their clothes, get rid of lice, shave and have their hair cut.

Prisoners who had some money in their account could buy certain food in the canteen such as beets and potatoes but also water, cigarettes, a toothbrush, toothpaste, stationery, stamps and so on.[71] There were also vouchers to go to the brothels. The first floor of Block 24 was converted into a large number of small rooms in the summer of 1943. *Kapos* in particular took advantage of this. The women lived in appalling conditions there, having sexually transmitted diseases and being forced to work as sex slaves. Every fifteen minutes a bell rang and the women had to change client.[72] Although they received better than the average food for prisoners, for some suicide was still preferable.

Jews were not allowed to send letters. Others prisoners were, twice a month. Pre-printed cards existed for this with '*Konzentrationslager Auschwitz*' printed in the top left corner together with the rules of the camp. These stipulated that the prisoners could receive money. Visiting was prohibited and a request for release was never acted on. Letters had to be written in German and were censored. The prisoners were obliged to write in each letter the sentence '*Ich bin gesund und fühle mich gut*' (I am in good health and feeling fine). At first the prisoners were not allowed to receive packages but that changed following a directive on 29 October 1942. From that date a great number of packages began to arrive, so more food was available. The sending and receiving of letters and mail took place via Block 25. Any money that was not stolen as a result of the 'censorship', would end up in the accounts of the relevant people who were then able to buy things with it in the canteen.

Remarkably, we also find in the archive, lists of bonuses that were regularly paid out to some *kapos* and to certain prisoners. There are payouts from two up to a maximum of nine Reichsmark. Several books on Auschwitz state that this did not apply to the Jews but on a list dated 19 October 1944 under the title '*Prämienscheine*' (Rewards coupons) there are in fact details of the payment of bonuses to tailors, amongst whom there are several Jews, including Mandelbaum, who was on the same transport as Ide. His good friend Samuel Berliner also received a bonus. On other lists the name Ignaz Szołtsyk, the *kapo* of Block 1 regularly appears. He often received bonuses.

Most prisoners were stick thin from a lack of enough calories. They looked like walking skeletons in their vertically striped jackets, shirts and trousers. The clothing was inadequate in protecting them from the cold and, when combined with malnutrition, meant that many were unable to cope with the conditions. The prisoners couldn't wash their clothes because of the lack of sanitation and water. They became dirty, were covered in fleas and smeared with excrement and urine. Occasionally, there were delousing sessions but the prisoners were often only given different clothes after a few months. For fear of disease, the SS men avoided as much physical contact as possible with the prisoners. Typhus in particular was very much feared. The *kapos* or Jews with designated tasks acted as a link between the SS men and the prisoners. They had to wash and disinfect their clothing much more regularly, including with the disinfectant Zyklon B.[73]

Some tailors, such as Ide, probably belonged to these 'privileged' few who were allowed to have contact with the Aryan guards. They sometimes worked on clothes from SS men or had to take their measurements. It was vital for them to keep their own clothes as clean and smart as possible. For that reason they had a laundry, dry cleaning and a disinfectant space in and next to their Block 1, while other prisoners had their poorly washed clothes returned damp, having to dry them with their own body heat. That must have been terrible in periods of extreme cold. Even more problematic was the footwear. After a certain time clogs would cause painful blisters and festering abrasions on the feet.[74] Some people died from it.

After the morning roll call, Ide and his companions worked in their block. There they were protected from the harsh weather conditions. The external work units were much less fortunate. They marched in rows past the camp orchestra. That was set up to the left of them, on a platform next to the entrance gate and with their backs to the kitchen. Even when the work units returned exhausted in the evening, the camp orchestra played cheerful marching music. Czech Jewess Edith Baneth described this spectacle:

> We were stood in front of the main gate of Auschwitz, with that famous *Arbeit Macht Frei*, and in front of that the orchestra was playing famous music by Strauss – and all the SS men were watching us there. We had to listen to that music for a long time and without warning we felt a little human again, listening to music we knew from when times were normal.[75]

The Auschwitz I camp orchestra originally consisted of seven members and rehearsed in Block 24 from 6 January 1941, but it quickly grew into a group of about a hundred musicians. Later there were also orchestras in Birkenau and Monowitz. In addition to popular songs and uplifting marches, they played classical music by Mozart and Grieg. Poland's Jewess Helena Dunicz Niwińska played the violin in the *Mädchenorchester* (Girls' orchestra) in Birkenau. It was led by Alma Rosé, a niece of Gustav Mahler. According to Niwińska, the orchestra played to re-assure the newly arrived Jews, so avoiding panic. She was amazed at the impact it had on both the prisoners and the SS guards. It reminded those who listened of the pre-war period in which they could enjoy music at home or in the theatre. Ide was also aware that the dozens of SS officers in the headquarters, a building next to Block 1, listened to the music and relaxed after their day job. On Christmas Eve he and his fellow prisoners heard the Germans singing carols, temporarily oblivious to the existence of the tens of thousands of malnourished and hypothermic detainees, many of whom would not survive the night.

The Nazis' indifference to the fate of the prisoners is also evident from their diaries; for example, the diary of SS doctor Johann Kremer, who arrived in the main camp a few days after Ide. On 2 September 1942 he wrote the following: 'Was present for first time at a "special action" at 3 am. By comparison Dante's Inferno seems almost a comedy. Auschwitz is justly called an extermination camp.'[76] About 761 French Jews who had arrived from Drancy that day with Convoy XXVII had been selected to be gassed.[77] On 5 September Kremer continued:

> In the morning attended a special action from the women's concentration camp (Muslims); the most dreadful of horrors. Master-Sergeant Thilo (troop doctor) was right when he said to me that this is the anus mundi. In the evening towards 8:00 attended another special action from Holland. Because of the special rations they [SS men] get a fifth of a litre of schnapps, 5 cigarettes, 100 g. salami and bread, the men all clamour to take part in such actions.[78]

This time it was 661 Dutch Jews who arrived from Westerbork with Convoy XVI and were gassed.[79] On 6, 9 and 10 September Kremer attended further such special actions, without showing any kind of compassion for the victims in his diary. The doctor enjoyed his stay in the camp. For example, on 20 September he wrote,

> This Sunday afternoon from 3 pm to 6 pm I listened to a concert of the prisoners' band in glorious sunshine; the bandmaster was a conductor of the Warsaw State Opera, 80 musicians. At 8 o'clock in the evening supper in the Home with *Obergruppenfuhrer* Pohl, a truly festive meal.

We had baked pike, as much of it, as we wanted, real coffee, excellent beer and sandwiches.[80]

On the same day 590 Dutch and 659 French Jews were gassed.[81]

The other SS officers also had no sense of shame or compassion. In 2007, 116 photographs by *SS-Obersturmführer* Karl Höcker came to light. The assistant of camp commandant Höss had taken photographs of SS officers and *SS-Helferinnen* [female helpers of the SS] having fun in the *Solahütte*, a leisure resort on the Sola river, near the town of Żywiec, some 40 kilometres east of Auschwitz. In these photos from the summer of 1944 they were making music and partying. At that time, the killing machine was running at full capacity and hundreds of thousands of Hungarian Jews were being gassed in Birkenau.

In September 1943 a group of 500 Jews was selected in Auschwitz-Birkenau to clear the rubble in Warsaw after the complete destruction of the ghetto and to salvage re-usable building materials. This was a very difficult task both mentally and physically, as shown in a testimony by Yaakov David Alchec, 'They were taking people to clean out the ghetto ... to clean the bricks .... And they found a woman and a girl alive, inside a bunker. The Germans took them and brought them into our camp. Then they took them away... . And I don't know what they did with them.'[82] The Germans chose mainly Greek Jews for this task. By opting for a work unit that did not speak Polish, they prevented the prisoners from communicating with the locals and the Polish resistance. But there were not enough Greeks. The Germans needed more manpower and looked for it among the Jews in Auschwitz-Birkenau who were still physically strong. The selection from Block 1 was done by *kapo* Ignac, according to the prisoner Jozef Szerman Szyja, who ended up in Auschwitz on 25 October 1942. After the war Szyja testified about the selection: 'I contacted Tobiasz, who worked at the *Schneiderei* Kommando. In 1943 the transport of prisoners selected for the clean-up of Warsaw left. Amongst them from the tailors' *Kommando* was Tobiasz and other communists chosen by *kapo* Ignac.'[83]

That last statement is consistent with David Mandelbaum's testimony. He said he spent thirteen months in Auschwitz until the large selection for Warsaw took place in September 1943. He arrived there a few days later to clear debris.[84] Interestingly, Ide also spoke about this when he answered the question 'Do you remember prisoners being transferred from Auschwitz to Warsaw?' His reply was, 'Yes, I even lined up to go to Warsaw.' Ide also had communist sympathies and possibly knew Mandelbaum, Tobiasz and Szyja. Apparently, he couldn't or wasn't allowed to leave, maybe because he was a Pole and spoke the language. But it is also possible that *kapo* Ignaz wanted to keep the best people from his *Kommando* or at least those who served him best when he did business with the Germans.

This is apparent from another testimony that archivist Kowalski gave us about the Jew Markus Lustbader (camp number 117613). In April 1943 he worked as a tailor in the *Kommando* in Block 1, but he was later employed as a road worker and as a help in the old laundrette. When asked if he had arranged anything for camp commandant Höss, Lustbader replied, 'Not me but *Kapo* Ignac had. That *kapo* was an ethnic German from Silesia. He had some favourite tailors who did the work for him but he was the one rewarded for it.'[85]

Privileged?

The various testimonies give us a better picture of Ide's plight in the camp. During his captivity in Auschwitz he worked in Block 1 under the watchful and probably protective eye of *kapo* Ignac Szołtsyk. Ignac did business with the SS guards and even with the deputy commandant Hans Aumeier. The *kapo* was given extra food for that, which he probably shared with the people who were useful to him. Both Benno Kartuz and his daughter Ellen's boyfriend, Luc Leemans, testify that Ide was given extra bread for certain services. That gave him a greater chance of surviving. But does that count as him being privileged? At first glance, yes. Literature shows that skilled craftsmen, such as tailors, had a greater chance of surviving. Professional people such as these were useful in the camp and they did not have to work like many others in the most extreme of conditions. They were spared from breaking, lugging or laying rocks, filling swamps, working in mines and building roads, often in the icy cold or under a sweltering sun. Good tailors for the most part worked in sheltered workshops where they were less vulnerable than the average prisoner to the brutality of the guards and the *kapos*. They did have it better than prisoners who, in the eyes of the Nazis, had no use and were beaten, shot or gassed without any scruples.

Did Ide enjoy certain privileges? Primo Levi writes in his book *If this is a man* about the desperate struggle of the Muselmänner (prisoners who were doomed and had often given up all hope of survival), who had nothing at all. In a sense he describes the *survival of the fittest* in the camp.

> The result of this pitiless process of natural selection could be read in the statistics of Lager population movements. At Auschwitz, in 1944, of the old Jewish prisoners (we will not speak of the others here, as their condition was different), *'kleine Nummer'* low numbers less than 150,000, only a few hundred had survived; not one was an ordinary prisoner, vegetating in the ordinary *Kommandos*, and subsisting on the normal ration. There remained only the doctors, tailors, shoemakers, musicians, cooks, young attractive homosexuals, friends or compatriots of some authority in the camp; or they were particularly pitiless, vigorous and inhuman individuals, installed (following an investiture by the SS command, which showed itself in such choices to possess satanic knowledge of human beings) in the posts of *Kapos*, *Blockaltester*, etc.; or finally, those who, without fulfilling particular functions, had always succeeded through their astuteness and energy in successfully organizing, gaining in this way, besides material advantages and reputation, the indulgence and esteem of the powerful people in the camp. Whosoever does not know how to become an 'Organizer,' 'Kombinator,' 'Prominent' (the savage eloquence of these words!) soon becomes a 'Muselmann.' In life, a third way exists, and is in fact the rule; it does not exist in the concentration camp.[86]

Does Ide match this description? He definitely had, as Levi writes, a low number (61979). He was in one of the deadliest concentration camps from 27 August 1942 to 19 January 1945, almost twenty-nine months. He was a tailor; to do this he must have had certain materials at his disposal. Fabrics such as leather, lace, buttons, shoe laces and even baleen. And, of course, also a tape measure, glue and fine sewing utensils. This means that Ide had access to one of the most coveted things in the camp – textiles. According to Primo Levi, textiles were a precious rarity in Auschwitz.

> It has to be realized that cloth is lacking in the Lager and is precious; and that our only way of acquiring a rag to blow our noses, or a pad for our shoes, is precisely that of cutting off the tail of a shirt at the time of the exchange.[87]

This access to precious goods meant Ide had a major advantage over other prisoners. His professional dexterity undoubtedly offered him protection but also the chance to keep or steal certain articles. If he produced quality work, he was given 'special' assignments that protected him from selections for other work units and the gas chambers.

However, that does not mean that he lived a safe, comfortable or quiet life. Like the other prisoners, he had to deal with the unpredictable cruel behaviour of the guards and *kapos*. His skills didn't spare him from violent entertainment. He too had to march past hanged corpses and he, too, was terrified when the SS men would shoot at him.

One day Kartuz and five other Jews were told to come with them very early one morning because it was a feast day. The tailors hurried, not out of curiosity, but out of fear. The SS men shouted that he and his friends must come forward. 'It's a feast day,' the Nazis said, 'and you can stand in the front row to get the best experience.' Around the corner, however, was a long beam from which three Jews, still alive, were hanging. While they were being hanged Kartuz and his companions were ordered to watch their death struggle.[88]

Kartuz was also mistreated. Several testimonies show that Ide was badly beaten by SS men and *kapos*. 'They would pound their heavy boots into his stomach and lower abdomen.' Ide suffered from gastro-intestinal problems as a result of these abuses until his death. Getting sick was a great danger in Auschwitz. Every prisoner tried to stay away from the hospital blocks B19, B20 and B21 which were on the opposite side of Block 1. B19 infirmary was the *Schonungsblock*, intended for prisoners who had recovered from an illness and were still healthy enough not to be sent to the gas chambers. Infirmary B20 took prisoners with not only infectious diseases such as typhoid, tuberculosis, meningitis and erysipelas, but also with hunger diarrhoea or general weakness. The camp was regularly hit by a typhoid epidemic, which caused fear among SS guards. On 14 February 1943 camp commandant Höss gave the order 'to keep an appropriate distance from individual prisoners and groups of prisoners'. By introducing this measure he tried to stop them from getting infected. Touching the prisoners was forbidden.[89] Any prisoners who suffered from typhoid had to register immediately in Block 20. Many of them became victims of the selections by the camp doctor. They were killed in the same block on the ground floor.

Infirmary 21 was a surgical block for prisoners who needed to undergo surgery. Even here, the bedridden prisoners were in grave danger of being selected. Blocks B10 and B11 in the southern corner of the camp, opposite Block 21, were even more dangerous. In Block 11, prisoners who committed an alleged offence were punished, tortured, starved and, if they survived all of that, executed. In Block 10 medical experiments were carried out under the direction of the notorious camp doctor Carl Cauberg who had been active there since December 1942. This professor of gynaecology at the University of Königsberg wanted to find a simple and inexpensive method of sterilising women on a large scale. He injected formaldehyde preparations into their wombs without anaesthetic. His guinea pigs were Jewesses and gypsy women. They sustained permanent damage and caught serious infections. Over the course of 1943 other doctors such as Josef Mengele, Horst Schumann and August Hirt also conducted their experiments on men, women and children alike.

Apart from what it says on Ide's card, we find no personal information on him in Auschwitz. He was reduced to simply a number and didn't exist for three years. If individual documents had existed on him, it is likely they were destroyed by the Germans as Russian troops approached from the East. Many individual documents went up in flames. It doesn't make the reconstruction of his story any easier. But thanks to expert and thorough research by deputy chief archivist Kowalski, we come across a rare document. It is a list of sick inmates who were treated in the infirmary of surgical Block 21 on 23 April 1943. Ide is amongst them! The box next to his name says the following: *Panaritium digiti v pedis distri*. Googling tells us that it was a painful infectious inflammation or phlegmon under a finger or toenail. It was the result of skin wounds caused by the hard footwear. Primo Levi described phlegmons, as well as diarrhoea, as the most common ailments in the concentration camp.[90] With regard to Ide it was a phlegmon under the little toe of his right foot. Such an inflammation is not only very painful, but can also cause high fever, necrosis and blood poisoning in the absence of treatment. At some point, either the pain must have been unbearable or his general condition worsened. That's why he would have taken the risk of having the inflammation treated.

Either of the two options were dangerous for Ide; if he didn't get treated, he could fall victim to the gas chambers and if he went to the infirmary he ran the risk of being subjected to experiments or of being replaced in his work unit. Still, he chose treatment. This consisted of the surgical removal of puss under the toenail and possibly also the removal of infected tissue under anaesthetic. The Polish doctor Władislaw Dering, who according to the document removed the abscess, was himself a prisoner (camp number 1723). He was involved in the experiments of gynaecologist Dr Carl Clauberg. Dering was a very controversial figure after the war. According to some ex-prisoners, he was a hero who smuggled medicine into the main camp, carried out life-saving operations and rescued numerous sick people from the gas chambers. Others saw in him a monster who steriliszed thousands of healthy men and women and took part in the selection of prisoners for the gas chambers. The discussions surrounding the doctor still exist today. Nevertheless, he was of great help to Ide who, thanks in part to the procedure, remained useful and survived the camp. He never spoke to anyone about the incident. Why Dr Dering helped a simple Jewish prisoner such as Ide is unclear. It may be that he was guided by the Hippocratic Oath, which requires a doctor to treat the sick to the best of their ability and to strive to heal. Another, more plausible, possibility is that he was ordered to save his patient. Maybe because Ide was so useful to certain *kapos*, guards or officers. In any case, Ide survived the infirmary.

Other prisoners were less fortunate. The Polish Jew Abram Moczydlinski (camp number 64187) came to Auschwitz on 14 September 1942 with Convoy X. He was also a tailor and knew Ide personally. They met in the main camp and probably worked there together. In the archive of the Dossin barracks we find one particular reference to Moczydlinski. He had not suffered any injuries and was not ill but was sent to the women's hospital in Block 30 of Birkenau in February 1943 along with other prisoners, including the previously mentioned Marian Gnyp. There, Dr Horst Schumann had set up an X-ray station. Men and women were forced to undergo X-rays on their genitals for several minutes which resulted in their sterilisation. Many died immediately and were cremated. Some survivors had their testicles removed which were sent to the University of Breslau for further examination. That was the case with Moczydlinski. Like Gnyp, he couldn't have children after the war. Ide was spared this. Dr Schumann did not go on trial for these heinous crimes until 1970 and was only jailed for one year.

Survival

Ide, like all prisoners in Auschwitz, had to follow the routine and rules of the camp in order to survive. At the morning roll call he probably had to stand at the front because he was small. This made him an easy target. The biggest problem was when someone who had escaped was missing from the count. Then there were collective punitive sanctions in which the SS men arbitrarily executed fellow prisoners and forced the others to squat or stand with their arms in the air for hours. In total about 700 prisoners tried to flee Auschwitz-Birkenau. More than 400 of them didn't succeed. Those still alive after such a failed escape were first tortured and then hanged. This happened to anyone who, in the eyes of the SS, had committed a serious offence.

The hangings took place in the central roll call courtyard (*Appellplatz*) between blocks 16 and 17. The whole camp had to watch. Simon Majzels talks about one such incident in his testimony. They had to watch the hanging of twelve Jews from a pole. Everyone had to watch how they died.[91] Austrian Jew Freddie Knoller, who was in Auschwitz from 1943, testified about three boys who were hanged after an escape attempt.

> They were marched to the gallows and we all had to stand at attention and watch them walking up the steps on to the gallows. The amazing thing is that one of them was courageous enough to shout down to us before the trap door opened. '*Kamaraden, wir sind die Letzten!*' – 'Comrades, we are the last ones!' Then the next one to him shouted down, '*Es lebe die Freiheit!*' – 'Long live Liberty!' This was really a defiance that we had never experienced from prisoners. The SS man who operated the trapdoor got all red

152

in the face and the *Kommandant* shouted 'Los!' – and the trapdoor opened and the three boys were hanged.[92]

Another important factor for survival was understanding and correctly interpreting the orders. They were mostly in German but guards and *kapos* also spoke other languages, as did their fellow prisoners with whom they bartered. Whoever spoke German, and Polish, French or Yiddish, as did Ide, was at an advantage compared to the others. The Polish-English Jewess Kitty Hart-Moxon pointed out the importance of language skills in the camp.

> I realised first of all that the camp had its own language and I was at an advantage because I could understand it: it was part German, part Yiddish, part Polish. You had to have the language to find your way around. And it had its own expressions: the most important was to 'organise'. This was a universal word for barter – to buy, to sell, to get food. And if you lived by this principle, you learnt how to get around certain situations – to try to get into a better work party, for instance. There were work parties where you couldn't survive and you had to get away from those. The better work parties were those that were within that camp compound. Those outside were a disaster because you were exposed to the elements, you were beaten, you had to walk to work in all conditions, in the rain and snow in winter, in the heat in summer.[93]

After the morning roll call Ide and his companions would go to work with their work unit inside the camp. The others would leave for their workplace outside the camp, often in sweltering heat. In rows of five, they would march through the main gate. On the right were the bodies of murdered prisoners who had tried to flee the camp or violated a camp rule. They were there to scare the others from trying the same.

The roll call itself had risks. Sometimes there were unexpected selections. Mandelbaum, for example, mentions a selection in August 1943 under the direction of Josef Mengele. The prisoners had to appear naked in front of him. Mengele pointed to the left or to the right with a stick. Those who were either too weak, could barely walk, looked pale or had a slight defect ended up in the gas chambers on the doctor's orders.

Although Ide suffered the same as the other Jewish prisoners there were three main differences. He talks about extra food which was necessary to keep up the gruelling work schedule, he had the opportunity to dress better as a tailor and he had people who relied on him for special services. In that sense Ide was privileged although his situation was anything but enviable. Any mistake he made was reason enough to send him to the gas chamber.

Another important factor in surviving was hope. Hope that the war would soon be over and this torment would finally end. Whoever lost hope was doomed. At the end of April 1943 Ide ran into Samuel Berliner (camp number 117468) in the main camp. Berliner was a Jewish tailor whom he had already met in Antwerp in 1941 and for whom he had made suits. Berliner came to Auschwitz from the Dossin Barracks with the twentieth convoy and arrived on 22 April 1943. 'In January 1943 I was arrested by the Germans and was transported to the Auschwitz camp. When I arrived at that camp I met Kartuz again,' Berliner declared after the war.[94] He told Ide about the German defeat at the battle of Stalingrad. The tide had turned dramatically in the war on the fronts and that must have given Ide and his fellow prisoners renewed courage. From the summer of 1943 the Red Army pushed the German troops ever further back. Furthermore, the Allies liberated Sicily in July and began their advance into Italy. In addition, there was a better flow of information on the extermination of the Jews, not only in the Allied countries, but also in Germany itself. On 18 February 1943 members of the resistance group *Die Weisse Ros*e, including Hans and Sophie Scholl, threw leaflets from the second floor of Munich University down to the lobby. It was their sixth leaflet. In it they renounced Hitler and the massacre of the Jews. Their second leaflet from the end of 1942 reads: '... we want to cite the fact that since the conquest of Poland *three hundred thousand* Jews have been murdered in this country in the most bestial way.'[95]

The young activists were found, arrested and guillotined but the Royal Air Force dropped their leaflets en masse over Germany. In fact *Die Weisse Rose* had not only distributed leaflets in Munich, they had also sent them by post to Frankfurt, Stuttgart, Vienna, Freiburg, Saarbrücken, Mannheim and Karlsruhe.[96] It is evident from this that many ordinary Germans, despite *'Wir haben es nicht gewusst'* were well aware of what was going on in their own country and beyond. There were the Jewish decrees, the pogroms, *Kristallnacht*. Most of the Jews in German cities had been arrested and disappeared. Few could say that he or she didn't know what was happening to them. Any reports on the constant deportations of the Jews would also have reached those who had been in the camp for a long time via any new prisoners. It led to hope and despair. Hope that the Russians would quickly liberate the camp near Krakow and free the prisoners. But at the same time fear and despair that the Nazis would retaliate even harder against the Jews by taking them with them to their graves and thereby preventing any future testimonies.

Their fear was justified. 'The heavier the fighting was and the longer the campaign lasted, the more the Germans became immune to feelings of pity,' says Holocaust researcher David Cesarani.[97] That was certainly the case from 1943 when the Germans were under increasing pressure from the advancing Red Army after the battle of Stalingrad. In the camps the Germans also became visibly more nervous and ruthless. Himmler continued to urge his people to liquidate the Jews without compassion. On 4 October 1943, in the Polish city of Poznań, he gave a three-hour speech to SS officers and some senior Nazi leaders.

> I also want to speak to you here, in complete frankness, of a really grave chapter. Amongst ourselves, for once, it shall be said quite openly, but all the same we will never speak about it in public. ... I am referring here to the evacuation of the Jews, the extermination of the Jewish people. ... This is one of the things that is easily said: 'The Jewish people are going to be exterminated,' that's what every Party member says, 'sure, it's in our programme, elimination of the Jews, extermination – it'll be done.' And then they all come along, the 80 million worthy Germans, and each one has his one decent Jew. Of course, the others are swine, but this one, he is a first rate Jew. Of all those who talk like that, not one has seen it happen, not one has had to go through with it. Most of you men know what it is like to see 100 corpses side by side, or 500 or 1,000. To have stood fast through this – and except for cases of human weakness – to have stayed decent, that has made us hard. This is an unwritten and never-to-be-written page of glory in our history. ... We had the moral right, we had the duty towards our people, to destroy these people that wanted to destroy us.[98]

The more the Germans lost ground, the harder they used their propaganda in the press to vilify the Jews as the worst enemies of the German people.

In September 1943, the Belgian Jewish trader Israel Joseph Feld ended up in Auschwitz after his imprisonment in many other camps. He had been in contact with Ide before his arrest as a member of the resistance. In a police report of 24 December 1949 he stated that he met tailor Ide Leib Kartuz in the camp and spoke to him about what was happening in the war. In Italy, Benito Mussolini was deposed by the Fascist Grand Council in the summer of 1943. That news was also a blow for the Nazis and so gave hope to the prisoners in the concentration camps.

Meanwhile, the extermination of the Jews continued more ruthlessly than ever. The Majdanek and Birkenau extermination camps were running at full capacity. In Birkenau, about 300,000 people were gassed in 1943. Ide would not have seen much of that in the main camp of Auschwitz because Birkenau was 2.5 kilometres away. But the rumours in the camp were undoubtedly rampant. The surviving Jews must have known what was going on there because, although a lot of newcomers were immediately transported to Birkenau, new Jews were regularly added to the main camp and IG Farben in Auschwitz III. They needed doctors, carpenters, bricklayers, street layers, electricians, welders and also tailors. They were used to supplement the *Kommandos* from where many prisoners had disappeared as a result of exhaustion or death and therefore needed to be replaced. Among these were tailor Berck Lachman (camp number 117605) and his son David (camp number 117604), who arrived in Auschwitz with Convoy XXV from Belgium on 21 May 1944. David was an apprentice tailor and ended up on the first floor of Block 2 where he remained in quarantine. He testified after the war that his father was in Block 1 in a workshop of tailors.

> There they had certain advantages over other prisoners because sometimes they did little jobs for one or another. Almost all prominent people who had certain privileges in the camp had a 'pantalon (trousers)' or a 'veston (jacket)' made or alterations done. When the tailors finished the task they got some extra bread. Father had certain contacts for jobs which gave him that little extra.[99]

At the end of August 1944 there were 104,878 detainees working in Auschwitz-Birkenau, 18,419 of them in Auschwitz I; 484 of them were Belgian Jews.[100] The newcomers talked about their arrest in raids, the destruction of the ghettos, the inhumane deportations, the selections on arrival at the camp, the separation of parents, wives and children. Those who had been there for some time on the other hand knew what was going to happen to them; the stench of the crematoria made the ultimate goal of the camp obvious. Ide said after the war that he and many others had realised on what scale the Jews were being annihilated. Although the newcomers brought snippets of information about the progress at the front, it remained particularly difficult for the Jews in the main camp to make a proper assessment of the war in general and their chances of survival.

It is difficult to estimate the impact these events had on Ide. We can only assume that it was now even more important for him to focus on his work in Block 1 and attract as little attention as possible, for him to avoid diseases and mistreatment and to protect himself from the cold. On top of that, he had to 'organise' enough food and try to survive from day to day. Whoever didn't was doomed.

According to Polish prisoner Witold Pilecki (camp number 4859) there was only one way to survive and that was not to stand out: 'Don't get yourself noticed, don't be the first or the last, don't be too fast or too slow. Avoid contact with the kapos but if that is unavoidable be submissive, helpful, friendly.'[101] Primo Levi also described how prisoners could survive the camp.

> We have learnt other things, more or less quickly, according to our intelligence: to reply '*Jawohl*' never to ask questions, always to pretend to understand. We have learnt the value of food; now we also diligently scrape the bottom of the bowl after the ration and we hold it under our chins when we eat bread so as not to lose the crumbs. ... We have learnt that everything is useful: the wire to tie up our shoes, the rags to wrap around our feet, waste paper to (illegally) pad out our jacket against the cold. We have learnt, on the other hand, that everything can be stolen, in fact is automatically stolen as soon as attention is relaxed; and to avoid this, we had to learn the art of sleeping with our head on a bundle made up of our jacket and containing all our belongings, from the bowl to the shoes.[102]

In order to survive, you had to be clever and cunning, properly assess the mood and behaviour of the *kapos*, stand up for yourself and not associate with those who let themselves go.

> With the *Muselmänner*, the men in decay, it is not even worth speaking, because one knows already that they will complain and will speak about what they used to eat at home. Even less worthwhile is it to make friends with them, because they have no distinguished acquaintances in camp, they do not gain any extra rations, they do not work in profitable Kommandos and they know no secret method of organising. And in any case, one knows that they are only here on a visit, that in a few weeks nothing will remain of them but a handful of ashes in some near-by field and a crossed-out number on a register.[103]

Auschwitz-Birkenau lived up to every expectation of the Nazi leaders. It grew into the ideal camp, where working and then killing people went hand in hand.

The pace of the extermination of the Jews accelerated again in 1944 and continued relentlessly despite the military defeats. Eichmann demanded as many trains and freight wagons as necessary to make Hungary *Judenfrei* (Jew-free) which, from a military strategic point of view, was completely absurd. The trains were needed for military transports, to provide a defence against the advancing Red Army. 'The "war against the Jews" had this time precedence over the war on the front line,' said historian Guido Knopp.[104] The *Endlösung* remained the highest priority.

In the spring of 1944, the Germans extended the train tracks on the *Judenrampe* to Birkenau closer to the gas chambers. This made the killings even more efficient and is where the typical image of trains entering the gate of death originates from. From 15 May to 19 June several trains ran daily between Hungary and Auschwitz-Birkenau bringing 12,000 new prisoners to the camp every day, ready to be gassed. In a six-week period 437,402 Hungarian Jews were deported and murdered. A number of women were allowed to live to help sort the clothes, shoes and other belongings of the murdered Jews. One of them was the survivor Trude Levi. She arrived in Birkenau on 7 July 1944 and later testified about the fateful deportations. 'The normal load for the trucks was 60-90 people, we were 120. ... This was June 1944, a very hot summer and there was very little air in the truck. It meant people went into hysterics, people went mad, and people died.'[105]

Most Jews were immediately taken to the gas chamber. Then their bodies were burned in the crematoria. The *Sonderkommando* was extended to 900 working Jews and was busy day and night. But the ovens became overloaded. They were not designed for this huge influx of corpses and so the architects of death decided to burn the bodies in big pits by pouring petrol over them. To stoke the fire they would also throw methanol over them.

Almost all transports end up in the gas chamber: men, women and children. The labour camps are bursting at the seams; there is no need for more labourers ... . The gas chambers run twenty-four hours a day at top speed. We hear from Birkenau that they first burned 3,000, then 3,500 and last week up to 4,000 bodies a day. The new *Sonderkommando* has been doubled to make the interplay between the gas chambers and the ovens run smoothly. From the chimneys there are flames blazing ten metres into the air; they can be seen from miles away at night and the vile stench of burnt meat can be smelled as far away as Buna, said Jewish prisoner Paul Steinberg (camp number 157239).[106] Above Birkenau there was a constant red glow and the smell was unbearable.

Vrba-Wetzler

On 7 April 1944 the roll call in Auschwitz-Birkenau lasted much longer than usual. Two Slovak Jews, Rudolf Vrba (camp number 44070) and Alfred Wetzler (camp number 29162), had escaped. All access roads to and from Auschwitz were closed indefinitely. The two had hidden themselves under building material during the construction of the new sorting camp 'Mexico'. They hid there for three days and waited for the blockade to be lifted. Then they managed to flee to Slovakia where they made contact with leaders of the Jewish community. Vrba and Wetzler told them about what was happening at Auschwitz-Birkenau extermination camp. They gave details of the transports that had arrived since 1942 and based on this calculated how many people had been killed.[107] They described how the prisoners were selected for work or the gas chamber upon arrival. They made sketches showing the size of the gas chambers, the places where the prisoners had to undress, and the locations of the crematoria. They had received the information on the gas chambers and the crematoria from the Slovak Jewish prisoner Filip Müller, a member of a *Sonderkommando*. Their escape and their statements led to a forty-page report, the so-called *Auschwitz Protocols*, which was translated into German and Hungarian and passed on to the Allies. Now there was no doubt that the deported Jews were not sent to labour camps, as the Nazis would have led us to believe. The reality was that they were systematically exterminated in enormous numbers. *The New York Times* had published such information back in November 1942, but it was not taken seriously. On 4 June 1944 the newspaper published details of the Vrba-Wetzler report. On 16 June it was covered by the BBC. Meanwhile, the Hungarian Holocaust continued unabated. The Allies encouraged Hungarian leader Miklós Horty to stop the transports, which happened on 7 July 1944.

The summer of 1944 was sunny and warm. Unlike in Birkenau, where the extermination of Jews was a priority, life in Auschwitz I remained more or less the same. Because the rumours about the Allies approaching had persisted for so long, no one believed them anymore. But that changed in the summer. The white contrails of the Allied aircraft gave the prisoners renewed hope. After a few weeks, however, it became clear that these planes were not coming for them. British historian Martin Gilbert quotes Hugu Gryn, a Jewish-Hungarian survivor who was 15 years old in 1944 and regularly saw Allied planes flying over Birkenau. 'One of the most painful things for those in the camp was the feeling of being completely abandoned.'[108]

On 20 August 1944 hopes were raised again. American aircraft bombed IG Farben's synthetic oil production plant in Auschwitz III, near the Buna-Monowitz concentration camp. There, 11,000 Jewish prisoners were forced to work in extreme conditions every day. The SS guards denied them access to bomb shelters, leaving them with just their wooden barracks for protection. The future Nobel Peace Prize winner, Elie Wiesel, who worked in Buna, described what it was like that day.

> At around ten o'clock, the sirens started to go off. Alert. The *Blockälteste* gathered us inside the blocks. while de SS took refuge in the shelters. ... To watch that factory go up

in flames – what revenge! While we had heard some talk of German military defeats on the various fronts, we were not sure if they were credible. But today, that was real![109]

Wiesel argued that none of the prisoners were afraid and that every bomb that fell gave them hope. That was an exaggeration. Most of the survivors were grateful that their barracks were not hit and that they might still be able to survive until the impending liberation.

Yet to this day, the question remains why Britons and Americans did not bomb the train tracks going to Auschwitz-Birkenau. The Allies were aware of the Vrba-Wetzler report and knew the fate of the Hungarian Jews who were transported to the extermination camp from 15 May 1944. But even before that, people in the West were well aware of what was happening in Auschwitz. The *Washington Post* wrote on 22 March 1944, that the Nazis had built gas chambers and crematoria in 'a concentration camp in Oświęcim (Auschwitz), southwest of Krakow, with "a capacity for tens of thousands of bodies a day"'.[110] When Michael Dov Weissmandel, a Slovak orthodox rabbi, realised that the Hungarian Jewish leaders did not use the Vrba-Wetzler report, he sent a coded telegram from Bratislava to Swiss orthodox Jews on 16 May 1944. They in turn forwarded it to the United States and requested the bombing of the railways between Košice and Prešov.[111] On 18 June 1944 Jacob Rosenheim, president of the Agudath Israel World Organisation, sent a letter to Secretary of the Treasury Henry Morgenthau, who headed the US War Refugee Board. In the letter he called for the train tracks between Hungary and Poland to be bombed. On 24 June 1944 Roswell McClelland, the US Representative to the War Refugee Board in Switzerland, repeated this request in a telegram. At the same time the Czech underground movement was able to find out the timetable for the trains. The telegram said the following:

> It is urged by all sources of this information in Slovakia and Hungary that vital sections of these lines, especially bridges along one [along the line Sap-Košice-Prešov-Ľubotín-Nowy Sącz towards Oświęcim] be bombed as the only means slowing down or stopping future deportations. ... There is little doubt that many of these Hungarian Jews are being sent to the extermination camps of Auschwitz

(Oświęcim) and Birkenau (Rajska) in eastern upper Silesia where according to recent reports, since early summer 1942 at least 1,500,000 Jews have been killed. There is evidence that already in January 1944 preparations were being made to receive and exterminate Hungarian Jews in these camps.[112]

This important telegram eventually ended up with John McCloy, a senior aide to the US Secretary of War. Until the end of August 1944 he had rejected any proposal to bomb the supply lines to the gas chambers and the crematoria of Auschwitz. He considered the plan unworkable because 'the target was too far off for dive bombers and fighter-bombers'.

However Auschwitz was already within their reach; but it had not yet been identified as an extermination camp for the deported Jews. On 4 April 1944 a de Havilland Mosquito photo-reconnaissance aircraft from the South African Air Force took off from Foggia. At an altitude of 26,000 feet, the aircraft took pictures of the rubber factory in Monowitz owned by IG Farben and situated four kilometres from Auschwitz. The pilot activated the camera as he approached his target and switched it off six kilometres further on.[113] The report and the photos ended up with American and British intelligence agencies. Three of the twenty photographs showed the Auschwitz I camp. A second flight over the area followed on 31 May. Two detailed photographs show images of not only Monowitz, but also parts of Auschwitz I and Birkenau, from an altitude of 27,000 feet.

Nevertheless, the British and American authorities were not interested in the clearly visible barracks in the concentration camp, but only in the industrial sites where synthetic rubber was made and oil was refined. The Allied bombers' main objective was a military one and precedence was given to the elimination of, or at least damage to, the German production centres for rubber and oil. On 26 June 1944 more than 100 aircraft, both bombers and fighters, flew over the east of Poland to destroy military production units which were located even further inland. During the return flight they flew over the main deportation railways.[114] By 17 August there had already been twenty-two flights over Warsaw. The pilots themselves didn't know what was beneath them when they approached their target.

Some historians argue that a possible bombing of Auschwitz did not take place because the deportations of Hungarian Jews had stalled at the beginning of July 1944. But that reasoning doesn't make sense. From August the Allies were aware of new deportations. For example, the Germans deported 60,000 Jews from the Łódź ghetto to Auschwitz-Birkenau and, later, tens of thousands of Jews from other territories. The Allies knew what was happening in that camp but McCloy rejected any requests from the Czech and Polish governments in exile to bomb the extermination camp and its supply lines. As mentioned before, on 20 August 1944, the Allies bombed the Monowitz synthetic oil production plant. Five days later, on 25 August, photos of that place were taken again. As a result, they had even more details at their disposal of the Auschwitz main camp and especially of Birkenau. The pictures give a grim portrayal of rows of Jews walking from the train to the gas chambers. By refusing to bomb the access roads to the camp, the Allies bear a certain responsibility for the deaths of all the Jews who were gassed from that moment onwards.[115]

On 13 September 1944, the British and Americans again attacked Monowitz. Some of the bombs that also fell on Auschwitz I resulted in casualties amongst both the SS men and the prisoners. Block 6, a clothing unit, was only a few dozen metres from Block 1 and was badly hit. In the process, sixteen SS men lost their lives and twenty-eight others were seriously injured. In the clothing workshop forty prisoners died, twenty-three of whom were Jews.[116] At the end of 1944 the Polish Government announced from its exile in London that the Germans were increasing their extermination activities in all Polish concentration camps.[117]

The survivors had mixed feelings about the air strikes. The impact was mostly psychological as none of the prisoners' circumstances had actually improved. To the contrary, the tenacity and cruelty of the SS guards only increased. The bombing caused resentment which they took out on the Jewish prisoners in the camp. The Nazis saw it as proof that there was such a thing as international Judaism, which was made up of a global collaboration of Americans, British and Bolsheviks against their heimat Germany. And so the extermination continued to the end.

Endgame

Members of the *Sonderkommando* who worked in crematoria III and IV realised that they would soon be eliminated. There were killings every two weeks. Some brave Jewesses who worked in a weapons' factory had secretly supplied them with a quantity of explosives. On the morning of 7 October 1944 members of the *Kommando* killed the *Blockälteste* and fired at the SS guards. With the explosives they disabled the installations in crematorium IV and damaged them irreparably. Members of the other *Sonderkommandos* also participated. They cut the wires of the electric fence and fled. However, most were quickly re-captured and shot. The damage was limited but the action of the *Sonderkommando* led to a delay and a hitch in the systematic extermination of the Jews. However, transports continued to arrive from Slovakia and Theresienstadt. On 30 October 1944 a transport of 2,038 Jews arrived from Theresienstadt, 949 men and boys and 1,089 women and girls.[118] From this transport 1,609 deportees were immediately gassed. In November the procedure was halted. On 26 November 1944 Himmler ordered the destruction of the gas chambers and crematoria of Auschwitz-Birkenau.[119] However, that didn't mean the killings stopped. Almost all members of the various *Sonderkommandos* were executed.

The news of the uprising spread to every corner of the camp and Ide must have heard of it. Later he said that, at the end of 1944, although some SS men were even more brutal than usual, others began to realise that they might be punished at a later date for their crimes. The number of prisoners in Auschwitz-Birkenau and Monowitz fell from 135,000 in July 1944 to 65,000 in January 1945, partly due to evacuations but also to the extremely high death toll in the camp.[120] Along the length of the barracks in Auschwitz I were corpses of prisoners who had been murdered by ruthless SS men.

At the beginning of January 1945, the prisoners heard the rumble of the Red Army artillery beyond the horizon. Scraps of burning paper drifted through the streets of the Auschwitz main camp. The SS guards had been ordered to burn as many documents as possible which could be used in evidence.[121] They used large fire-pits. The crematoria buildings had been dismantled so that they could be blown up and corpses had been cleared away. All this served to cover up evidence of the massacres. Several trains quickly transported the stored possessions of the Jews from the *Kanada* camp to the interior of the Third Reich. Another special train came to collect the senior SS officers and their relatives. Fear of the Red Army was great. Only the thousands of prisoners hoped for the quick arrival of the Soviets. They only wanted one thing: survival.

Part Four

Mauthausen

Death March

When the Red Army broke through the German defensive line on 12 January 1945 and advanced into Poland, the Auschwitz SS commanding officers gave the order to start the evacuations. From 17 to 21 January 1945 the Nazis removed more than 58,000 prisoners from the camps and sub-camps of Auschwitz-Birkenau and forced them to walk in the freezing cold to the stations in Gleiwitz and Loslau. Prisoners who couldn't keep up were ruthlessly murdered by the SS escort. More than 15,000 prisoners did not survive the journey. They died of starvation, froze to death or were shot along the way. When they arrived at these stations the Nazis forced their victims to squeeze into crowded freight wagons. Most of the wagons had open tops. During the journey thousands more died from exhaustion and hypothermia, and their bodies were thrown out to make more room.

On 20 January 1945 the SS blew up the gas chambers and most crematoria and set fire to Kanada's warehouses. The watch towers remained manned until 21 January. A day later the last guards left their posts in Auschwitz. Some took off their uniforms while others put on civilian clothes to avoid being recognised.[1] Retreating *Wehrmacht* soldiers drove through Auschwitz in search of valuables left in the half-destroyed warehouses. In crematorium V, which was not blown up by the SS until 25 January 1945, executions were still taking place. Two days later the Red Army freed the remaining 7,500 prisoners. They were in the infirmary or had been able to hide at the last minute. One of them was Jewish Primo Levi. In the remaining warehouses the Russian soldiers found '836,525 women's dresses, 348,820 men's suits, seven tons of women's hair – collected for the manufacture of mattresses – spectacles, shoes and dentures in piles the height of a man'.[2] Part of that find can be seen in Blocks 4 and 5 of the Auschwitz-Birkenau State Museum.

We search for a long time for the date when Ide began his death march. Finally, we find the answer with the help of Krzysztof Antończyk of the Auschwitz-Birkenau State Museum. He wrote his PhD on the death marches that left Auschwitz and its various sub-camps. His records show that on 19 January at 1:00 am a group of 2,500 prisoners had left for Mauthausen. The group first walked 63 kilometres to the station of Loslau, now Wodzisław Śląski in Poland. In the village of Rajsko, 1,000 prisoners from Birkenau joined them and later some 833 prisoners from the Charlottengrube coal mine. Finally, 1,948 prisoners from the Jawischowitz sub-camp joined the 'walking dead' past the village of Brzeszcze. *SS-Obersturmführer* Wilhelm Reischenbeck commanded this last major evacuation march from Auschwitz-Birkenau.

In a temperatures of minus-15- to minus-20-degrees Celsius and a biting headwind, the 5,714 prisoners marched through the snow to the station. Many of them were physically exhausted and were barely able to make any headway in their wooden and cloth footwear.

David Lachman, who was in Ide's group, testified about the foot march: 'The death march was terrible. It was very cold, almost 20 degrees below zero. My feet hurt a lot. At the back were SS men who shot the Jews who couldn't keep up.'[3] The SS guards constantly hurried them on and shouted at them to walk faster. The reason they were in a hurry was obvious. Months before, on 24 July 1944, the Soviets liberated the Majdanek concentration camp. They immediately executed as war criminals the SS guards left behind. Those who were able to flee ended up in Auschwitz and testified about the cruelty of the Red Army. No guard wanted to fall into the hands of the Russians and they therefore pushed the prisoners to the limit.

After two days they finally reached Loslau. From there they were transported in open train carriages to Mauthausen in Austria. Several survivors testified that the Jews had to climb into wagons with half a metre of snow in them. Lachman described the scene, 'That night we arrived at open freight wagons. In a temperature of minus 20 degrees 120 of us were pushed into one wagon. It was snowing. We travelled for three days and three nights. They threw some bread into the open wagons and the prisoners started fighting.'[4]

Felix Müller also testified about this torture on the train:

> In open cattle wagons, exposed to a biting cold, we travelled for several days from Loslau to Mauthausen.

We were strictly forbidden to leave our trucks. No rations were handed out. Under these harsh conditions it was not surprising that many died from cold or hunger during the transport. Some tried to escape by jumping from the moving train during the night, risking not only injury but also being picked off by the SS who had machine guns and swivelling searchlights set up all along the train.[5]

Some Jews died of hunger and thirst or froze to death. Their bodies were simply thrown out. A total of 567 prisoners lost their lives in this transport. After six days the survivors arrived at Mauthausen station. There they went again on foot up the hill to the camp. The steep climb through the snow must have been utter torture for the exhausted and hungry prisoners. The Austrian inhabitants saw the Dantesque death march go past from behind their windows. David Lachman witnesses:

> Arrival in Mauthausen. We were very hungry. We had to get out and go up in lines. ... At the entrance to the camp we had to wait outside. We were with a group of fellow prisoners from Antwerp. Eventually we were allowed in. ... I managed to go into a barrack where it was warm, it was full of dying people. I undressed and went under a hot shower. Then they threw us out again in the freezing cold. Many died. ... The survivors then went to another block, where we got clothes and some hot soup.[6]

We know with certainty that Ide was on this march and also in this transport because this group arrived in Mauthausen on 26 January 1945 and the survivors of the death march from the Auschwitz main camp had the camp numbers 116,501 to 120,400.[7] Ide Leib Kartuz's number was 118,890.

Austria

We've covered quite a few kilometres for our research. We drove to Germany, Poland and Bulgaria, and flew to Florida. But it doesn't stop there. It is impossible to tell Ide's story without having some idea of his stay in Mauthausen. That's why we get back in the car and set a course for Austria via the wide German motorways.

The road is being widened to three or four lanes so there are road works everywhere. On 23 September 1933 Hitler put the first spade in the ground here to build *Reichsautobahn* 3. It runs from the Dutch border through Cologne, Frankfurt, Nuremberg, Regensburg to Passau on the Austrian border. We pass Linz, where the Führer spent his teenage years, and we drive a further 20 kilometres to the town of Mauthausen on the Danube. From our hotel we have a view of the river that has its source in the Black Forest and then winds through Central and South-Eastern Europe for 2,829 kilometres. Before the Danube empties into the Black Sea it passes through Linz, Vienna, Bratislava and Budapest. River cruises are particularly popular there. But in the hotel there are also brochures about the city's main draw: the *KZ-Gedenkstätte Mauthausen.* That's where we need to be.

We meet our guide, Daniel Tscholl. The stone fort is situated on a hill near a granite quarry and was the largest concentration camp in Austria. It was established on 9 August 1938, a few months after the Anschluss of the country to the Third Reich. Prisoners brought in from Dachau built the camp. From all over the Reich, and later from the occupied territories, opponents of the regime, political dissidents, criminals, anti-socials, gypsies and Jews were imprisoned here. In 1940, 7,000 members of the International Brigades, who had fought in the Spanish Civil War and were hiding in France after its occupation by German forces, were also sent here.[8] According to the motto *Vernichtung durch Arbeit* (annihilation through work) they were forced to do hard labour. Over the entirety of the war, nearly 200,000 people were imprisoned here. Of the approximately 120,000 people who did not survive the camp, 38,000 were Jews. In 1942 Heydrich classified the camp as Category III, 'camps of no return'.[9] Many prisoners arriving in Mauthausen were sent to one of the forty-nine sub-camps in Austria. They were scattered all over the country and mainly served the German arms industry. Companies produced aircraft and missiles there, among other things.

Daniel takes us to the entrance of the imposing building. We pass two massive watch towers and arrive at the roll call area. Around the whole camp there is a 1,600-metre-long wall which is over two-and-a-half-metres high. On top of the wall there is electrified barbed wire. On the right were the buildings for the kitchen, laundry, the camp brothel, the camp prison and the infirmary. Underneath, the gas chamber where thousands of prisoners were murdered with Zyklon B. But there was also an execution room where prisoners were shot or hanged. The bodies were then burned in one of the two crematoria. To the left of the roll call area were wooden barracks, each of which could accommodate 300 prisoners, although sometimes they were crammed with more than 1,000 unfortunates. Daniel explains that the newcomers had to line up along the camp wall. They had to hand in their clothes and possessions. In the basement they were then shaved, showered and given their striped prisoner uniform to put on. They then spent two to four weeks in separate, overcrowded quarantine barracks. The intention was to keep out infectious diseases. As the camp grew, new buildings were added. In October 1941 ten additional wooden barracks, fenced with electrified barbed wire, were erected outside the main building for Russian prisoners. From 1943 onwards it became a place where the ill were brought to die. The SS also held regular selections in this so-called 'hospital camp'.

According to the camp register Mauthausen held 6,969 male and 399 female prisoners on 17 October 1944. Around that time thousands of Jews arrived from Auschwitz. As a result the population in the main camp increased to nearly 20,000. The risk of disease increased enormously. To cope with this influx of new prisoners, the SS leadership ordered the construction of a tented camp in a field behind the barracks. There, too, the living conditions were absolutely horrendous. As the Red Army approached Auschwitz-Birkenau in January 1945, the pressure on Mauthausen increased. At that time, an additional 25,000 prisoners had been added to the camp. Most of them immediately ended up in the hospital or tented camp where they had to survive with primitive sanitation and a great shortage of food. Between January and May 1945, 45,000 prisoners died. Those who still had sufficient strength after a few weeks had to join the forced labourers for the war industry in one of the sub-camps.[10]

Hitler's megalomaniacal structures required a lot of resources. He envisaged developing the nearby town of Linz, where he spent his youth, into a cultural capitol of the Third Reich. This is why the SS had established a company which had to supply the stones, among other things. To meet the demand, the company deployed the prisoners to dig out with pick-axes blocks of granite which they then carried on their backs out of the quarry via the 'stairs of death'. This *Todesstiege* was made up of 186 steps, on which the prisoners regularly slipped, fell or were pushed by the guards, often falling to their deaths in the quarry. Other prisoners were deliberately starved or sprayed with water in winter so they froze to death during the night. A disturbing example of this were the deaths of 200 physically weak and elderly prisoners from Sachsenhausen. On the night of 16/17 February 1945 they had to wait outside naked for their registration. They were then sprayed with water while it was minus-2 to minus-7 degrees Celsius outside.[11] No one survived.

Many prisoners chose suicide, others tried to flee. One of them was the Austrian Hans Bonarewitz, who hid in a crate in June 1942 and managed to escape. Sometime later, he was arrested again and sentenced to death by hanging. The SS put him on a cart that was pulled to the scaffold from the roll call area in the presence of all the prisoners. The camp orchestra accompanied this with music.

From the roll call area our guide Daniel points to houses in the distance where ordinary Austrians lived during that period. They were able to see what was happening in and around the camp. But they didn't care about the fate of the prisoners. They mainly complained about the crematoria, which spread a bad smell and ashes all over the city. A striking example of this indifference was a written complaint by Eleonore Gusenbauer:

> In the concentration camp Mauthausen at the work site inmates are being shot repeatedly; those badly struck live for yet some time, and so remain lying next to the dead for hours or even half a day long. My property lies upon an elevation next to the Vienna Ditch, and one is often an unwilling witness to such outrages. I am anyway sickly and such a sight makes a demand on my nerves that in the long run I cannot bear. I request that it be arranged that such inhuman deed be discontinued, or else done where one does not see it.[12]

The locals benefited from the camp. Several women had relationships with the guards and supported the SS football team, which played in the regional league. Daniel shows us the site of the football field outside the walls of the main camp. It was right next to the camp hospital and there were stands around it. Even the press followed these matches and reported on them in the newspapers. We stare at the field. It's unreal. We can't understand how people happily played football here and supporters would cheer while there were people dying in the worst of conditions right next to it.

Ide and other survivors arrived at Mauthausen on 26 January 1945. There they were shaved again, disinfected and numbered. On his prisoner card he is described as being a Belgian Jew, originally from Poland, 157 centimetres tall, 'slim build', with an oval face, blue eyes, a common nose shape, a normal mouth, normal ears, irregular teeth, dark hair and Flemish and German speaking. For the first few weeks he was quarantined. However, the barrack was overcrowded with 1,000 prisoners and most detainees had no beds or blankets. Many succumbed to the freezing temperatures, exhaustion and hunger. As more prisoners arrived the pressure increased by the day during February 1945, leading the authority to send useful Jews to sub-camps as forced labourers.

Sub-camps

From 1945 the Third Reich gradually collapsed. Both the Soviets in the East and the Allies in the West advanced towards Berlin. The Allied air forces bombed the German cities day and night. The aim was mainly to eliminate the war industry of the Nazis, but its effect on industry was minimal. Under the leadership of Albert Speer, Minister of Armaments and Munitions from 1942, arms production continued to run at full speed. Large companies such as Hirtenberg Patterns-Fabrik, Steyr-Daimler-Puch, Messerschmitt, Heinkel Werke and Herman Göring Reichswerke were able to continue to produce weapons, ammunition, armoured vehicles, aircraft and missiles in the Mauthausen sub-camps until 1945. In St Georgen, Gusen II, Ebensee and Melk, forced labourers had dug underground corridors and tunnels to protect the production from possible bombing. Other camps were located in wooded areas and were difficult to detect from the air. There, too, thousands of prisoners died from exhaustion, hunger and disease. There was, therefore, a constant demand for new prisoners to keep the industry going.

After three weeks of quarantine Ide was sent to the Sankt Aegyd am Neuwalde sub-camp in Lower Austria. He arrived there on 21 February 1945. It could accommodate 300 prisoners who lived in barracks built around a roll call area. The exact purpose of this camp remains unclear. It may have been intended as a production department for the infamous V-2 missiles.

However, the rapid advance of the Russians thwarted these plans. While the war was still going on, the prisoners had to dig out a cave. The camp was led by *SS-Hauptscharführer* Willi Auerswald. Together with the help of forty-eight SS men he was in charge of the camp. Many prisoners could not cope with the heavy work and died on the spot or were sent back.

In the Mauthausen-Memorial archive we find a *Transportliste* that includes the names Jules (Ide) Kartuz, Samuel Berliner and Abram Moczydlinski, all Belgian Jews, who had to work there as *Hilfsarbeiter*, unskilled workers. In addition, the convoy included masons, electricians, carpenters, roofers and other craftsmen. Because Ide could no longer work as a tailor and now had to do heavy physical work, his chances of survival decreased considerably.

On 1 April 1945, the Nazis decided to shut down the camp and send the 297 survivors back to the main camp.[13] Amongst them was Ide who by then had lost a lot of weight. At 40 years old, he was one of the older survivors of this horror. But there was no room for them in the main camp because of the constant influx of prisoners from the satellite camps. Ide and the other prisoners from Sankt Aegyd ended up in the tent camp. This must have been one of the dirtiest places he'd ever been imprisoned. About 12,000 Hungarian Jews and Jews who had returned from the disbanded sub-camps lived like animals here. They slept in the mud, there were no toilets, there was hardly any food and drink and rotting corpses lay covered with rags next to the sick.

To make room, the SS decided to send the 22,000 Jews in the tent camp to other more westerly camps. Ide's personal notes show that he was put back on a transport after only a week. This time the destination was Gunskirchen, where he arrived on 14 April 1945. That journey, too, must have been terrible. We don't have a testimony from Ide himself but we know with certainty that marches took place on an almost daily basis from Mauthausen to Gunskirchen from 10 April 10 – 55 kilometres, again on foot. It is estimated that a total of about 6,000 Jews did not survive this evacuation.

Liberation

The story and our search don't end here. As a consequence of the decisions taken by the Germans who were now panicking, Ide's trail at the end of the war leads us to Gunskirchen. We take the back roads and pass small, charming villages, meadows and rolling forests. Unknowingly, we follow the river Traun, which empties into the Danube near the city of Linz.

We don't have a precise address for the sub-camp in Gunskirchen but thanks to historian Angelika Schlackl and archaeologist Yvonne Burger we do have an idea of where we have to be. They are specialists in the study of the site. It is surrounded by pine trees. The researchers did not give us an address, but co-ordinates: 48°06'50.1'N - 13°56'23.8'E. Our GPS suddenly leads us from the road onto a narrow path that, according to the map, runs between the trees in the direction of the village of Saag. The path gets narrower and around a bend we see a small open space. It must be here! Here was the entrance to the camp. There's a somewhat dilapidated memorial stone and a metal sign with some explanation. At the bottom we read the statement *Den Toten zum Gedenken. Den Lebenden zur Mahnung. Nie Wieder Faschismus!* (In memory of the dead. To warn the living. Never again Fascism!) From here, an almost completely overgrown path leads us deeper into the forest. According to Angelika and Yvonne, there is hardly anything left apart from the concrete foundation of a barrack and two latrines. Everything is overgrown. After two hours of searching we're close to despair; we don't find anything. We carry on a bit deeper into the woods. Miraculously, near an uprooted tree, we discover the only material evidence that at some point there had been a camp here: the foundations of the latrines. We take pictures and leave.

Later we receive an e-mail from Angelika and Yvonne. They send us a scanned brochure they made together in 2017. It contains information, photos, descriptions and testimonies about the camp.[14] Yvonne carried out excavations here two years before and found rusty dishes and spoons, broken toothbrushes, shoes and rags, as well as glass bottles, cups, boxes of medicine and so on, evidence of a human presence here seventy-five years ago.

Polish and Soviet prisoners started building ten wooden barracks in Gunskirchen in December 1944 to relieve the pressure on an overcrowded

Mauthausen. Only six barracks were completed. The overall capacity had been calculated at 3,000 people, but this was quickly exceeded. By the end of April more than 15,000 prisoners were living there in the direst of conditions. There was one latrine with twenty holes, which was only allowed to be in use for six hours a day. For a lot of prisoners with dysentery and diarrhoea, this was torture. Those who went to the toilet outside these hours or relieved themselves outside their barracks among the trees, were shot dead by the SS guards. The prisoners were barely fed – at most a piece of black bread and some watery soup. Many were completely broken and perished.[15] Once a day, a fire engine passed with 1,500 litres of water, totally insufficient for so many prisoners.[16]

After all this time Ide became seriously ill for the first time and got typhoid fever. With rashes and a high temperature, he lay on a simple bale of straw. Almost all detainees were malnourished or seriously ill. On average 200 people died every day. Their corpses were piled up in the barracks or left scattered on the ground in the mud among the trees in the forest. By the end, there were 2,500 prisoners in each barrack. No one could lie down anymore. The unfortunates had to crouch down between the knees of the person in front of them.[17] Often they found that the person in front or behind them had died during the night. There was hardly any food which, according to witnesses, even led to cannibalism.[18]

Five days before liberation panic broke out among the SS guards. When they noticed that the prisoners no longer even had the strength to bury their deceased inmates, they shot dead several of these poor souls out of frustration. On 4 May 1945 they fled from the approaching US military with some putting on civilian clothing to disappear into the masses. What they left behind was a scene of unbelievable horror.

Soldiers from 71st Infantry Division of the US Third Army reached the camp a day later and couldn't believe their eyes. There were rotting corpses all around the camp. The survivors were squeezed together and could barely stand on their feet. The 'strongest' dragged themselves to the exit. American Captain J.D. Pletcher described how he drove his jeep in the direction of the camp and was approached by living skeletons, 'Hundreds of starving, half-crazed inmates lining the roads, begging for food and cigarettes. Many of them had been able to get only a few hundred yards from the gate before they keeled over and died.'[19] Pletcher also spoke about the stench in and around the camp:

Of all the horrors of the place, the smell, perhaps, was the most startling of all. It was a smell made up of all kinds of odors: human excreta, foul bodily odours, smoldering trash fires. German tobacco – which is a stink in itself – all mixed together in a heavy dank atmosphere, in a thick, muddy woods, where little breeze could go. The ground was pulpy muddy throughout the camp, churned to a consistency of warm putty by the milling of thousands of feet, mud mixed with faeces and urine. The smell of Gunskirchen nauseated many of the Americans who went there. It was a smell I'll never forget, completely different from anything I've ever encountered. It could almost be seen and hung over the camp like a fog of death.[20]

Sergeant Alan Moskin, who was one of the first Americans to arrive at the camp, also testified about this horrific experience:

There were dead bodies everywhere in Gunskirchen. We were sickened by a terrible smell. We knew Hitler had done terrible things but we hadn't heard anything about any concentration camps. There were bodies to the left and right of the road and in the forest. The survivors looked like living skeletons. They wore dirty pyjamas with grey and white stripes. They begged for water, food and cigarettes. The barracks were full of dead bodies and you couldn't stay in them because of the smell. Piles of corpses, dead horses. Survivors began to eat the raw horsemeat. Everyone shouted 'Essen, essen essen!' We gave them food but they couldn't swallow it. Many died.[21]

The US Army and the Red Cross immediately began handing out food, but many were unable to tolerate it and died in the hours and days after the liberation. Of the more than 15,000 prisoners, the Americans recorded 5,419 survivors. German prisoners of war were made to bury the corpses in mass graves behind the stinking barracks. The survivors were taken to nearby houses and hospitals.

As did Ide, who weighed 38 kilograms and ended up in the Wels State Hospital. As the entire Allied world celebrated victory, Gunskirchen's sick fought for their lives. They lay in a real bed for the first time in a long time, on freshly-ironed white sheets and with a warm blanket over their cold bones. The doctors and nurses measured out the food so their stomachs and intestines could slowly get used to processing food again. To reduce his fever, Ide was given high doses of antibiotics. He hovered between life and death for days, but eventually recovered and was able to stand up on his own after three weeks. Like most other survivors, he had only one wish: to get away from there and look for surviving family or acquaintances in Antwerp. Perhaps he was hoping to see his wife and children again against all the odds. Perhaps that hope had kept him alive..

The repatriation of the prisoners was chaotic at first. Those who were strong enough were taken to the station, from where they could travel home by train. In the chaos this often took weeks, sometimes even months.

Ide did manage to be repatriated via Paris by military plane on 28 May 1945. There he swapped his prison uniform for civilian clothes. From Paris he took the train to Belgium and so back to Antwerp.

Part Five

Antwerp

Repatriation

After they returned many Jews had to fend for themselves. Once repatriated they would look for surviving relatives and friends as well as try to regain their identity. Many had to get used to their newfound freedom and learn to become human again after the Nazis had destroyed even their souls.

Jewish organisations in particular were involved in the re-uniting of survivors. The Jewish Community set up a kind of displaced persons' camp at the Brussels-South station, where repatriated people could go for meal vouchers and a place to sleep. There were also lists of missing persons and of others who were known to have died. It was chaos. Hundreds of people walking up and down clinging desperately onto photos as they approached others who were all, in the hope of seeing them again, searching for a son, daughter, husband, brother, sister. Most of the time they found no answers which resulted in heartbreaking scenes.

Ide wasn't in the displaced persons' camp. After his repatriation to Belgium he stayed in the Brussels St Pieter Hospital until 15 June 1945. According to a bulletin he filled out, he was helped financially and materially by relatives in Brussels. That must have been the Litman and Deborah Artman-Zucker family. It was the only family he had left.

At the bottom of the document was his picture. He was wearing a classic dark suit with a black tie. His face was skinny, his cheeks still hollow. His ears seemed bigger and his hair was very short. He looked right into the lens. His eyes were deep in their sockets. Around that time his niece Mimi was allowed to see him again 'when he was no longer a skeleton'. Ide then rehabilitated for two months in a retirement home in the Ardennes in French-speaking Belgium.

Back in Antwerp

From the autumn of 1945 Ide must have known some peace again. He received a temporary identity card, issued in Antwerp and valid until 22 August 1947. This allowed him to stay in Belgium again. Its validity was later extended twice more. It gave him some breathing space. From 24 September 1945 Ide rented a house in Antwerp in the Jewish neighbourhood.

For most Jews though, it was clear that they would never see their families again. Many never overcame their loss and felt guilty for surviving when their loved ones had died. They had mental health problems, suffered from depression or even committed suicide years later. Others learned to cope with their loss and held on to what precious life was left for them.

Ide took up his profession as a tailor again and tried to rebuild his life. He wore his own tailored suits, looked groomed to perfection and re-established social contacts. In the private archives of his granddaughter Cathy we find a picture from the spring of 1946. He sits at a table with Joséphine Vervloet, a 19-year-old girl he must have made an impression on. Ide, now over 40, looks amazingly well in the photo. Only a year earlier, he was almost dying in the excrement and mud of Gunskirchen. Anyone who's been through hell probably looks at life differently. His appearance and his acquaintance with this young, good-looking woman is therefore a statement. 'My dignity will never be taken from me again.'

The two became a couple and soon had children. Ellen was born in 1947, Benno in 1948. In the margin of their birth certificates it states that the father and mother were unmarried at the time of birth of both children. That was not unusual for that time. Because Joséphine's parents opposed marriage, they had no choice but to accept it. Joséphine was not yet 25. They eventually married on 24 July 1952, legitimising the two children.

In their wedding photos, the couple look loving and pose arm in arm in front of the Antwerp Town Hall. Joséphine wore an expensive suit and a coquettish hat on her luscious, dark curls. From her appearance and the testimonies we deduce that she certainly did not have any financial worries. Ide was a lot smaller than her and had to look up to her. He also looked dapper again in one of his tight tailored suits, with his hair combed back and an affectionate look. In a photo where they are sitting at a table in a café they both look directly into the lens. Joséphine, with her back against the wall, smiles broadly. Ide, opposite her, is wearing a smart suit and looks over his shoulder at the photographer. His gaze is lively and relaxed again. Each holds a cigarette in their hands; later he would have bad coughing fits from his excessive smoking.

Ide made sure his young bride had everything she wanted. He bought a large, dark blue Goliath from the former Borgward car brand. They drove to Koksijde at the Belgian coast, and sometimes they took the plane to Nice, where they posed arm in arm on the Promenade des Anglais, he in a beautiful outfit and she in a Dior suit, with an expensive handbag, stylish shoes and a gold necklace. They slept in nice hotels, ate in expensive restaurants and shopped in the upmarket shops in the coastal city along the Mediterranean.

There followed trips to the Vorarlberg in Austria and to a friend of Joséphine in England. It must have cost him a fortune, but he apparently thought it was worth it. Many of the photos of Nice and Koksijde also show an unknown woman. According to Benno, she was a nanny who took care of the children. That, too, indicates that they were well off.

It's unclear where Ide got so much money from so soon after the war. In any case, he spent money easily, as if he wanted to make up for lost time and to enjoy life. But he also worked hard for his new family as a master tailor, however without a permit. He also wanted to assert his rights as a victim of the Nazi regime. Indeed, he saw how his remaining friends, resistance men and camp prisoners were entitled to various government schemes. Many were officially recognised as an activist, as a distributor for the underground press, as a political prisoner, as a forced labourer or as a victim of other Nazi crimes. From the 1950s Ide started applications in four areas: for recognition as a political prisoner, for recognition as a member of the resistance, for recognition as a survivor and – most importantly – in obtaining Belgian nationality. For these four causes he fought a long battle with the Belgian government over the rest of his life.

It was not until 15 December 1955 that the Comité International de la Croix Rouge in Geneva recorded a *Certificate of Incarceration and Residence* with number 322546, in the name of Ide Kartuz. It contains the official dates on which he was deported from Mechelen to Auschwitz, his transfer to Mauthausen, then to Sankt Aegyd and back to Mauthausen. It also refers to the transport list of the Dossin barracks in Mechelen, his personal prisoner card in Auschwitz and Mauthausen's registration and number book. On 10 July 1952 he had already received a certificate from the Office of the United Nations High Commissioner for Refugees.. On 25 July 1950 Kartuz was officially recognised as a political prisoner and later as a war invalid. These documents were important to him because no one could dispute that he had been in the concentration camps. It would also help him get compensation later.

Meanwhile he received a favourable opinion with regard to exercising his trade as a 'tailor – craft activity'.[1] But, apparently, the professional card was not immediately awarded to him or Kartuz failed to pick it up and pay the necessary fees while continuing to trade independently. This led to a third court hearing at the end of 1950. The police were tipped off about his 'illegal activities' and a new report followed which showed that 'the defendant is exercising a profitable business for his own account without being in possession of a professional card'.[2] This offence was passed on to the public prosecutor for notification by the Immigration Police and would have consequences for his request to become Belgian.

Naturalisation

Ide had been in Belgium since 1929 and absolutely did not want to return to Poland. As was the case for many other Jews, it was obvious that a permanent passport would ensure security and stability. On 14 March 1951 he applied to the Ministry of Justice for Belgian nationality. The letter was written in the third person singular, indicating that Ide's application had been processed and written by someone else. The content reads like a plea.

> The person concerned has the honour to base his application first and foremost on the legal grounds of a continuous, exemplary stay in Belgium since April 1929. This stay was interrupted only by a three-year deportation by the Nazis to the German concentration camps, where his behaviour was exemplary and where it was possible for him to save the lives of many deportees. The person concerned has the honour to bring to your kind attention that he was

recognised as a beneficiary of the status of political prisoner for his exemplary, selfless and patriotic activity during the occupation. ... Like every prisoner he suffered greatly and returned to Belgium in a shocking physical condition. He regularly and dutifully fulfilled his civic duties in Belgium and regularly paid the taxes he owed to the state treasury. Through his long stay in Belgium he has learned to appreciate and love the Country and the People more and more; he rightly considers Belgium to be his real homeland. All the more so as all of his family in Poland were murdered and he no longer has any connection with his country of birth. He speaks and writes the Dutch language fluently and knows enough of the French language to be able to use it.[3]

Legally, nothing stood in the way of his naturalisation.

An investigation into his person was next. On 19 February 1952 the Justice of the Peace in Antwerp sent a damning ruling.

I have the impression that following the applicant's explanation to justify his unusual circumstances, his situation is not serious. In addition, the applicant is not a highly deserving person. He has been repeatedly prosecuted and convicted. He is part of or has until recently been part of institutions with political (communist) tendencies. I consider that, in respect of the aforementioned, the Belgian community has no interest in accepting him with open arms.[4]

Three months later the verdict was upheld. In a reasoned report of 13 May 1952, the Public Prosecutor's advice to the Procurator-General was unfavourable. According to him, the applicant had not adapted our morals, he spoke our national languages only poorly, and seemed to have assimilated little into Belgium. 'Furthermore, the applicant seems to have no respect for our legislation – in addition to the convictions he has received, he has twice entered into unlawful family unions.' Here the prosecutor is referring to the fact that Kartuz only had a religious marriage ceremony to an Israelite woman before the war. From that marriage two illegitimate children were born, Charles-Victor and Simone. With his second wife he also had two children, Ellen and Benno. But because they weren't married initially, the prosecutor considered that relationship an illegitimate family. 'With regard to a foreign national staying here, this must not be allowed,' the prosecutor concluded.[5]

The report also stated that Ide did not own real estate and that he was practising the profession of tailor, when his professional card was only valid until 30 June 1952. This negative advice must have weighed hard on him. It hung over his head like the sword of Damocles. As long as he was not Belgian, he remained vulnerable and at the mercy of officials. Three days after the negative advice of the Public Prosecutor, the Procurator-General of the Court of Appeal in Brussels backed the negative advice and passed the report on to the Minister of Justice.[6]

Ide's reaction and emotions are hard to assess, but after the deaths of his family, his wife and his children, the horror in the camps and its physical consequences, this must have been a major blow to him. His world collapsed again.

But Ide persisted. The Minister of Justice had to present such requests to parliament. On 1 August 1952 Joséphine, who was now married to Ide, told the civil registry of the City of Antwerp that she wished to 'retain the status of Belgian'. That made his case for naturalisation stronger.

In the end the Commission for Naturalisations granted Ide Leib Kartuz ordinary citizenship. This decision became final after King Baudouin signed the document for his naturalization on 14 April 1956. A few weeks later, on 3 May 1956, Ide received his passport from the Antwerp Civil Registry Councillor. This was an important step for Ide, who could finally feel completely safe and at home in Belgium. In 1964 he also received his War Invalid Identity Card from the Belgian State, which gave him a 75 per cent discount on Belgian railway fares.

Resistance fighter

Since his return in 1945 Ide had also been trying to be recognised as a civil member of the resistance. He first turned to the resistance group 'Independence Front' Antwerp. They provided him with a Declaration that he had 'been working in the movement since July 1941 and had duly fulfilled his duty, as a member of the Patriotic Militias unit in the province of Antwerp'. It also stated that he had been 'arrested for selfless patriotic activity on 22 July 1942'.[7]

But the Belgian state was not convinced. A police commissioner wrote the following strange and somewhat flawed letter to the state commissioner:

> We have not found anyone here who could confirm to us that the person concerned has actually carried out acts of resistance or that he was indeed affiliated with the aforementioned resistance group (according to Ide, the Independence Front) during the occupation. However, if he has carried out such acts, it is doubtful – and it seems to us to be highly unlikely – that the reason for his arrest had anything to do with the resistance, since the concerned party was treated only as if he had been detained for racist reasons.[8]

Ide has always disputed that he was arrested because he was a Jew. According to him the German *Feldgendarmen* were aware of his membership of the resistance and that was the reason for his arrest on 22 July 1942. The reason is unclear but, no matter what it was, on 15 February 1952 the Control Committee decided that Ide could not be accredited with the title of civil resistance fighter. It was only many years later that he would submit a new application, with more supporting documents and testimonies from former allies. One of these was from Jozef Holzer who stated under oath on 28 April 1969 that Ide Kartuz had been involved in (1) raising funds for people in hiding; (2) receiving funds; (3) the distribution of illegal press and pamphlets; and (4) collecting intelligence which he forwarded to Joseph Feld, the person who had recruited him as a resistance fighter.[9] Ide was known to them as Jules, his pseudonym in the resistance. This is evident from the post-war testimonies of several other resistance members who made statements to the authorities that Ide was indeed part of the resistance.

Ide submitted all these statements to the National Appeals Control Committee in Brussels on 10 May 1971. They had the authority to make the final judgement about the Status of civil resistance fighters. At its session on 26 April 1973 the Commission overturned the previous ruling and decided that Ide Kartuz should be accredited with the title of civil resistance fighter.[10]

Compensation

In addition to his struggle for official recognition as a civil resistance fighter, Ide also made a claim for the status of political prisoner that would entitle him to compensation for the suffering inflicted on him in the concentration camps.

He was also entitled to the status of political prisoner. In the questionnaire from the Consultative Committee for Political Prisoners for Recognition as a Political Prisoner of 17 December 1947, he wrote that he had been imprisoned from 22 June 1942 to 5 May 1945 (a total of thirty-four months). When asked if he had been abused, he replied 'Yes'. He later told his son Benno that he had often been kicked in the stomach with heavy boots which had caused him to have frequent pain in his intestines.

On 27 July 1950 the Acceptance Committee gave him the green light and he was given the rights associated with it. The decision contained four elements: '

> The person concerned (1) may enjoy the status of political prisoner; (2) is entitled to the exceptional remuneration calculated on the basis of 34 months x 1,500 Belgian francs; (3) is entitled to an additional allowance, corresponding to 6 six-month prison terms; he will receive the value in capital on the basis of an annual amount of 6 x 3,000 francs for 4 years, subject to the decision of the Justice of the Peace, which 'will decide as advantageously as possible on his claim'; (4) is entitled to all other benefits as stipulated by the Law of 26/2/1947, in accordance with the modalities laid down there.[11]

This meant that, in addition to his income as a tailor, Ide had a steady income for a period of almost three years. Another document from 1951 states that he did not have any real estate but he owned other assets in the value of 130,000 francs which 'the party concerned received as a beneficiary of the Status of Political Prisoner'.[12] He probably spent a large part of it on the holidays, clothes and other wants of his wife Joséphine. According to testimonials from his children, grandchildren and others who knew him, he worked hard as a tailor. According to Benno, his father usually worked well into the night.

184

Ide also relied on funding for medication. According to his granddaughter Cathy he had eczema on his hands from handling fabrics and clothing in Auschwitz. He often suffered from that throughout his later life. Sometimes he asked Cathy to buy him ointment from the pharmacist. She had to look after the receipt 'because the Germans had to pay it back to him'.[13]

Ide also tried to claim compensation from a completely different area. After he was arrested in his street on 22 July 1942 and deported with his wife and children, the Occupiers emptied his home and seized it. All the possessions and assets of the Jews then became the property of the Germans. *Reichsleiter* and Nazi leader Alfred Rosenberg was put in charge of the large-scale Operation *EINSATZSTAB*. From its seat in Paris it was responsible for the embezzlement and shipping of valuable artefacts, libraries and other cultural goods to Germany. This included the so-called *Möbelaktion,* in which the entirety of a household and its furniture were transported to the Reich. Many Jews tried to sell their furniture quickly but this was soon forbidden under a new regulation of early June 1942. As a result, Jewish goods fell completely into the hands of the Occupiers. A total of 4,015 Jewish homes was seized and of those 3,868 were emptied. From 1 October 1942 large ships and trains loaded with confiscated furniture left Antwerp for Hamburg and Cologne. There the items were sold or distributed among the German families who had lost their homes and belongings in the Allied bombings. Some removal companies in Antwerp played a dubious role in this and made money for themselves at the expense of the victims of the Holocaust.

One of those firms was Arthur Pierre's. He used his trucks not only to transport the arrested Jews to the Dossin barracks in Mechelen for a fee but also for the transportation of their seized goods. Pierre regularly complained about wear and tear on his vehicles because they were overloaded. He also worried about Jews relieving themselves in his crammed trucks when they were deported. He asked in a letter to the Occupier if he could get any financial compensation for this. At a time when fuel was rationed, he was given the necessary extra fuel cards to keep his vehicles running. The removal company is said to have earned a total of about 4.6 million francs from the Germans, doubling its turnover.[14]

After the war a lot of people didn't come back from the camps. Those who did return found that their household contents had disappeared.

To begin with, no one paid it any attention but in the 1950s demands for restitution became stronger. On 11 October 1961 Ide received a letter from the mayor of Antwerp. The letter confirmed that the couple's furniture and household goods were removed on 5 April 1944 by order of the Germans and transported to an unknown destination. It continued, 'In the 26 Vestingstraat building, the Kartuz-Artman family had four rooms, namely a drawing room, a dining room, a bedroom and a kitchen.'[15] It seems as if someone wanted to make some sort of estimate of the material loss he had suffered during the war. It is not clear whether Ide eventually received compensation for this and nothing can be found about it in the National Archives. What is certain is that he was helped by Roger Op De Beeck, a teacher and journalist from Berchem who specialised in tracking down Jewish property as a second job. In the National Archives we find several letters in which he acted as Ide's representative. Op De Beeck, according to witnesses, worked on commission. If he didn't find anything, he would not be paid. If he found something, he got a percentage of the value.

Under pressure from the Allies the German government also organised a system of *Wiedergutmachung* (compensation) after the war. This involved paying money to Holocaust survivors for material and non-material damage suffered. To this end Ide also had to fill out all kinds of documents and make statements. On 20 July 1955, for example, he wrote a letter to the Chairman of the Commission International Tracing Service, detailing where and for how long he had been in the camps. He requested that compensation be made for his moral and material suffering through the Government president of North Rhine-Westphalia to the Ministry of *Wiedergutmachung* in Cologne. According to Benno, after much form filling, paperwork and red tape, he received a monthly amount (a kind of pension) of 4,000 Belgian francs from 1948 onwards. In 1956 a one-off cash payment of 200,000 Belgian francs followed. He hid it in a bag in his bedroom. It was quite a sum for that time. As part of the *Wiedergutmachung* he was also given the opportunity to go regularly to a medical spa in Germany to treat his tuberculosis and stomach problems. During the 1960s he stayed several times in Bad Nauheim and Bad Kissingen in Central Germany.

Documents in the Belgian National Archives show that, like other victims, he also sought compensation for the loss of his wife and children. However, he was never granted this, because the children did not have his name and a civil wedding to Chaja had never taken place. However, in Poland we found an official marriage certificate between Ide and Chaja from 1929. In a document from 1930 the Antwerp rabbi M. Amiel wrote that the couple was indeed married, albeit according to Jewish ritual. The couple officially lived in Belgium at the same address. Chaja received a letter from the Occupier 'as a wife' that she had to register in the Dossin barracks. If she didn't 'it would have consequences for her husband'. An extract from the Jewish Register lists Charles-Victor and Simone as his children. In the framework of the deportations Chaja and the children were considered family. But in terms of compensation for their deaths, this evidence was not legal for the Belgian state and the *Wiedergutmachung*.

We can at least question the double standards for the award of compensation. Anyone who loses someone through crime must be able to enter into legal proceedings regardless of their legal relationship with the victim(s).

Nightmares

Despite receiving compensation, Ide continued to work as a tailor. At home he received his clientele. In the finished suits and jackets he sewed a 2-centimetre-high and 6-centimetre-wide logo with the words 'Kartuz' and 'master tailor' underneath. He made a good living from it. According to his son Benno, he made beautiful men's jackets for diamond dealers, doctors and lawyers. He used to spend a week on a suit and would ask 5,000 francs for it.

In the meantime things were going less well with Ide's marriage. Quarrels with Joséphine became more frequent and often deteriorated into blinding rows. Joséphine visited the cinema and often went to cafés, as did Ide who also liked to drink a beer outdoors. Benno remembers many discussions. 'When they had been drinking, they could be very aggressive verbally. Dad used to get up early and start working on his costumes by 8:00 am, while my mom slept until noon and did nothing.' Joséphine's brother, François Vervloet, had a café in Antwerp. She met a new man there, a sailor. According to Benno, while Ide was recovering from his medical problems at a sanatorium, Joséphine stole the remaining money from the *Wiedergutmachung*. Inevitably, divorce followed in 1958. Joséphine left very suddenly. Benno stayed with his father and Ellen went with her mother.

After the divorce Kartuz lived very frugally. He even had to borrow money for a trip. Sometimes he would go to a café to drink a beer and play billiards. He was a member of a billiards club. He regularly mourned for Charles-Victor and Simone, calling them his 'golden children'. He described Charles-Victor as super intelligent and Simone as a very beautiful and sweet girl. But he often had nightmares. He had lost his last ounce of belief in the existence of God, like many other ex-prisoners, in the camps.

Ann Van Turnhout, the youngest sister of David, remembers that Ide would sit in a beige folding chair around Christmas and New Year and talk about his family being taken away and gassed in Auschwitz. Then he would cry. 'My family was murdered, after that I never really had a family,' he said.[16] Ann, who was 12 or 13 at the time, understood. She had read *Anne Frank's Diary* at school. Ide was a pleasant person. Ann describes him as a small, cute, stylish, quiet man, who spoke bad Dutch but fine Yiddish.

Ide, however, could not let go of the past. He and his son Benno visited Fort Breendonk three times. He wanted to show him where he had been imprisoned but he never came back feeling any happier. He spent hours talking to family members and friends, often ex-camp prisoners, about his experiences in the camps. After the war, he followed the trials of the major Nazi criminals in the press, especially those who had harassed him and massacred his family.

On 11 March 1946, British soldiers arrested Rudolf Höss on a farm near Flensburg, where he worked as a servant. At first he denied that he was the former camp commandant of Auschwitz. He gave a false name, 'Franz Lang', but was given away by his wedding ring, which had his first name and his wife's engraved on it. After further questioning, he eventually revealed his true identity. In 1947 Ide followed the trial against Höss, who had to appear in court in Warsaw, in the newspapers. The SS officer acknowledged no guilt and showed no remorse: 'We SS men were not supposed to think about things; that didn't even occur to us. We took it for granted that the Jews were to blame for everything.' When he testified as an exculpatory witness for *SS-Obergruppenführer* Ernst Kaltenbrunner, the head of the *Reichssicherheitshauptamt* (RSHA), who supervised the *Einsatzgruppen* and the persecution of the Jews, he stated that he had only carried out orders from above:

In the summer of 1941 I was summoned to Berlin to Reichsfuehrer SS Himmler to receive personal orders. He told me something to the effect – I do not remember the exact words – hat the Führer had given the order for a final solution of the Jewish question. We, the SS, must carry out that order. If it is not carried out now then the Jews will later on destroy the German people. He had chosen Auschwitz on account of its easy access by rail and also because the extensive site offered space for measures ensuring isolation.[17]

According to his estimate, approximately 2.5 million victims were killed by gassing and execution. At least half a million others succumbed to malnutrition and diseases (these estimates were incorrect; according to historians between 1.1 and 1.4 million people were murdered in Auschwitz-Birkenau). On 2 April 1947 he was sentenced to death by hanging by the Supreme Court of Poland. The execution took place two weeks later on a purpose-built gallows next to the Auschwitz I crematorium. Only years later did a photo of the hanged Höss appear in the press.

A few months later, on 24 November 1947, the first Auschwitz trial started in Krakow. Only forty of the many thousands of SS officers and camp guards were on trial there. Hans Aumeier, the main war criminal who was prosecuted there, had regularly been inside Block 1. In February 1942 Aumeier became a sub-commandant in the Auschwitz main camp. He was extremely violent towards the prisoners, let the *kapos* do their own thing and shot numerous prisoners himself at the execution site between Blocks 10 and 11. He had business dealings with *kapo* Ignac of Block 1 and obtained jewellery and money through him that the tailors found in the clothes of the gassed prisoners. Because of this corruption, theft and personal enrichment, he was transferred to a concentration camp in Estonia a year and a half later by Höss. The Polish Supreme Court sentenced him to death and in 1948 he was hanged in Krakow prison.

Two other commandants in Auschwitz-Birkenau, Karl Möckel and Arthur Liebehenschel, who were also responsible for mass gassings of the Jews, were hanged. SS physician Johann Kremer, who witnessed the gassings and murders of prisoners with phenol injections in the heart, claimed in court that he himself had not killed anyone. He was found guilty and sentenced to death but this was later commuted to life imprisonment. He was released in 1958.

Ide must also have known the defendant *SS-Unterscharführer* Franz Romeikat. He worked in the clothing and administration department of the camp. He treated the prisoners cruelly, stole belongings from the murdered people and was instrumental in many other punishments. It is quite possible that he had kicked Ide in the stomach. According to his son Benno, that had happened when Ide brought some suits to the clothing department. Romeikat received a fifteen-year prison sentence but was released after nine years.

SS-Obersturmführer Wilhelm Reischenbeck, who was in charge of the death march to Mauthausen and had many prisoners shot dead during that march, was sentenced to ten years in prison in 1958, but was released early. Twenty other convicts also walked free again after only a short time. *Kapos* who had killed prisoners with canes or even their bare hands were left untouched. Many camp survivors were disillusioned with this unpalatable outcome, but the onset of the Cold War made further trials against these war criminals virtually impossible.[18] As a result, the entire denazification process almost stopped.

It was not until 1963 that a number of former SS executioners were tried. This happened under the direction of Fritz Bauer, a driven German-Jewish public prosecutor and head of the Frankfurt Public Prosecutor's Office. Despite all opposition, he persevered and managed to get eighteen defendants convicted. Among these was Emil Bednarek, a *kapo* who was sentenced to life for the murder of several prisoners. But he, too, was released after ten years. There were some trials behind closed doors against the SS men of the camp after this. 'Out of the 6,500 or so members of the SS who worked in Auschwitz between 1940 and 1945 and who are thought to have survived the war, only around 750 ever received punishment of any kind,' said Laurence Rees.[19] Usually, the sentences were particularly mild.

During the cross-examination of Höss and the other defendants, the name Adolf Eichmann regularly came up. He was well informed about the activities in the camp and he had visited it several times. He had primary responsibility for the deportation of the Jews, gypsies, homosexuals and others to the death camps. Eichmann was arrested by the Americans in May 1945 but they had no idea he was such a major war criminal, principally because he had given a false name. He escaped from prison and in 1950 with the help of bisschop Alois Hudal, head of the Austro-German Congregation of Santa Matina dell'Anima, he fled to South America, where he lived a carefree life for ten years under the pseudonym Ricardo Klement. Eventually, Eichmann was arrested and taken to Israel by members of the Israeli secret service. There he stood trial before a court in Jerusalem. The arrest and trial of one of the most important architects of the Holocaust was world news and was discussed extensively in the press. From this Ide and the other survivors finally were able to get a good insight into the deportations to the concentration and extermination camps. Eichmann was the main organiser of the deportations of Polish Jews to the death camps in the east. Treblinka, where Ide's family and friends were all exterminated, was one of the main destinations.

On 11 June 1942 the heads of the German security forces from Belgium, The Netherlands and France met. Eichmann chaired the meeting. During this meeting, the decision was made to 'evacuate' the Belgian Jews from the Dossin barracks in Mechelen. Ide was a direct victim of this decision. During the trial a total of 116 witnesses testified, including many Holocaust survivors. For the first time, a detailed picture was put together of the unimaginable extent of the extermination of the Jews. Eichmann was charged with war crimes, crimes against humanity, crimes against the Jewish people, crimes against Poles, Slovenes, Czechs and gypsies. Eichman himself pleaded innocent. His defence was that he was obeying the orders of Adolf Hitler and his other superiors such as Heinrich Himmler, Reinhard Heydrich and Ernst Kaltenbrunner. 'I was only an intermediary ... I received orders and had to fulfil them in spite of my reluctance.'[20] But in the memoir that Eichmann had dictated a few years earlier, he said, 'When I was given the order to fight the Jews I acted with the greatest degree of fanaticism.'[21]

Numerous documents, testimonials and statements, however, showed that Eichmann himself had actively collaborated in the extermination of as many Jews as possible. This was clear from his informal statements at the Wannsee Conference. Different murder methods were openly discussed there. He discussed the construction of gas chambers for exterminating Jews which he implemented very early on, for instance in Chełmno where he personally witnessed the massacres, as well as in Majdanek and Auschwitz. He organised train transports to the camps and was well aware that the victims were killed there. His active role during the Hungarian Holocaust, in which hundreds of thousands of non-Aryans were transported to Auschwitz, was also very important. Eichmann showed no regrets or repentance during the trial. He was finally found guilty by the judges and was hanged on 31 May 1962. His body was burned and the ashes scattered over the Mediterranean Sea.

What did become clear during the Eichmann trial was the purpose of the Treblinka death camp. The train schedules and the transport lists read out at the trial showed that huge numbers of Jews were taken to the extermination camp and were immediately gassed there. During the trial Israeli prosecutor Gideon Hausner read lists of Jewish transports from various cities to the extermination camps of Bełżec, Sobibor and Treblinka in particular. It then became clear to Ide what had happened to his family. Camp Commandant Franz Stangl was arrested by the Americans in 1945 and later handed over to the Austrian authorities because of his contribution to the T4 Programme at Hartheim Castle. He stayed there in an open prison from where he soon escaped and fled to Rome. Renegade Catholic Bishop Alois Hudal gave him a visa and money to flee to Syria. From there he emigrated to Brazil in 1951. The Brazilian police arrested him in 1967. After his extradition to the Federal Republic of Germany, Stangl was tried three years later in Düsseldorf. The charge was serious: complicity in the murder of 900,000 people. Stangl also defended himself on the grounds of someone who was just following orders. In a long conversation with journalist Gitta Sereny he stated, 'My conscience is clear about what I did, myself.'[22] As regards Treblinka, he admitted that, as a camp commandant, he had seen and been aware of everything that had happened, but added that he had never intentionally harmed anyone himself. Even so, he had been directly in charge of the camp where so many people had been exterminated.

Sing mei a lieder

Ide regularly went to spas in Germany and Switzerland to recover further. When he came back from one in 1963 he decided to give up dressmaking due to his eczema. His friends made good money in the diamond industry and urged him to do the same. On 13 April 1963 he wrote in the register of Merchants and Commercial Companies that, apart from being a master tailor, he was also a diamond broker. However, that didn't last long. Brokers are not in high esteem within the diamond sector and are often ridiculed by manufacturers and salesmen. One day Ide was waiting with some stones in a diamond merchant's office when the salesman said: 'Sing mei a lieder' (Sing me a song). Ide really disliked being at the mercy of third parties. 'I was in the camps too long to be insulted like that,' he said. With his anti-capitalist ideas, he didn't fully trust the rich diamond traders. He quit the next day and focused again on making suits. He would rather work with a skin condition than suffer an attack on his dignity. At home he often worked on his tailor's table, even well into the night.

His health went up and down. His lungs were affected from inhaling dust and he also periodically smoked a lot. When he left the house, he often tied a scarf over his mouth because he found the air too dirty. He was again diagnosed with TB. On 31 July 1969, at the age of 64, he stopped working. He often had visits from old mates as well as from his grandchildren.

His health remained fragile. Ide took eight pills a day. He had dizzy spells and one day he tripped and hit his head against a wall. In the hospital doctors diagnosed a brain tumour. In 1992, through one of his earlier contacts with the resistance, he ended up in the retirement home in Dilbeek near Brussels, which after the war was set up as a nursing home for retired veterans. His son Benno visited him there but Kartuz was no longer aware of very much. He died on 8 September 1995, with his granddaughter Cathy by his side, the last person to have had contact with him. He was buried as a political prisoner at the military honorary park of Schoonselhof Cemetery Antwerp, bizarrely enough without any mention of him being Jewish.

Epilogue

Little stone

According to a Jewish saying, a man is not dead while his name is still spoken. When I told Dirk that my grandfather survived Auschwitz but nobody really knew the full story, we decided to do research together and write a book about it. That way we could ensure that his story was not lost but lived on.

When I found Ide's grave in Antwerp in 2006 I put a stone on his grave in accordance with the old Jewish custom. Dirk and I did the same at the many Jewish cemeteries and mass graves we visited in Poland. Although I received no Jewish education and am certainly no follower of any faith, by following a tradition he knew and appreciated it is a tribute to him. According to Jewish tradition, it goes back to the time when the Jews crossed the desert. Marking the graves with stones made it easier to find them later. Unlike flowers, stones do not wilt. They symbolise a lasting memory of the next of kin. Dirk emphasised that they are not only in remembrance of my grandfather but are used as a general symbol in memory of the Holocaust in books, films, documentaries. They help ensure that we will never forget what happened in the heart of our European civilisation in the 1930s and 1940s.

The atrocities in the camps were so horrifying and inhumane that many survivors were aware that others would not believe them. In the preface *The Drowned and the Saved*, Primo Levi refers to a statement by SS camp guards, as recorded by Simon Wiesenthal:

> However this war may end, we have won the war against you; none of you will be left to bear witness, but even if some of you survive, the world would not believe him. There will perhaps be suspicions, discussions, research by historians, but there will be no certainties, because we will

destroy the evidence together with you. And even if some proof should remain and some of you survive, people will say that the events you describe are too monstrous to be believed: they will say they are the exaggerations of Allied propaganda and will believe us, who will deny everything, and not you. We will be the ones to dictate the history of the camps.[1]

Despite frantic efforts by negationists to colour or erase the memory of the Holocaust, the mass murder by the Nazis has been proven. Historical material, publications and testimonials have unequivocally demonstrated the extent to which the concentration camps of the totalitarian Nazi regime served to destroy 'man'. But with the disappearance of the last first-hand witnesses, there is a danger that the memories will fade. 'I was frightened by the terrible strength of man, his desire and ability to forget,' wrote Russian dissident Varlam Sjalamov, who had been locked up in the Russian Gulag camps for seventeen years.[2] Forgetting is indeed part of life. That is one of the greatest tragedies in history. There is a risk that in roughly a hundred years Hitler will be as abstract as Napoleon, namely that future generations will only see the German dictator as an eccentric figure with a crazy moustache.

Despite the access to a multitude of information via the internet and other means of communication, the power of forgetting is very real. Ask students what Auschwitz, Treblinka, Mauthausen or the Gulag mean and you encounter a staggering lack of knowledge amongst many of them. That is not only unfortunate, but also dangerous. It is important that young people of every new generation continue to learn about the dangers of totalitarian ideas and regimes. Its consequences are detrimental to democracy and freedom. That is why it is so important that this also has an important place in education and that the terrible events of the first half of the twentieth century are explained in lessons of history.

Forgetting does not advance us morally; on the contrary. Forgiveness, on the other hand, is an important quality that combines moral aversion with the curbing of revenge, breaking the spiral of violence and making people understand each other again. To be able to forgive one must remember the facts. By so doing memories are not only useful, they are also necessary so that we may understand where we have come from and the trials we have had to endure and overcome on the way. 'Without history, there are no memories, and without memories, there is no future. If we don't learn from our mistakes, we will repeat them,' said Holocaust survivor Max Eisen.[3]

Remembering is a prerequisite for true reconciliation and peace. Without memories we would still be fighting each other. So we must withstand the power of forgetting, resist dividing people into good and bad. To understand what nationalism and Nazism have wrought on society, every student and citizen should visit the museums dealing with the two world wars and the Holocaust.

Wir Sind Zurück

'Crushing the sense of dignity and humanity in mankind may have been the greatest tragedy of the past century,' said Hungarian writer György Konrád, who experienced nationalism, Nazism and communism first-hand. He warned that following the deaths of the last witnesses, this awareness may quickly disappear, 'Because others cannot have access to what they experienced,' he wrote. As a result, nationalist, far-right and far-left parties everywhere in the world, and certainly in Europe, are re-surfacing and trying to fill any gaps in people's memories with their utopian ideas, which have led to so much human suffering in the past. This gap is filled with anti-semitic sentiments, where the past is downplayed and where Jews and other faiths and populations also, are identified as being a danger to our society and even civilisation in general.

The recent displays of anti-semitic behaviour in several European countries is particularly worrying. Jewish graves were defaced with swastikas. These findings strengthened our determination to prevent these reminders of the consequences of totalitarianism and anti-semitism from before and during the Second World War from disappearing into the mists of time.

At the end of our research for this book, Dirk and I went together to the grave of Ide Leib Kartuz and we each placed a stone on his gravestone. As long as we speak of him, as long as people read this book, the tailor of Auschwitz is not dead.

Bibliography

Abicht, Ludo: *De Joden van Antwerpen* (Vrijdag, Antwerpen, 2018)

Allen, Michael, Thad: *The Business of Genocide. The SS, Slave Labor, and the Concentration Camps* (The University of North Carolina Press, Chapel Hill NC, 2002)

Angrick, Andrej: *Besatzungspolitik und Massenmord, Die Einsatzgruppe D in der südlichen Sowjetunion 1941-1943* (Hamburger Edition, Hamburg, 2003)

Anstadt, Milo: *Polen en Joden* (Uitgeverij Contact, Amsterdam, 1989)

Antończyk, Krzysztof: *Transport of prisoners between KL Auschwitz and KL Mauthausen, on the background of the general policy of displacing prisoners in the concentration camp system in the Third Reich* (Pedagogical University, Krakow, 2012)

Arad, Yitzhak: *The Operation Reinhard Death Camps: Bełzec, Sobibor, Treblinka* (Indiana University Press, Bloomington, 1987)

Bacior, Josef: *Jewish Żarki. Lost photographs* (Fundacja Brama Cukermana, Będzin, 2016)

Barth, Rüdiger, Friederichs, Hauke: *The Gravediggers* (Profile Books, London, 2019)

Bartrop, Paul: *Modern Genocide: A Documentary and Reference Guide. Holocaust: The Gerstein Report* (Greenwood, Santa Barbara, 2019)

Bauer, Yehuda: *The Death of the Shtetl* (Yale University Press, New Haven, 2009)

Bauer, Yehuda: *American Jewry and the Holocaust: The American Jewish Joint Distribution* (Wayne State University Press, Detroit, 2017)

Bauman, Zygmunt: *Modernity and the Holocaust* (Polity Press, Milton, 2013)

Bergen, Doris: *War and Genocide: A Concise History of the Holocaust* (Rowan & Littlefield Publishers, Lanham, 2009)

Bernadac, Christian: *Camp for Women: Ravensbrück* (Ferni Publishing House, Geneva, 1978)

Blatman, Daniel: *The Death Marches. The Final Phase of Nazi Genocide* (Harvard College, Cambridge, 2011)

Bohler, Jochen: *'Größte Härte...': Verbrechen der Wehrmacht in Polen September/Oktober 1939* (Fibre, Osnabrück, 2005)

Breitman, Richard: *Heinrich Himmler. The Architect of Genocide* (Knopf, New York, 1991)

Bridgman, Jon: *The End of the Holocaust. The Liberation of the Camps* (B.T. Batsford Ltd., London, 1990)

Bronstein, Michael, Holinstat, Debbie: *Survivors Club: The True Story of a Very Young Prisoner of Auschwitz* (Farrar, Straus and Giroux, York, 2017)

Browning, Christopher: *Ordinary Man. Reserve Police Battalion 101 and the Final Solution* (Harper Perennial, New York, 2017)

Cesarani, David: *Eichmann. His Life and Crimes by David Cesarani* (William Heinemann Ltd, London, 2004)

Cesarani, David: *Final Solution. The Fate of the Jews 1933-1949* (Macmillan, London, 2016)

Chot, Joseph: *De la défaite a la victoire* (Librairie Vanderlinden, Bruxelles, 1949)

Citroen, Hans: *Auschwitz – de Judenrampe* (Verbum, Almere, 2014)

Citroen, Hans, Starzyńska Barbara: *Auschwitz-Oświęcim* (Post Editions, Rotterdam, 2011)

Cohen, Rob: *Niet klein gekregen. Mijn overwinning op de nazi's* (Verbum, Almere, 2005)

Czech, Danuta: *Kalendarz wydarzeń* w KL *Auschwitz* (Muzeum w Oświęcimi, Brzezince, 1992)

Datner, Szymon: *Zbrodnie Werhmachtu na jeńcach wojennych w* II *Wojnie Swiatowei* (Wydawn. Ministerstwa Obrony Narodowej, Krakow,1961)

Dederichs, Mario, R.: *Heydrich. The Face of Evil* (Greenhill Books, London, 2006)

Doetzer, Oliver: *'Aus Menschen werden Briefe': die Korrespondenz einer jüdischen Familie zwischen Verfolgung und Emigration, 1933-1947* (Hohlau Verlag, Wien, 2002)

Evans, Richard: *The Third Reich at War*, Part 3 (Allen Lane, London, 2008)

Fairweather, Jack: *The Volunteer. The True Story of the Resistance Hero who Infiltrated Auschwitz* (Virgin Digital, London, 2019)

Fisher, Jacob: *Death and destruction of Jewish* Żarki, in *Kehilat Żarki,* Icchak Lador (in Yiddish) (Tel Aviv, 1959/1960)

Fisher, Joseph: *Die Himmel waren vermauert. The Heavens were Walled In* (New Academic Press, London, 2017)

Friedländer, Saul: *Nazi Germany and the Jews 1933-1945* (Harper Perennial, New York, 2009)

Georgi, Matthias, Kamp, Michael: *Lodenfrey in der ns-Zeit 1933-1945* (August Dreesbach Verlag, München, 2012)

Gilbert, Martin: *Auschwitz and the Allies* (Random House, London, 2001)

Gilbert, Martin: *Kristallnacht. Prelude to Destruction* (Harper Perennial, New York, 2007)

Glazar, Richard: *Trap with a Green Fence: Survival in Treblinka* (Northwestern University Press, Illinois, 1999)

Greenfeld, Martin: *Measure of a Man. From Auschwitz Survivor to Presidents' Tailor* (Regnery History, Washington D.C., 2014)

Greif, Gideo, Siebers, Peter: *Death Factory Auschwitz* (Emons Verlag, Köln, 2016)

Gross, Jan, Tomasz: *Neighbors: The Destruction of the Jewish Community in Jedwabne*, (Princeton University Press, Princeton, 2001)

Gross, Jan, Tomasz: *Fear: Anti-Semitism in Poland After Auschwitz* (Princeton University Press, Illinois, 2007)

Gryn, Hugo: *Chasing Shadows* (Penguin Books, London, 2001)

Gutman, Yisrael, Berenbaum, Michael: *Anatomy of the Auschwitz Death Camp* (Indiana University Press, Bloomington, 1998)

Heinz, Hohne, *Der Totenkopf. Die Geschichte der SS* (Sigbert Mohn Verlag, Gütersloh, 1967)

Heller, Celia S., *On the Edge of Destruction. Jews of Poland between the Two World Wars* (Wayne State University Press, Detroit, 1994)

Helm, Sarah: *Ravensbrück. Inside Ravensbruck: Hitler's Concentration Camp for Women* (Little Brown Book Group, London, 2015)

Hilberg, Raul: *The Destruction of the European Jews* (Martino Fine Books, Eastford, 2019)

Hirsch, Michael: *The Liberators: America's Witnesses to the Holocaust* (Bantam, New York, 2010)

Höhne, Heinz: *Der Orden unter dem Totenkopf: Die Geschichte der SS* (Orbis, Berlin, 2002)

Holden, Wendy: *Nacidos en Mauthausen: La lucha por la vida de tres madres y sus bebés en el horror de los campos nazis* (RBA Libros, Madrid, 2015)

Holzinger, Gregor, Kranebitter Andreas (Ed.): *Mauthausen. The Concentration Camp 1938-1945* (New Academic Press, New York, 2013)

Höss, Rudolf: *Commandant of Auschwitz* (The World Publishing Company, Cleveland, 1959)

Iwaszko, Tadeusz: *Auschwitz 1940-1945, Volume II, The Organization and Exploitation of Auschwitz Concentration Camp Prisoners as Laborers* (Auschwitz-Birkenau State Museum, Oświęcim,2002).

Kaienburg, Hermann: *Die Wirtschaft der SS* (Metropol Verlag, Berlin, 2002)

Klee, Ernst, Dressen, Willi, Riess, Volker: *The Good Old Days. The Holocaust as Seen by Its Perpetrators and Bystanders* (Konecky & Konecky, Connecticut, 1991)

Klee, Ernst: *Euthanasie im NS-Staat* (Fischer Verlag, Frankfurt am Main, 2004)

Klukowski, Zygmunt: *Diary from the Years of Occupation 1939-1944* (Urbana, III, University of IllinoisPress, Illinois, 1993)

Knopp, Guido: *Hitler's Holocaust* (The History Press, Gloucestershire, 2005)

Kogon, Eugen: *Der SS-Staat Das System Der Deutschen Konzentrationslager* (Frankfurter Hefte, 1946)

Krakowski, Shmuel: *A Small Village in Europe Chełmno (Kulmhof), The First Nazi Mass Extermination Camp,* (Yad Vashem Jeruzalem, 2001)

Kranz, Tomasz: *Extermination of Jews at the Majdanek Concentration Camp* (Państwowe Muzeum na Majdanku, Lublin, 2007)

Laks, Szymon: *Music of Another World*, Northwestern (University Press, Illinois, 2000)

Laqueur, Walter: *The Terrible Secret: Suppression of the Truth About Hitler's "Final Solution"* (Rootledge, Oxfordshire, 2017)

Lanzmann, Claude: *Shoah: The Complete Text Of The Acclaimed Holocaust Film* (Da Capo Press, Boston, 1995)

Laureyssens, Stan: *Adolf Eichmann. Boekhouder van de dood* (Uitgeverij Van Halewyck, Leuven,2010)

Lehnstaedt, Stephan: *Der Kern des Holocaust*, (C.H. Beck Verlag, München, 2017)

Levi, Primo: *If This is A Man* (Abacus, London, 2014)

Levi, Primo: *The Drowned and the Saved* (Abacus, London, 2013)

Levi, Primo: *Survival in Auschwitz* (Simon & Schuster, London, 1996)

Levi, Primo: *Auschwitz rapportage* (Meulenhoff, Amsterdam, 2008)

Lewis, Brenda, Ralph: *Hitler Youth. The Hitlerjugend in War and Peace (1933-1935)* (Amber Books, London, 2019)

Lifton, Robert: *The Nazi Doctors: Medical Killing and the Psychology of Genocide* (Basic Books, New York, 1986)

Lipstadt, Deborah: *Beyond Belief. The American Press & the Coming of the Holocaust 1933-1945* (The Free Press, New York, 1993)

Losh, L. (ed.): *Radomsko Yizkor Book , Sefer yizkor le-kehilat Radomsk ve-ha-seviva*, Memorial book of the community of Radomsko and vicinity, (Former residents of Radomsko, Radomsko, 1967)

Lulas, Richard: *The Forgotten Holocaust: The Poles under German Occupation 1939-1944* (Hippocrene Books, New York, 2001)

Marsalek, Hans: *The History of Mauthausen Concentration Camp* (Austrian Society of Mauthausen Concentration Camp, Linz, 1995)

Martin, Gilbert: *Kristallnacht. Prelude to Destruction* (Harper Perennial, New York, 2007)

Megargee, Geoffrey P.: *Encyclopedia of Camps and Ghettos, 1933-1945* (Indiana University Press, Bloomington, 2009)

Melching, Willem, Stuivenga, Marcel: *Ooggetuigen van het Derde Rijk* (Bert Bakker, Amsterdam, 2006)

Minerbi, Sergio: *The Eichmann Trial Diary: A Chronicle of the Holocaust* (Enigma Books, New York, 2011)

Morris, Heather: *The Tattooist of Auschwitz* (Zaffre Publishing, London, 2018)

Morse, Arthur D.: *While Six Million Died: A Chronicle of American Apathy* (The Overlook Press, New York, 1998)

Moutier, Marie: *Lettres de la Wehrmacht* (Tempus Perrin, Paris, 2018)

Müller, Filip: *Eyewitness Auschwitz. Three Years in the Gas Chambers* (Rowman & Littlefield,Lanham, 1999)

Neufeld, Michael, Berenbaum, Michael: *The Bombing of Auschwitz. Should the Allies Have Attempted It?* (University Press of Kansas, Lawrence, 2003)

Nissim, Gabriele: *Der Mann, der Hitler stoppte: Dimitar Pesev und die Rettung der bulgarischen Juden* (Siedler Verlag, Berlin, 2000)

Pajer, Rajmund: *Ich war I 69186 in Mauthausen* (Kitab Zeitgeschichte, Klagenfurt am Wörthersee, 2010)

Pfeffer, Georg: *My Escape from Majdanek* (Arc Foundation of Monroe, Rochester, NY, 2006).

Piper, Franciszek: *Auschwitz 1940-1945*, Volume II, *The Prisoners— Their Life and Work* (Auschwitz-Birkenau State Museum, 2000)

Pohl, Dieter: *Holocaust. Holocaust. Die Ursachen, das Geschehen, die Folgen* (Herder-Spektrum, Wien, 2000)

Poliakow, Leon, Wulf, Josef: *Das Dritte Reich und die Juden, Documente und Aufsatze* (Arani Verlags-GmbH, Berlin-Grunewald, 1955)

Rabl, Christian: *Das KZ-Aussenlager St. Aegyd am Neuwalde* (Bundesministerium fur Inneres, Mauthausen Studien, 2008)

Rees, Laurence: *Auschwitz* (Public Affairs, New York, 2006)

Rees, Laurence: *The Nazis* (The New Press, New York, 1998)

Reich-Ranicki, Marcel: *Mein Leben* (Pantheon, München, 2012)

Richie, Alexandra: *Warsaw 1944: Hitler, Himmler, and the Warsaw Uprising* (Farra, Straus and Giroux, York, 2013)

Rosengarten, Israel: *Survival: The Story of a Sixteen-Year Old Jewish Boy* (Syracuse Univ PR, Syracuse, 1999)

Saerens, Lieven: *Vreemdelingen in een wereldstad. Een geschiedenis van Antwerpen en zijn Joodse bevolking (1880-1944)* (Lannoo, Tielt, 2000)

Schmidt, Barbel: *Geschichte und Symbolik der gestreiften KZ-Häftlingskleidung* (Carl Von Ossietsky Universitat, Oldenburg, 2000)

Schmidt, Ephraim: *Geschiedenis van de joden in Antwerpen* (Uitgeverij S.M. Ontwikkeling, Antwerpen, 1963)

Scholl, Inge: *Students against tyranny: the resistance of the White Rose* (Wesleyan University Press, Connecticut, 1970)

Scholl, Inge: *The White Rose. Munich 1942-1943* (Wesleyan University Press, Connecticut, 1983)

Schram, Laurence: *Dossin. Wachtkamer van Auschwitz* (Lannoo, Tielt, 2018)

Schulte, Jan Erik: *Zwangsarbeit und Vernichtung: Das Wirtschaftsimperium der SS. Oswald Pohl und das SS-Wirtschafts-Verwaltungshauptamt 1933-1945* (Schoeningh Ferdinand, Paderborn, 2001)

Sereny, Gitta: *Into That Darkness: An Examination of Conscience* (Vintage, Benton Harbor, 1983)

Shalamov, Varlam: *Kolyma Tales* (Penguin Books, London, 1994)

Sluszny, Marcel: *Twee Antwerpse Diamantairs. Het verhaal van Irena* (Les iles, Ellezelles, 2012)

Smith, Lyn: *Forgotten Voices of the Holocaust* (Ebury, Princeton, 2006)

Snyder, Timothy: *Black Earth: The Holocaust as History and Warning* (Random House, New York, 2015)

Spector, Shmuel, Wigoder, Geoffrey: *The Encyclopedia of Jewish Life Before and During the Holocaust* (New York University Press, New York, 2001)

Steinbacher, Sybille: *Auschwitz: A History* (Harper Perennial, New York, 2006)

Steinberg, Maxime: *De ogen van het monster. Volkerenmoord dag in dag uit* (Hadewijch, Groningen, 1992)

Steinberg, Maxime, Schram, Laurence: *Mecheln-Auschwitz: de geschiedenis van de transporten 1942-1944, Deel I* (VUB Press, Brussels, 2009)

Steinberg, Paul: *Speak You Also: A Survivor's Reckoning* (Holt and Company, New York, 2000)

Struk, Janina: *Photographing the Holocaust. Interpretations of the Evidence* (Tauris, London, 2004)

Strzelecka, Irena: *Hefte von Auschwitz 18* (Verlag Staatliches Auschwitz-Museum, Oświęcim, 1990)

Strzelecka, Irena, Setkiewicz, Piotr: *Auschwitz 1940-1945, Volume I, La construction et l'organisation du camp* (Musee d'Etat d'Auschwitz-Birkenau, Oświęcim, 2011

Strzelecka, Irena: *Auschwitz 1940-1945, Volume II, The Prisoners— Their Life and Work* (Auschwitz-Birkenau State Museum, Oświęcim, 2000)

Strzelecki, Andrzej: *The Evacuation, Dismantling and Liberation of KL-Auschwitz* (Auschwitz-Birkenau State Museum, Oświęcim, 2001)

Świebocka, Teresa: *The Architecture of Crime. The 'Central Camp Sauna' in Auschwitz II-Birkenau,* (Auschwitz-Birkenau State Museum, Oświęcim, 2001)

Allen Michael Thad, Allen, Michael: *The Business of Genocide. The SS, Slave Labor, and the Concentration Camps* (The University of North Carolina Press, Chapel Hill, 2002)

Thone, Georges: *De Jodenvervolging in België* (Commission of Inquiry into violations of International Law, 1948)

Timm, Uwe: *Am Beispiel meines Bruders* (dtv Verlagsgesellschaft, München, 2005)

Tooze, Adam: *Ökonomie der Zerstörung: Die Geschichte der Wirtschaft im Nationalsozialismus* (Pantheon Verlag, München, 2018)

Tych, Feliks: *The History of Częstochowa Jews during the Holocaust and After as Documented in the Archives of the Jewish Historical Institute* (The American Association for Polish-Jewish Studies, New York, 2000)

Vandecandelaere, Ronny: *Natan Ramet. Mens, kampnummer, getuige* (Epo, Antwerpen, 2015)

Van den Wijngaert, Mark (red.): *België tijdens de Tweede Wereldoorlog* (Standaard Uitgeverij, Antwerpen, 2015)

Van Doorslaer, Rudi (red.): *Gewillig België. Overheid en Jodenvervolging tijdens de Tweede Wereldoorlog* (Meulenhoff/Manteau, Amsterdam, 2007)

Vandormael, Herman: *Verborgen oorlogsjaren. Ondergedoken Joodse kinderen getuigen* (Lannoo, Tielt, 2009)

Vandormael, Herman: *Kinderen van Theresienstadt. De laatste overlevenden van de concentratiekampen getuigen* (Lannoo, Tielt, 2012)

Van Eck, Ludo: *Zo was het in Mauthausen* (Libertas, Leuven, 1985)

Van Goethem, Herman: *1942. Het jaar van de stilte* (Polis/Cossee, Antwerpen, 2019)

Van Pelt, Robert, Jan, Dwork, Deborah: *Auschwitz* (W. W. Norton & Company, New York, 2002)

Van Pelt, Robert, Jan, Dwork, Deborah: *Auschwitz* (W. W. Norton & Company, New York, 1997)

Verbeken, Pascal, Selleslags, Hermn: *Tranzyt Antwerpia. Reis in het spoor van de Red Star Line* (De Bezige Bij, Amsterdam, 2013)

Verhofstadt, Dirk: *Pius XII en de vernietiging van de Joden*, (Houtekiet/Atlas, Antwerpen/Amsterdam, 2008)

Vogelaar, Jacq: *Over kampliteratuur* (De Bezige Bij, Amsterdam, 2006)

Vrba, Rudolf: *I escaped from Auschwitz* (Simon and Schuster, New York, 2020)

Wachsmann, Nikolaus: *KL. A History of the Nazi Concentration Camps* (Farrar, Straus and Giroux, York, 2016)

Wette, Wolfram, Karl Jager: *Mörder der Litauischen Juden* (Fisher Verlag, Frankfurt am Main 2011)

Wiesel, Elie: *A Jew Today* (Random House, London, 1978)

Wiesel, Elie: *Night* (Hill and Wang, New York, 2017)

Wiesenthal, Simon: *Justice Not Vengeance: Recollections* (Grove Pr, New York, 1990)

Willenberg, Samuel: *Surviving Treblinka* (Blackwell Pub, London, 1989)

Winstone, Martin: *The Holocaust Sites of Europe: An Historical Guide* (Tauris, London, 2010)

Wolfson, Leah: *Jewish Responses to Persecution 1944-1946* (Rowman & Littlefield Publishers, Lanham, 2015)

Thanks to Els Wouters, Vé Bobelyn, Mathieu Morret and Muriel Rappaport of the publishing house Houtekiet, to Kristien De Wulf and Jane Camerea for the translation, to Joseph Pearce and Leo De Haes for their comments. Finally, Anne Beeckman for her support, and to Elaine and Tine for their boundless patience.

Endnotes

Part One: Treblinka

1. Czestochowa-Radomsko Area Research Group, https://www.crarg.org/
2. Bauer, *The Death of the Shtetl*, p. 15.
3. Pohl, *Holocaust. Mass murder of European Jews*, p. 29.
4. Remigiusz Okraska, *Daw-ne Zarki*, p. 16.
5. Vatican.va, *Homily of his Holiness Pope Frances*, Częstochowa, 28 July 2016.
6. Bauer, op. cit., p. 17.
7. Lulas, *The Forgotten Holocaust: The Poles under German Occupation 1939-1944*, p. 3.
8. Evans, *The Third Reich At War*, p. 76.
9. Fisher, *Death and destruction of Jewish Zarki*, in *Kehilat Zarki*, Icchak Lador (in Yiddish), pp. 223-81.
10. Bronstein, Holinstat, *Survivors Club: The True Story of a Very Young Prisoner of Auschwitz*, p. 16.
11. Vandormael, *Verborgen oorlogsjaren. Ondergedoken Joodse kinderen getuigen*, p. 45.
12. Bohler, *"Größte Härte ...": Verbrechen der Wehrmacht in Polen September/ Oktober 1939*, Ausstellungskatalog, Fibre Wydanie, 2005.
13. Tych, *The History of Częstochowa Jews during the Holocaust and After as Documented in the Archives of the Jewish Historical Institute*, 2000.
14. Bauer, *American Jewry and the Holocaust: The American Jewish Joint Distribution*, p. 188.
15. Brief von der Burgermeister der Gem. Plawno, gez. Karl Rusche (stamp), 22. Januar 1942.
16. *Radomsko Yizkor Book, Sefer yizkor le-kehilat Radomsk ve-ha-seviva*, Memorial book of the community of Radomsk and vicinity, Edited by L. Losh, pp. 379-81.
17. Ibid, p. 347.
18. Ibid, p. 350.
19. Ibid, p. 351.
20. Ibid, p. 354.
21. Rees, *The Nazi's: A Warning from History*, p. 133.
22. Pohl, op. cit., p. 51.
23. Knopp, *Hitler's Holocaust*, p. 18.

24. Friedländer, *The Years of Extermination. Nazi Germany and the Jews, 1933-1945*, p. 202.
25. Bauer, op. cit. , pp. 82-3.
26. Wette, *Karl Jäger. Mörder der Litauischen Juden*, p. 78.
27. Friedlander, op. cit., p. 223.
28. Cited in Vandormael, *Verborgen oorlogsjaren*, p. 48.
29. Friedländer, op. cit., p. 225.
30. Wette, op. cit., p. 118.
31. Ibid, p. 119.
32. Ibid, Anhang, Blatt. 7.
33. Buchbender, Sterz, *Das andere Gesicht des Krieges. Deutsche Feldpostbriefe 1939-1945*, p. 173.
34. Auszüge aus Briefen von Walter Mattner, eines Polizeisekrets in Mogilev, an seine Frau. 5. Oktober 1941, Zentrale Stelle der Landesjustizverwaltungen, Ludwigsburg, Band 396, copy YVA O.5/38.A.
35. Höhne, *Der Orden unter dem Totenkopf: Die Geschichte der SS*, p. 332.
36. Cesarani, *Final Solution. The Fate of the Jews 1933-1949*, p. 387.
37. Browning, *Ordinary men. Reserve police battalion 101 and the Final Solution in Poland*, p. 65.
38. Cesarani, op. cit., p. 475.
39. Klee, Dressen, Riess, *The Good Old Days. The Holocaust as Seen by Its Perpetrators and Bystanders*, p. 60.
40. Ibid, pp. 66-7.
41. Christian Ingrao in the documentary film by Michael Prazan, *Einsatzgruppen, The Nazi Death Squads*, Part III, *Funerals Pyres* (1942-1943), 2009.
42. Testimony by Dr. Mieczysław Sękiewicz. Krakowski, *A Small Village in Europe Chełmno (Kulmhof), The First Nazi Mass Extermination Camp*, pp. 19-21.
43. Dederichs, *Heydrich. The Face of Evil*, p. 106.
44. Angrick, *Besatzungspolitik und Massenmord, Die Einsatzgruppe D in der südlichen Sowjetunion 1941-1943*, p. 370.
45. Statement by August Becker in Klee, Dressen, Riess, *The Good Old Days. The Holocaust as Seen by Its Perpetrators and Bystanders*, p. 68.
46. Klee, *Euthanasie im NS-staat*, p. 103.
47. Sereny, *Into That Darkness*, p. 53.
48. Lifton, *The Nazi Doctors: Medical Killing and the Psychology of Genocide*, p. 75.
49. Baupläne der Mordfabrik Auschwitz gefunden, Welt, 08.11.2008.
50. Melching, Stuivenga, *Ooggetuigen van het Derde Rijk*, p. 136.
51. Friedländer, op. cit., p. 341.
52. Lehnstaedt, *Der Kern des Holocaust*, p. 35.
53. Dederichs, *Heydrich. The Face of Evil*, p. 138.
54. Bergen, *War and Genocide: A Concise History of the Holocaust*, p. 183.
55. Knopp, *Hitler's Holocaust*, op. cit., p. 99.

56. Confession of Adolf Eichmann noted by journalist Wilhelm Sassen, in Life, November 28, 1960, p. 104.
57. Ibid, p. 104.
58. Pfeffer, *My Escape from Majdanek*, 63.
59. Friedländer, op. cit., p. 559.
60. Kranz, *Extermination of Jews at the Majdanek concentration camp*, p. 14.
61. Klukowski, *Diary from the Years of Occupation 1939-1944*, p. 214.
62. Paul R. Bartrop, *Modern Genocide: A Documentary and Reference Guide. Holocaust: The Gerstein Report*, p. 90.
63. Ibid, pp. 90-1.
64. Stephan Lehnstaedt, op. cit., p. 81. The graves contain thick layers of human fat, unburned human remains and large pieces of human bone mixed with carbonised wood and grey ashes.
65. Sonderkommandos were groups of prisoners, almost exclusively Jews, who were required by the SS to assist them in the extermination process. They had to reassure the newly arrived prisoners, guide them to the gas chambers, remove the corpses, extract the gold teeth from the mouths, remove the corpses from the mass graves and burn them in the crematoriums.
66. Klee, Dressen, Riess, *The Good Old Days. The Holocaust as Seen by Its Perpetuators and Bystanders*, p. 231.
67. Arad, *Bełżec, Sobibór, Treblinka: The Operation Reinhard Death Camps*, p. 76.
68. Losh, L. (ed.), *Radomsko Yizkor Book*, testimony of Simka Hampel and Yisokhar Minski, p. 358.
69. Ibid, p. 358.
70. Ibid, p. 359.
71. Ibid, testimony of Abraham Buchman and Yehuda Waksman, p. 363.
72. Cesarani, op. cit., p. XXV.
73. Lanzmann, *Shoah – The Complete Text of the Acclaimed Holocaust Film*, p. 44.
74. Der Gerstein-Bericht, *Augenzeugenbericht über Massenvergasungen*, Tubingen (Wurttemberg), Gartenstrase 24, den 4. Mai 1945, Rottweil, Vierteljahrshefte fur Zeitgeschehen, 1953, nr. 2, April, pp. 185-96.
75. Lanzmann, *op.cit.*, pp. 46-7.
76. Sereny, op. cit., pp. 157-8.
77. Glazar, *Trap with a Green Fence: Survival in Treblinka*, pp. 5-6.
78. Lanzmann, op. cit., p. 37.
79. Glazar, op. cit., p. 12.
80. Willenberg, *Surviving Treblinka*, Blackwell Publishers, p. 60.
81. Arad, *Bełżec, Sobibór*, op. cit., p. 373.
82. *Sonderkommando 1005* refers to the one thousand ordinary prisoners working together with five experienced prisoners whom Paul Blobel considered experts in extermination actions.
83. Gross, *Fear, Anti-Semitism in Poland After Auschwitz*, p. 81 and next.
84. Gross, op. cit., p. 261.
85. Friedländer, op. cit., 150.

86. Smith, *Forgotten Voices of the Holocaust*, p. 121.
87. *Ringelblum Notes* quoted in Cesarani, op. cit., p. 348.
88. Richie, *Warsaw 1944: Hitler, Himmler, and the Warsaw Uprising*, p. 572.

Part Two: Antwerp

1. Schmidt, *Geschiedenis van de joden in Antwerpen*, p. 108.
2. Saerens, *Vreemdelingen in een wereldstad. Een geschiedenis van Antwerpen en zijn Joodse bevolking 1880-1944*, p. 16.
3. Evans, op. cit., p. 49.
4. Gross, *Neighbours: The Destruction of the Jewish Community in Jedwabne*, Penguin Books, p. 38.
5. Heller, *On the Edge of Destruction. Jews of Poland between the Two World Wars*, p. 3, 48.
6. Ibid, pp. 101-5.
7. Anstadt, *Polen en Joden*, p. 86.
8. Bauer, op. cit., p. 21.
9. Heller, op. cit., p. 239.
10. Ibid, p. 245.
11. The Danish Jews were informed at the end of September 1943 of an impending raid. They were then transported to Sweden with help from the Danish population in fishing trawlers and small boats.
12. Friedländer, op. cit., p. 452.
13. Nissim, *Der Mann, der Hitler stoppte: Dimitar Pesev und Die Rettung der bulgarischen Juden*, p. 211.
14. Document 214184, City of Antwerp, drawn up on 22 December 1932. Source: State Archives.
15. Cesarani, op. cit., p. 29.
16. The letters KZ stand for *Konzentrationslager* (concentration camp).
17. The *Sturmabteilung (SA)* was founded in 1921 and was a sort of Nazi fight team that was responsible for securing party meetings against political opponents. Later, the SA would operate as a terror group that acted extremely violently towards Jews, Communists, Socialists, and other opponents of the Nazi regime. The members were mainly war veterans and unemployed workers, who wore brown uniforms with a swastika on their arms.
18. Swear word for a French speaking person living in Flanders who advocates French as the national language.
19. These *Protocols* were a falsification prepared by the Ochrana, the Russian secret service. They concerned a nonexistent secret gathering of Jewish leaders purporting to have hatched a plan to conquer the world and overthrow Christianity. It was quickly exposed as a work of fiction. Yet it has been and is still being cited by all kinds of antisemitic groups, including the Nazis.
20. Saerens, op. cit., p. 421.
21. Morse, *While Six Million Died: A Chronicle of American Apathy*, p. 201.
22. 'The Best Protest', *The Christian Science Monitor*, 15 November 1938, p. 20.

23. *The New York Times*, 8 July 1938, quoted in Lipstadt, *Beyond belief. The American Press & the Coming of the Holocaust 1933-1945*, p. 95.
24. Martin, *Kristallnacht. Prelude to Destruction*, p. 131.
25. Morse, op. cit., pp. 205-6.
26. Ibid, p. 145.
27. Lewis, *Hitler Youth: The Hitlerjugend in War and Peace, 1933-1945*, p. 215.
28. Doetzer, *'Aus Menschen werden Briefe': die Korrespondenz einer jüdischen Familie zwischen Verfolgung und Emigration, 1933-1947*, p. 126.
29. Van Goethem, *1942. Het jaar van de stilte*, pp. 22-3.
30. Lieven Saerens, op. cit., p. 426.
31. Ibid, pp. 471-7.
32. City of Antwerp, Police Station 6th District, File 214.184, 7 June 1938.
33. Court of First Instance Antwerp, Aliens Police, No. 109712, 11 December 1940.
34. Court of First Instance Antwerp, Aliens Police, No. 26917, 30 May 1942.
35. Van Doorslaer (Ed.), *Gewillig België. Overheid en Jodenvervolging tijdens de Tweede Wereldoorlog*, p. 494.
36. Thone, *De Jodenvervolging in België*, p. 20.
37. Van Goethem, op. cit., p. 69.
38. Schmidt, op. cit., p. 157.
39. Lieven Saerens, op. cit., pp. 573-4.
40. Thone Publisher, op. cit., p. 22.
41. Lieven Saerens, op. cit., p. 501.
42. Ibid, p. 503.
43. Ibid, p. 504.
44. Vandecandelaere, *Natan Ramet. Mens, kampnummer, getuige*, p. 62.
45. Immigration and Naturalization Service in Philadelphia, Board of Immigration Appeals, Washington DC, File 99666-327.
46. Letter from Jacob J. Singer to Mr. John W. Pehle, Acting Executive Director of the War Refugee Board, Washington DC, 29 March 1944.
47. Letter from Joseph Savoretti, U.S. Department of Justice, Immigration and Naturalisation Service, Philadelphia, 14 November 1944.
48. Schram, *Dossin. Wachtkamer van Auschwitz*, p. 57.
49. Van den Wijngaert (red.), *België tijdens de Tweede Wereldoorlog*, p. 236.
50. Van Goethem, op.cit., p. 71.
51. Pro Justitia, Stad Antwerpen, Politie Zesde Wijk, Ide Leib Kartuz, 8 februari 1949.
52. Verslag, Stad Antwerpen, Politie Bijzondere Opdrachten nr. 2717, Ide Leib Kartuz 26 november 1949.
53. Verslag, Stad Antwerpen, Politie Bijzondere Opdrachten nr. 2717, Ide Leib Kartuz 26 November 1949.
54. Schram, op.cit., p. 58.
55. Schram, op.cit., p. 59.

56. Ibid, p. 98.
57. Ministry of Justice, Public Security, Prison in Antwerp, Declaration of 11 September 1940 No 7254 – Source: State Archives Brussels.
58. Schram, op. cit., pp. 59 & 119.

Part Three : Auschwitz

1. Steinbacher, *Auschwitz. A History*, p. 9.
2. Fairweather, *The Volunteer: One Man's Mission to Lead an Underground Army in Auschwitz and Expose the Greatest Nazi Crimes*, p.82.
3. Strzelecka, Setkiewicz, *The Establishment and Organization of the Camp, Auschwitz 1940-1945*, p. 89.
4. Knopp, *op. cit.*, p. 176.
5. Gutman, Berenbaum, *Anatomy of the Auschwitz Death Camp*, p. 16.
6. Piper, *Auschwitz 1940-1945*, p. 90.
7. Helm, *Ravensbrück. Live and Death in Hitler's Concentration Camp for Women*, p. 202.
8. Höss, *Commandant of Auschwitz*, pp. 134-5.
9. Snyder, *Black Earth. The Holocaust as History and Warning*, p. 197.
10. Rudolf Höss, op. cit., p 146.
11. Ibid, pp. 146-147.
12. Greif, Siebers, *Death Factory Auschwitz*, Emons Verlag, 2016, p. 125.
13. Müller, *Eyewitness Auschwitz. Three Years in the Gas Chambers*, p. 30.
14. Rees, *Auschwitz*, Ambo/Anthos, p. 102.
15. Wachsmann, KL. *A History of the Nazi Concentration* Camps, p. 315.
16. Müller, op. cit., p. 62.
17. Höss, op. cit., p. 187.
18. Czech, *Kalendarz wydarzeń* w kl *Auschwitz*, pp. 147-8.
19. Ibid, pp. 149-51.
20. Ibid, p. 196.
21. Smith, op. cit., p. 176.
22. Steinbacher, op. cit, p. 100.
23. Rudolf Höss, op. cit., pp. 148-9.
24. Ibid, p. 150.
25. Rudolf Höss, statement under oath in Nurenberg on 5 April 1946.
26. The latter is true. Helena Hycz-Wola, the grandmother of Kamila Sokalska who translated texts from Polish for our research, was four years old at the time and lived almost five kilometres from the camp. She remembered very well the filthy burning smell from Birkenau.
27. Steinberg, Schram, *Mecheln-Auschwitz, 1942-1944*, p. 43.
28. David Mandelbaum, Foundation Auschwitz, 9 December 1992, DVD No. 1/1.
29. Czech, op. cit., p. 238.
30. Vrba, *I escaped from Auschwitz*, 163.
31. Citroen, *Auschwitz – de Judenrampe*, p. 54.
32. Ibid, p.48.

33. Wachsmann, op. cit., p. 309.
34. Citroen, op. cit., p. 32.
35. Van Pelt, Dwork, *Auschwitz – 1270 to the Present*, p. 302.
36. David Mandelbaum, Foundation Auschwitz, 9 December, 1992, DVD No. 1/1.
37. Simon Majzels, USC Shoah Foundation, The Institute for Visual History and Education, Interview Code 29228, May 21, 1997, Disc I, Part II, 00'30".
38. David Mandelbaum, Foundation Auschwitz, 9 December 1992, DVD No. 1/1.
39. Archives of the Auschwitz-Birkenau State Museum in Oswiecim, Testimonies, Wladyslaw Czajkowski, Volume 32, p. 12.
40. Georgi, Kamp, *Lodenfrey in der* ns-*Zeit 1933-1945*, August Dreesbach Verlag, 2012, p. 22. In this publication is shown that the company Lodenfrey used forced labourers.
41. Schmidt, *Geschichte und Symbolik der gestreiften kz-Häftlingskleidung*, p. 101.
42. Thad, *The Business of Genocide. The SS, Slave Labor, and the Concentration Camps*, p. 74.
43. Bernadac, *Camp for Women: Ravensbrück*, p. 145.
44. Helm, op. cit., pp. 215-16.
45. Testimony of Alfredine Nenninger- Wawcziniak, Mahn- und Gedenkstätte Ravensbrück, RA Bd.26, Bericht zu 392, S. 3.
46. Schmidt, *op. cit.*, pp. 107-8.
47. Helm, *op. cit.*, p. 219.
48. Testimony by Maria Wiedmaier, Mahn- und Gedenkstätte Ravensbrück, RA Bd. 25, Bericht 383, S. 1.
49. https://www.tracesofwar.nl/articles/1824/Konzentrationslager-Ravensbruck.htm?c=gw
50. Schulte, *Zwangsarbeit und Vernichtung: Das Wirtschaftsimperium der SS. Oswald Pohl und das SS-Wirtschafts-Verwaltungshauptamt 1933–1945*, S. 131 ff.
51. Barbel Schmidt, op. cit., p. 65.
52. Ibid, p. 66.
53. Ibid, p. 130.
54. David Mandelbaum, Foundation Auschwitz, 9 December 1992, DVD no 1/1
55. https://collections.ushmm.org/search/catalog/vha15269
56. Greif, Siebers, Todesfabrik Auschwitz, 2016.
57. Archives of the Auschwitz-Birkenau State Museum in Oswiecim, Testimonies, Marian Gnyp, Volume 111, pp. 116-7.
58. Archives of the Auschwitz-Birkenau State Museum in Oswiecim, Testimonies, Stanislaw Dorosiewicz, Volume 126, p. 132.
59. Ibid, p. 132.
60. Ibid, p. 133.
61. Interview with Benno Kartuz, 25 July, 2019.
62. Testimony Nadine, 19 August, 2018.
63. Testimony by Luc Leemans, 21 September 2018.

64. Höss, op. cit., pp. 195-6.
65. Smith, op. cit., pp. 178-9.
66. Archives of the Auschwitz-Birkenau State Museum in Oswiecim, Testimonies, Antoni Slapinski, Volume 49, p. 15.
67. Archives of the Auschwitz-Birkenau State Museum in Oswiecim, Testimonies, Adam Jerzy Brandhuber, Volume 76, p. 111.
68. Archives of the Auschwitz-Birkenau State Museum in Oswiecim, Testimonies, Volume 151, p. 267, Kurt Scholz, No. 92367, Relacja b.więźnia KL Auschwitz, 18.1.1988, p. 3.
69. Strzelecka, *Auschwitz 1940-1945*, p. 71.
70. Laks, *Musik in Auschwitz*, p. 30.
71. Ibid, p. 67.
72. Laurence Rees, op. cit., p. 250.
73. Ibid, pp. 63-4.
74. Iwaszko, *Auschwitz 1940-1945, Volume II, The Organization and Exploitation of Auschwitz Concentration Camp Prisoners as Laborers*, p. 65.
75. Smith, op. cit., p. 180.
76. Knopp, op. cit., p. 183.
77. Czech, op. cit., p. 242.
78. Knopp, op. cit., p. 183. The morning action involved the gassing of 800 female detainees who were completely exhausted and had been selected to be gassed.
79. Czech, op. cit., pp. 243-4.
80. Knopp, op. cit., p. 184.
81. Czech, op. cit., p. 252.
82. Testimony of Yaakov David Alchec, Yad Vashem Archive, 0.3/8619
83. Archives of the Auschwitz-Birkenau State Museum in Oswiecim, Testimonies, Jozef Szerman Szyja, Volume 53, p. 165.
84. David Mandelbaum, Foundation Auschwitz, 9 December 1992, dvd no 1/1.
85. Archives of the Auschwitz-Birkenau State Museum in Oswiecim, Testimonies, Markus Lustbader, Volume 78, p. 160.
86. Levi, *If this is a man*, p. 105.
87. Ibid, p. 90.
88. Interview with Gerta De Voeght, August 12, 2018.
89. Czech, op. cit., p. 347.
90. Levi, *Auschwitz rapportage*, pp. 64-5.
91. Simon Majzels, USC Shoah Foundation, The Institute for Visual History and Education, Interview Code 29228, May 21, 1997, Disc I, Part II, 01'25".
92. Smith, op. cit., p. 182.
93. Ibid, p. 173.
94. Municipality of Sint-Gillis-Op-Brussels, Police Service, Administrative Act No 768, 15 December 1949.
95. Scholl, The *White Rose. Munich 1942-1943*, Wesleyan University Press, 1983, pp. 78-9.
96. Ibid, pp. 40-5.

97. Cesarani, op. cit., p. 685.

98. Documents on the Holocaust, Selected Sources on the Destruction of the Jews of Germany and Austria, Poland and the Soviet Union, Yad Vashem, Jerusalem, 1981, Document no.161, pp. 344-5.

99. Fondation Auschwitz, David Lachman, 29 avril 1992, DVD No. 1-2, from 26'17".

100. Iwaszko, *Central Issues in the History of the Camp*, Volume II, *The Prisoners: Their Life and Work*, p. 44-5.

101. Fairweather, *The Volunteer: One Man's Mission to Lead an Underground Army in Auschwitz and Expose the Greatest Nazi Crimes*, p. 66.

102. Primo Levi, op. cit., p. 34.

103. Ibid, p. 104.

104. Knopp, op. cit., p. 289.

105. Smith, op. cit., pp. 212-3.

106. Steinberg, *Speak You Also: A Survivor's Reckoning*, pp. 97-8.

107. Cesarani, op. cit., p. 743.

108. Gilbert, *Auschwitz and the Allies*, p. 301.

109. Wiesel, *Night*, p. 58-59.

110. The Washington Post, March 22, 1944, p. 2, quoted in Lipstadt, *Beyond Belief. The American Press & the Coming of the Holocaust 1933-1945*, p. 233.

111. Neufeld, Berenbaum (Ed.), *The Bombing of Auschwitz. Should the Allies Have Attempted It?*, p. 80-1.

112. Gilbert, op. cit., p. 246.

113. Ibid, p. 190.

114. Ibid, p. 249.

115. Laqueur, *The Terrible Secret*, p. 211.

116. Danuta Czech, op. cit., p. 757.

117. Gilbert, op. cit., pp. 301-20.

118. Danuta Czech, op. cit., p. 797.

119. Ibid, p. 811.

120. Bridgman, *The End of the Holocaust. The Liberation of the Camps*, p. 23.

121. Polish historian Andrzej Strzelecki describes how prisoners who worked at the *Erkennungsdienst* managed to save many documents and the negatives of 40,000 identification photographs taken from the prisoners between 1940 and 1944. Those negatives are now in the possession of the Auschwitz-Birkenau State Museum. Strzelecki, *The Evacuation, Dismantling and Liberation of KL Auschwitz*, p. 210.

Part Four: Mauthausen

1. Strzelecki, op. cit., pp. 207-8.

2. Knopp, op. cit., p. 296.

3. Fondation Auschwitz, David Lachman, 29 April 1992, DVD No. 1-2, from 1h08'16".

4. Fondation Auschwitz, David Lachman, 29 April 1992, DVD No. 1-2, from 1h08'43".

5. Müller, *Eyewitness Auschwitz: Three Years in the Gas Chambers*, p. 179.
6. Fondation Auschwitz, David Lachman, 29 April 1992, DVD No. 1-2, from 1h19'47" to 1h25'34".
7. Antończyk, *Transport of prisoners between kl Auschwitz and KL Mauthausen*, p. 174.
8. Holzinger, Andreas Kranebitter (Ed.), *The Concentration Camp Mauthausen 1938-1945*, 2013, p. 127.
9. Winstone, *The Holocaust Sites of Europe*, p.153.
10. Holzinger, Kranebitter (ed.), op. cit., pp. 175-200.
11. Marsalek, *The History of Mauthausen Concentration Camp*, p. 245.
12. Friedländer, op. cit., 295.
13. Rabl, *Das KZ-Aussenlager St. Aegyd am Neuwalde*, p. 57.
14. *Waldlager Gunskirchen in Edt bei Lambach 1945-2017*, Fotodokumentation, Yvonne Burger, Angelika Schlackl, 2017.
15. Megargee, *Encyclopedia of Camps and Ghetto's, 1933-1945*, p. 918.
16. Hirsch, *The Liberators: America's Witnesses to the Holocaust*, p. 219.
17. Blatman, *The Death Marches. The Final Phase of Nazi Genocide*, p. 240.
18. Ibid, p. 241.
19. https://remember.org/full_version.html
20. Hirsch, op. cit., p. 220.
21. Moskin's testimony can be found here: https://www.youtube.com/watch?v=qlj2BbBjH6g.

Part Five: Antwerp

1. Letter from the Ministry of Economic Affairs and Trade, Council for Economic Research on Foreigners, Bundle No 3534/6187, 10 March 1949.
2. Ministry of Economic Affairs and Trade, Council for Economic Research on Foreigners, Bundle: PL 3534/12908, 23 February 1951.
3. Letter from Ide Kartuz to the Minister of Justice, via the Public Prosecutor in Antwerp, 14 March 1951.
4. Letter from the Justice of the Peace of the Second canton of Antwerp to the Public Prosecutor, 19 February 1952.
5. Rechtbank van 1ste Aanleg te Antwerpen, Parket van de Procureur des Konings, nr 3778, 13 mei 1952.
6. Excerpt of the Procurator General's letter to the Justice Minister, No. C 2898/51, 16 May 1952.
7. Independence Front Provincial Committee Antwerp, Declaration, 17 February 1949.
8. Ministry of Reconstruction – Control Committee for Civil Resistance Fighters, Chamber 1, Antwerp 15 February 1952, first page – file no. 740.704/1454/1423.
9. Civil resistance fighter, Statement Jozef Holzer, Antwerp, 28 April 1969.
10. Ministry of Welfare, Health and Family, Status of civil resistance fighters, National Appeals Control Committee in Brussels, File No. 740.704/2016/2016, Session of April 26, 1973.

11. File Beneficiary of the Status of Political Prisoner, No. 31.370/1322/1279, 27 July 1950.
12. Document 6, Biographic note, Subject: Kartuz, 1951.
13. Interview with Cathy Eyletters, 21 April 2019.
14. 'Antwerp mover became rich from Jewish transports, *Joods Actueel,* 13 April 2019.
15. Stad Antwerpen, Centraal Bestuur 2de Directie, Oorlogsschade, The deputy councillor Wilms for the mayor. 11 October 1961.
16. Interview with Ann Van Turnhout, 22 July 2018.
17. https://avalon.law.yale.edu/imt/04-15-46.asp
18. Evans, op. cit., p. 747.
19. Rees, op. cit., p. 303.
20. Minerbi, *The Eichmann Trial Diary: A Chronicle of the Holocaust*, Enigma Books, 2011, p. 144.
21. Ibid, p. 144.
22. Sereny, op. cit., p. 364.

Epilogue

1. Levi, *The Drowned and the Saved*, p. 2.
2. Shalamov, *Kolyma Tales*, p. 393.
3. Max Eisen in the documentary *The Accountant of Auschwitz* (2018) by Matthew Shoychet about the trial of the Nazi criminal Oscar Groning.